A Longm

Chican@s in the Conversations

ELIZABETH RODRIGUEZ KESSLER
University of Houston

ANNE PERRIN
University of Houston

New York San Francisco Boston
London Toronto Sydney Tokyo Singapore Madrid
Mexico City Munich Paris Cape Town Hong Kong Montreal

Titles in the Longman Topics Reader Series

Translating Tradition
Karen E. Beardslee

Reading City Life
Patrick Bruch and Richard Marback

Diversity: Strength and Struggle
Joseph Calabrese and Susan Tchudi

Legends, Lore, and Lies: A Skeptic's Stance
Joseph Calabrese

The People and Promise of California
Mona Field and Brian Kennedy

Citizenship Now
Jon Ford and Marjorie Ford

The Changing World of Work
Marjorie Ford

Issues of Gender
Ellen G. Friedman and Jennifer D. Marshall

Youth Subcultures: Exploring Underground America
Arielle Greenberg

Education Matters: Exploring Issues in Education
Morgan Gresham and Crystal McCage

Science and Society
Richard W. Grinnell

International Views: America and the Rest of the World
Keith Gumery

Listening to Earth
Christopher Hallowell and Walter Levy

Chican@s in the Conversations
Elizabeth Rodriguez Kessler and Anne Perrin

Body and Culture
Greg Lyons

Writing Places
Paula Mathieu, George Grattan, Tim Lindgren, and Staci Shultz

Peace, War, and Terrorism
Dennis Okerstrom

The World of the Image
Trudy Smoke and Alan Robbins

The Hip Hop Reader
Tim Strode and Tim Wood

The Counterculture Reader
E. A. Swingrover

Discovering Popular Culture
Anna Tomasino

Music and Culture
Anna Tomasino

Ethics in the 21st Century
Mary Alice Trent

Considering Cultural Difference
Pauline Uchmanowicz

Language and Prejudice
Tamara M. Valentine

CyberReader, Abridged Edition
Victor J. Vitanza

Para *Gloria Anzaldúa*
In life and death, always part of the conversations

Senior Sponsoring Editor: Virginia L. Blanford
Senior Marketing Manager: Sandra McGuire
Production Manager: Denise Phillip
**Project Coordination and Electronic
Page Makeup:** TexTech International
Cover Design Manager/Cover Designer: John Callahan
Cover Image: © Getty Images, Inc.
Manufacturing Manager: Mary Fischer
Printer and Binder: Courier Corporation, Westford
Cover Printer: Coral Graphic Services

Library of Congress Cataloging-in-Publication Data

Rodriguez Kessler, Elizabeth.
Chican@s in the conversations / Elizabeth Rodriguez Kessler, Anne Perrin. —1st ed.
p. cm.
ISBN 0-321-39417-8
1. Mexican Americans—Ethnic identity. 2. Popular culture—United States. 3. Mexican Americans—Languages. 4. Mexican Americans—Education. 5. Mexican Americans—Social conditions. 6. Immigrants—United States—Social conditons. 7. Mexico—Emigration and immigration. 8. United States—Emigration and immigration. 9. United States—Ethnic relations. I. Perrin, Anne. II. Title. III. Title: Chican@s in the conversations.
E184.M5R595 2007
305.8968'72073—dc22

2007045231

Please visit us at www.ablongman.com

ISBN-13: 978-0-321-39417-0
ISBN-10: 0-321-39417-8

2 3 4 5 6 7 8 9 10—CRW—10 09

According to a May 10, 2001 article in *The New York Times* reporter Eric Schmitt asserts that, "the number of people of Mexican ancestry in the United States grew by 53 percent in the 1990s. . . ." Schmitt additionally states that "Mexicans are by far the largest Hispanic group in the United States, at 20.6 million, accounting for nearly 60 percent of the country's 35.5 million Latinos." Furthermore, Texas and California are not the only two states to report tremendous growth in the Mexican American population: Georgia, Nebraska, and North Carolina also show large increases. *Chican@s in the Conversations* speaks to and for this growing section of the American population and looks at the ways Hispanic individuals and communities are shaping the presence of the Hispanic culture in America on a daily basis.

Part of this shaping process is the recognition that the very words used to describe the Hispanic cultures in America carry multiple meanings that need to be addressed so that the writer does not offend anyone. For example, in this book the spelling "Chican@" in place of the more traditional spelling of "Chicano/a" is not a typo. As many of the articles in this work bring out, the issue of terminology—of the words one uses to represent the self—is often a highly volatile subject. Terms such as Hispanic, Latino, Tejano, Mexican, and Mexican-American (with or without the hyphen) convey associations of and to cultural and national identities. What such terms also carry, when word endings are involved, is preference in gender: linguistically, the "o" ending indicates the masculine and the "a" ending indicates the feminine. But which comes first, which is privileged? Even more importantly, is the use of the ending "o" as a generic application to all really all that generic? Would such general application work if the "a" was used instead of the "o"? We believe it would not. Instead, to avoid privileging of any kind, we, as other critics and writers preceding us, have adopted the "@" sign to indicate both the "a" and "o" combined in the hope that our readers will see all individuals, both female and male, simultaneously. However, when we intend to refer to one gender or the other, we use the appropriate ending.

Another issue of concern is how to recognize or identify the community and the individuals. Who are Mexican Americans? Chicanos? And how are they different from Latinos or Hispanics?

Because Chapter 1 deals extensively with this topic, we will begin with the term Chican@s. To display community pride in their heritage, many Americans with Mexican heritage became identified as Mexican-Americans. Unfortunately, bigotry and prejudice against Mexicans resulted in a number of pejoratives, among them the term *Chicano*. Before the student movement in the 1960s, many older Mexican Americans in different regions of the country considered *Chicano* a negative word, as the well-known n-word pejorative is to African Americans or queer is to homosexuals. The organizers of the college student movement in 1967 attempted to change this viewpoint by adopting the term as the name of their cause: The Chicano Movement, also known as *el movimiento*.

Since then *Chicano* has stood for a political position announcing one's solidarity with others who are fighting for better educational opportunities for Mexican Americans, improving working conditions for agricultural workers as well as for others, creating and supporting Chican@ studies departments in colleges and universities, and generally recognizing and acknowledging Americans with Mexican heritage, the contributions they make, and the revenue they generate in the United States.

Many of the authors in this text are well-known writers who have written extensively or who have made important contributions to their fields: Gloria Anzaldúa, Rudy Acuña, Sandra Cisneros, Richard Rodriguez, and others. Others are relatively new writers who are beginning to make their voices heard in the Chican@ community: Linda Rader Overman, RosaMaria Chacon, and others. Whether they are speaking through their fiction or raising their voices in nonfiction, these writers—as well as many whom we did not have room to include—are speaking out, challenging the accepted standards and stereotypes, and pointing out a positive, progressive presence of the Chicano culture in America.

This book explores five topics that concern the community: Identity, Popular Culture, Language and Education, Borders, and Everyday Issues. Certainly, there are other broad areas of interest to the Chican@ community, such as gender and legality, and their exclusion from this text as a major category is not meant to minimize their importance. Rather, the five broad areas of discussion were chosen because each possesses a quality of immediacy—of immediate importance—to the Chican@ community as it interacts with an ever-changing American society. The expanded nature of immigration into the United States, not just in terms of numbers but also from an ever-growing list of differing nationalities, not only serves to make the United States expansive in its perspectives and opportunities but also serves to shrink the pool of resources for education, for media attention, for federal dollars, and for living space. The more traditional approach to minority representation is shifting in terms of just whom one is competing with and what one can expect for one's efforts. As Haya El Nasser's article points out, "Hispanics . . . are projected to become the majority in California by 2040." How does a perception of culture change when one shifts from a minority to the majority? It is to these shifting borders of cultural representation and opportunities that this text directs its focus.

Because the topics are broad, we have broken down the general topic into smaller issues and chosen works that specifically address the areas that are of interest as well as articles that are excellent models for discovery. We have included three levels of questions at the end of each article:

- those that check for basic understanding of the article,
- those that ask students to use higher level thinking and reading skills to analyze each article,
- those that provide a broad topic for further investigation and/or personal response.

At the end of each chapter, we have provided additional topics for analysis and research. We have also taken the liberty of italicizing all Spanish words in all articles, whether the author did or not, and we have provided a Spanish–English glossary for both words and phrases/sentences. We hope that this text will pique the curiosity of readers and encourage them not only to continue reading and writing about these topics but also to raise their voices in these conversations and in others.

In reviewing the articles themselves, our readers will find that we have attempted to give our audience a wide variety of formats in terms of genres and topics from which to choose. From interviews and personal narratives involving life experiences to essays dealing with scientific facts regarding health, *Chican@s in the Conversations* offers a wide variety of voices speaking in a multitude of forms. We invite our readers to get comfortable and to join in the conversations.

ACKNOWLEDGMENTS

We are grateful to the following people who have helped us make this book what it is: Longman English Specialist Andrew Draa, whose insight into the need for a book of this nature and help in encouraging others to see the need, too, were invaluable; our editors at Longman, Lynn Huddon and Ginny Blanford; and the reviewers whose feedback helped shape the book's development, including Damian Baca, Michigan State University; Liz Ann Báez Aguilar, San Antonio College; Yvette Benavidos, Our Lady of the Lake University; Judith Broome, Austin Peay State University; Luis A. Contreras, Fresno City College; Vincent Piro Merced College; Cecilia Rodríguez Milanés, University of Central Florida; and Timothy J. Viator, Rowan University.

In closing, we have chosen to dedicate this text not to family or friends, or to colleagues or assistants, but to Gloria Anzaldúa who expanded the vision of so many and who helped us rethink our space in this world. At times the border space that Gloria described for all is a rather uncomfortable place to be in, a space filled with many of our old views and ways of thinking that keep poking us in the foot as we walk around, and we long for the quiet, soft comfort of complacency. Leave it to Gloria to shake things up! She is sorely missed, and her border space is now a little bit lonelier without her.

Elizabeth Rodriguez Kessler, Ph.D.
University of Houston

Anne Perrin, Ph.D.
University of Houston

Identity

Identity: is it static or dynamic? The issue of who we are ethnically seems to be pretty consistent to each of us. However, this is a conversation that has been in progress for decades. If you have ever had to self-identify your nationality/ethnicity on a job or college application and did not see the exact, correct category, you might have had some problems selecting the "right" box. You might be American with Mexican, African, and Chinese heritage. Which box did you mark? Which "identity" did you claim?

The articles in this chapter examine identity from various perspectives: family, gender, sexuality, politics, and ethnicity. All aspects subvert the claim that there is a simple answer to the question, for identity is complex in any of these areas, and adding the Mexican American culture as part of an identity also adds a new layer of requirements for behavior. In other words, being a woman or a man of Mexican heritage does not mean the same thing as being one of African or Asian descent. And being a woman or man of Mexican heritage does not ensure that the individual feels comfortable adhering to some of the traditional values and customs that are commonly practiced.

Before you begin reading the articles, take a private moment to self-identify, exploring what you believe about yourself, who you are in relation to others around you, who you want to become, and how satisfied you are with the person you are now. If you begin to question what you have always believed or if you feel uncomfortable, that is all right. It means you are now seriously examining many things that you have probably taken for granted. This is not a betrayal; it's an exploration. And when you finish, you might find that you return to where you began, accepting what you initially believed. Now, however, it will be because you have analyzed, considered, questioned, challenged, and chosen it rather than simply accepting it as received identity.

The authors of the articles in this chapter have made that journey, and they will open the conversations in this book with their discoveries about themselves and others. The readings have been grouped in a way that makes readers feel as if the authors are talking among themselves about the material. For example, the first three articles, "We Owe History," "What Is a Hispanic?" and "What's the Problem with 'Hispanic'? Just Ask a 'Latino'" have some common assumptions and conflicts running through them. "'New Urbanism' Embraces Latinos" moves from a global perspective to a more regional one and acts as a transition into the generally cultural articles: "'But Can She Cook?' Family Expectations Weigh Heavily on Latina Students" and "Creating the New Macho Man." The last two articles in the chapter "Family Pictures Shape Memory" and "Changing Names and Making Connections: *¿Cómo te llamas?*" are clearly written from and about personal experiences in identity. Thus, the conversations about identity do more than just question who I am individually; rather, the readings cover a broad range of issues about who I am in a personal, cultural, regional, and global context.

We Owe History

Rodolfo F. Acuña

A founding force in the development of Chicano Studies programs within the United States, Rodolfo F. Acuña strives to address the cultural and political inequities that continue to affect the Mexican American communities in the United States. His works include Occupied America: A History of Chicanos *(1976),* Anything But Mexican: Chicanos in Contemporary Los Angeles *(1996), and* A Community under Siege: A Chronicle of Chicanos East of the Los Angeles River, 1945–1975 *(1984), as well as numerous articles relating to the Chicano community and its day-to-day existence. Acuña currently teaches in the Department of Chicano/a Studies at California State University, Northridge, and remains an activist for the rights of Chican@s in America. Whether in the classroom, at a conference, in newspaper articles, or in books, Acuña's voice is welcomed in the conversations about the state of Chican@s.*

✦

A question often asked of me is, Why do you continue to use the word Chicano when even the *cholos* have stopped using it?

As probative a question is why do we continue to call the field of study of Mexican-origin peoples Chicano Studies, when the demographics of the community has so dramatically changed in the past 20 years? Shouldn't we broaden the term to include other brown people?

The fact that we ask these questions speaks about the complexity of forging a common identity, not only in the United States but in Mexico itself. The truth be told, Mexican origins have continuously changed their identity and even that of the field of study. Generally, it is to meet the fancy of *políticos* or the marketplace. In my opinion, this has worsened our intellectual schizophrenia.

What we call ourselves is important, and it has consequences. The name of the discipline determines the epistemology of the body of knowledge we study. It determines what questions we ask. It determines what we do with that knowledge.

Unfortunately, most of our leaders and politicians do not really think about the implications of their choices. Most of them do not read history, and consequently take the path of least resistance and select the sound bite of the moment. This is unfortunate because history is an important tool in testing our assumptions.

By not defining what we are going to study, we overrely on the deduction process in arriving at answers. This avoids testing popular assumptions, and the deduction reinforces distortions of history.

The term Chicano as we will see was selected as an oppositional term that encourages skepticism of established paradigms and societal inequalities. It questions the general assumption that we have always called Mexicans, Mexicans.

The truth is that Mexicans did not universally call themselves Mexicans for many years after Mexico's independence in 1821. This identity was problematic until the process of state formation was almost completed in the latter half of the nineteenth century. Even then the term was limited to the *mestizos* and *criollos* who controlled Mexico. The indigenous nations remained separate. Even today the Maya, Yaqui, Tarahumara, and other Mexican tribes coexist within the Mexican nation state as nations.

Spanish colonialism gave birth to a national schizophrenia. It imposed not only European but African and Asian blood on the indigenous peoples. It assigned different race and social categories to the various racial mixtures. Privileges flowed to the European, and the darker subjects were less equal. Eventually, colonialism stigmatized *lo indio* and erased the African.

Independence did not eliminate racist practices. Within the process of state building, some Mexicans wanted the new Mexican identity to be European rather than indigenous. They often called themselves Hispano, a term popular in the Southwest and throughout the Americas. The *gente de razón*, the civilized people, spoke Spanish as opposed to the indigenous who spoke their own languages.

The term Hispano persists, and it is still used in New Mexico and in other parts of the conquered territory. The universal identification as Mexicans was slow.

In the United States, the Mexican-origin population increased after 1900. The Mexican Revolution heightened the awareness of the indigenous past of Mexicans and many workers identified as Mexicans. U.S. racism framed nationalism among the first generation of Mexicans. Anyone from south of the border was Mexican to most North Americans and it didn't matter what they called themselves.

With the rise of the second and third generations of Mexicans and the formation of a small middle class, the identity puzzle entered another phase. The utility of identifying themselves as anything but Mexican was not lost on those wanting upward social and economic mobility.

After World War I, organizations with hyphenated names became more common, that is, Latin-American and Spanish-American. Unlike the *mutualistas,* mutual aid societies, and other U.S. Mexican organizations, the names of these new organizations were in English and demanded citizenship.

During the 1930s, a minority began to use the term Mexican-American. This term seems to have been the most popular among younger activists in California. It gained popularity after World War II. Generally, however, second-generation Mexican Americans continued to use just Mexican.

Race always played a role within the identity puzzle. Throughout the 1930s, organizations such as the League of United Latin American Citizens campaigned to pass legislation that designated Mexicans as Caucasian. They believed that the Treaty of Guadalupe Hidalgo gave them that right. Further, in the United States white has always been right. Many Mexican Americans believed that World War II gave them the right to be Caucasian.

The term Mexican-American with a hyphen crept into use in California and Arizona, for example, the Mexican-American Movement (1930s), *la asociacion mexico-americana* (*anma*) (1950s), and the Mexican-American Political Association (1959). Attempts in the aftermath of the Viva Kennedy presidential campaign of 1960 to organize a national Mexican-American organization failed.

Texans and New Mexicans refused to embrace the Mexican-American identity, forming instead the Political Association of Spanish-speaking Organizations (PASO). Although they called themselves Mexicans privately, they rejected the word Mexican publicly. Even with a hyphen, it seemed to compromise their Americanism as well as their right to be white.

The identity debate took on a new proportion during the 1960s when Mexican-Americans with a hyphen became Mexican Americans without a hyphen. This was a subtle change where Mexican became part of the noun, a coequal with American. A critical core of activists made it clear that they no longer wanted assimilation, which the hyphen symbolized. They, in other words, were Mexican and, unlike the European immigrant, would retain that identity.

By the end of the decade, Mexican American youth dominated the activist space. Youth manufactured movement symbols trying to motivate the community to action. Their struggles toward self-identity expressed themselves in the adoption of the term Chicano, which most of the older generation rejected.

The term Chicano by some calculations went as far back as the turn of the century. For some it meant *plebe* (plebeian), lower class—poor Mexican workers. For others, the word came from chicanery, meaning deceitful and immoral. For youth, Chicano symbolized the essence of being in college, which was to uplift and even transform the community.

The adoption of the word Chicano came at the Chicano Youth Conference in Denver in 1969. We applied it to the new Mexican American Studies program that same spring at Santa Barbara. I voted against its adoption because I felt Mexican American without a hyphen more fully expressed my identity. Putting Mexican in the face of the older *Tejano* and New Mexican activists and, more important, in front of the Euroamerican was essential to the process of liberation.

In Texas, youth had already made a break, with the formation of the Mexican American Youth Organization. However, when Chicano became our identity, I vowed to abide by the choice and respect the wishes of the majority. Even more important, for the sake of stability and the sake of forging a community, making a commitment to one identity was imperative.

Almost immediately, the private and public sectors led the assault on the new Chicano identity. There are varied reasons for the inability of the term Chicano to achieve hegemony. As mentioned, it had political baggage among older Mexicans. Certainly the government conspired to lump all Spanish-speaking groups under a common umbrella at the expense of Chicanos.

Although Mexican Americans comprised a growing market, it was even larger if it included all the other groups. Just as important, the private sector tended to look at everything in terms of the marketplace. For Mexican American *políticos* and business leaders, creating the illusion of a voting block rivaling that of African Americans became an obsession. For them it meant power.

The identity of choice of the 1970s was the word Hispanic, an identity that the media readily adopted, and frankly a word lacking epistemological skepticism.[1] The term was appealing to the new and larger middle class. The student militancy of the 1960s had created a space for Chicanos on the university campuses. However, most Mexican-American students did not participate in the student movement of the times. They did not have the benefit of Chicano studies and did not know the history of the changing identities, much less the significance of the word Chicano. Words such as liberation, and pretensions to the land had little meaning for them.

In all honesty, Chicano nationalists and leftists also functioned as cliques, alienating many of Mexican-American (with a hyphen) students. The word Hispanic allowed these students to feel part of the hype, without having to think or be committed to anything. Because of the lack of skepticism, few recognized the racial overtones of the word Hispanic and its throwback to the Hispano era.

The evolution of Latino is more complex. On one hand it was an attempt to unite those of Latin American origin under one umbrella. In San Francisco's Mission District and Oakland, where there were many Central Americans and Puerto Ricans, activists often used *la raza* and sometimes Latino, with varying success. There were tensions, and some Latinos accused Mexican Americans and later Chicanos of being nationalists when they were reluctant to shed their identity.

On the other hand, the adoption of Latino was an effort to head off the term Hispanic. There were former student activists in the mainstream media who recognized the contradictions inherent in the word Hispanic. Reporters such as Frank del Olmo of the *Los Angeles Times* influenced that newspaper to adopt "Latino" over Hispanic as a compromise.

Finally, the 1980s increased the pressure to adopt a general term as the migration of Central Americans swelled the *barrios*. Even former Chicano activists working with the Spanish-speaking groups wanted to be inclusive of the newcomers, and they suffered from the awkwardness of separating the disparate nationalities. Calling them all Latinos, they believed, would solve this dilemma.

By the 1990s, the death of the term Chicano was almost complete. A survey by the U.S. Department of Labor in October 1995 found that 57.88 percent of the Latinos surveyed preferred the term Hispanic as the racial or ethnic term that described them. 11.74 percent of them said they preferred Latino, 12.34 preferred "Of Spanish origin," and 7.85 percent (Chicanos were probably included under this category) preferred "Some other term." During this decade, the number of university programs calling themselves exclusively Chicano also declined.

In retrospect, the term Chicano has been kept on life supports by student organizations such as MEChA (*El Movimiento Estudiantil Chicano de Aztlan*) and Chicano nationalists. Marxist organizations such as the League of Revolutionary Struggle, through its analysis of the national question, supported the position that Chicanos comprised a nation, separate from the United States and Mexico. More important, the term has been kept alive by cultural workers. So what went wrong?

Much of the blame must be placed on a small minority of true believers who narrowly defined the word Chicano, often tolerating tendencies that were sexist, homophobic, and jingoists, often anti-Marxist, who excluded other Spanish-speaking groups. The true believers exuded a "Mexico Love It Or Leave It!" mentality. To dissociate themselves from these tendencies, many activists and academicians leaned toward the term Latino.

Although understandable, some of this distancing was disingenuous. Academicians who were never part of any struggle took the extreme positions of a minority of nationalists and used it as a pretext not to be committed to the process of change caused by the Chicano Movement. In this way, they could avoid any involvement or duty toward existing student or community structures.

Lastly, the Mexican immigrant never accepted the word Chicano and played a role in its demise.

With this said, Why do I continue to use the word Chicano when even the *cholos* have stopped using it? Because it is the term that most expresses what I believe that research is all about. I am not a Hispanic and only use Latino to avoid confusion, especially when dealing with statistics. I feel a special solidarity with Central Americans in their individual particulars. I believe that the Chicano experience and the questions raised by that movement will help them find their own identities and cause unity between themselves and Mexican Americans (without a hyphen). The term Latino, for example, makes them minorities whom the Chicano majority eclipses.

The term Chicano raises skeptical challenges to arguments made by mainstream social scientists. How and what knowledge we excavate is critical to understanding the coherence of Chicano studies as a discipline. For example, it ensures that alternative views of knowledge are presented as dialectical oppositions.

This would not be true if the name was Mexican-American with a hyphen. The name would assume that Chicano history followed in the footsteps of the European immigrant. It would ignore the common bond of colonialism that links indigenous peoples of the Americas. If we let go of the term Chicano, it would legitimatize the litany of identities—Hispano, Mexican, Latin-American, Spanish-American, Mexican-American with a hyphen, Hispanic, and even Latino.

In sum, every Spanish-speaking person in the United States owes a debt to Chicanos and to the history of activists that came before them. It is this civil rights history that has entitled them to equal protection. It is why they are in college.

Endnote

1. Questioning the meaning or definition.

Joining in the Conversation

1. Acuña provides his readers with an historical and cultural overview of several key terms used by various communities and governmental agencies to identify, and, thus, define individuals. Review the article for the various terms Acuña refers to and briefly gives a definition of what the terms mean and which part of the population supports its use.
2. Often, the subtle ways one writes out a word can determine a difference in meaning. Consider Acuña's argument regarding the use of the hyphen in the term "Mexican-American" versus removing the punctuation and only using "Mexican American." For Acuña, the hyphen is closely connected to the issue of "Americanism" for the individual. Do you agree? Defend your answer, giving specific examples to illustrate your points.
3. The United States is a country of multiple nationalities. Acuña addresses the Mexican-American community, yet he brings out issues that many other people from different nationalities would relate to, such as Asians, French, and Australian. Interview four individuals from one country not discussed in

Acuña's article and find out if there is a disagreement as to "name" and identity for those individuals as there is for the Mexican-American community. When your research is finished, list the similarities and differences between the ideas in Acuña's article and your interviewees and present them to the class.

What Is a Hispanic?

RICHARD RODRIGUEZ

Richard Rodriguez is an award-winning author, an editor for the Pacific News Service in San Francisco, an essayist for the MacNeil/ Lehrer News Hour, and a contributing editor for Harper's Magazine, U.S. News & World Report, *and the Sunday "Opinion" page of the* Los Angeles Times. *His most well-known book,* Hunger of Memory: The Education of Richard Rodriguez *(1982) received several awards, including the Gold Medal for Non-Fiction from the Commonwealth Club of California, the Christopher Prize for Autobiography, and the Anisfeld-Wolf Prize for Civil Rights from the Cleveland Foundation. He has also written two other autobiographical books:* Days of Obligation: An Argument with My Mexican Father *(1992) and* Brown: The Last Discovery of America *(2002). Always a controversial figure, Rodriguez has never ceased to join in the conversations about education, Affirmative Action, religion, sexuality, or other topics of interest. The following article is a revised version of the one published in the Spring/Summer 2000 issue of* Texas Journal: Ideas, History, and Culture. *Rodriguez adds his definition of identity, talks about what it means to be Hispanic, and updates many facts included in the original.*

✦

Source: "What Is a Hispanic?" by Richard Rodriguez. Copyright © 2000 by Richard Rodriguez. Adapted from a lecture given at the Institute for the Humanities in Salado. Originally appeared in the *Texas Journal of Ideas, History and Culture* (Spring/Summer 2000). Reprinted by permission of Georges Borchardt, Inc., on behalf of the author.

I remember when I was a boy—the young son of immigrants, of parents from Mexico—becoming an American. Very early I sensed, even before I knew English, that America was insinuating itself into my life, transforming me into an American kid.

A convertible passes on the street with music blasting. Elvis Presley is singing. Even though the boy does not know the singer's name, Elvis Presley goes into the boy's ear and lodges there with his cape and his shiny electric guitar. And there is no way for the boy to get him out.

Nowadays people ask me: "When did you decide to become so Americanized?" Or my critics sneer: "How could you give up your (Hispanic) culture?" But culture is not a thing, like a jacket that you take off on a hot summer day. Culture is not a suitcase you forget at the airport. Culture is something you breathe and it comes to you through your five senses—in the thump of hip-hop, for example, or the metallic smell of fast-food, or the impatient pace of traffic.

Growing up in America, I knew that I was not Mexican, as my parents were still Mexican. I was not "losing" my culture, as my mother often complained. I was growing up in Sacramento, California. My culture was Walt Disney and Martin Luther King, Jr.

Recently I was interviewed on a British radio program. The woman introduced me to her listeners as a man who is "in favor" of assimilation. And I thought to myself: that is not quite right. I am not in favor of assimilation any more than I am in favor of the Pacific Ocean or the wild flowers of Texas.

If I had a bumper sticker that summarized my opinion, it would read simply: ASSIMILATION HAPPENS.

I like the metaphor of the melting pot—the American melting pot—because of its suggestion of violence. As in a fairy tale, the child stumbles and falls into the bubbling brew. His soul is charred. The child emerges from the pot radically changed, as if by alchemy. The child ends up with a voice different from his parents, taller, and with an American disrespect toward anything that is old-fashioned.

Our immigrant parents—wherever they come from—are always pro-choice. They leave the past behind in search of a changed future. They choose to leave Mexico. They choose to leave China.

Our immigrant parents think that we, their children, can be similarly pro-choice and choose to leave America, or to moderate America's influence on our souls. They complain about how Americanized we, their children, are becoming. They didn't come here, they say, in order to raise American teenagers. But what do our parents expect? Do they expect their daughters and sons to grow up Peruvian or Vietnamese when we live in Dallas, Texas?

There are difficult, painful stories in America that come with assimilation. I keep remembering the silence that filled our immigrant home. There is no silence anywhere in America like the silence at home, when parents speak one way and their children are being schooled to speak another.

* * *

Though they neighbor each other, Mexico and America are starkly different countries. In Mexico (as in many other nations) the most important pronoun is the first-person plural pronoun, "We" (*nosotros*). The most important We in Mexico is the family. By contrast, America is a country where parents raise their children to leave home. (I remember in school, my teachers gave me a book about a kid named Huck Finn who took off one night on a raft on the Mississippi River with a runaway slave. It's an American classic, my teacher said.)

The pronoun that America trusts is the first-person singular pronoun, the "I." I think. I want. I believe. When I grow up, I am going to be . . .

The American I: No country in the world has given itself so fully to individualism as America. The reason Americans are so creative, so inventive is because of our I. Americans discard anything that seems old-tradition, the warnings of elders, an appliance that is two-years old. Americans are constantly throwing things away, moving on.

The price we pay for our clutch on the American I is loneliness. I sometimes think there is no country more lonely than America. I think loneliness is our great burden and neurosis, but also our grandeur. Our heroes, after all, are people who can stare [sic] loneliness or the rock star.

The allure of the American I prompts us to glorify the idiotic celebrity, checking in and out of rehab. We idolize the self-made billionaire. We honor youth and disrespect Homer Simpson, "the old man." The old man is a fool. It is the responsibility of every new generation to make its own way, even to remake the language, for example.

So how could I reconcile them? I would call myself a "Mexican American," when people asked. But in truth there was no easy way to balance the two national pronouns—"I" and "*nosotros*." Because I lived north of the border, I was governed by one and haunted by the other.

And yet, as much as I became a man of the United States, Latin America left its mark on me. Literally, Mexico marked my brown face.

The United States is a country where people see themselves distinct from each other. Mark your race in the box: White, Black, Asian, Hispanic. Latin America is much more aware of mixture. The architecture, religion, art, the food of Latin America results from a blended recipe of Europeans, Arabs, Asians, Africans, and the Indian—very hot, indeed.

The curious thing, the wonderful thing about Mexico, for example, is that Mexico speaks openly of its bastard birth. Insofar as I am related to Mexico, I trace my birth back to the sixteenth century, to the "rape" of the Indian by the Spaniard. My great-great-great grandfather was a hairy Spaniard. My great-great-great grandmother was a smooth Indian.

However the Indian and the Spaniard met, whether, in fact, one seduced the other or raped the other or romanced the other, I will never know for certain. What I see in my family, all these centuries later, is clear evidence of races meeting. I have a brother who looks Spanish. I have two sisters—one looks Polynesian, the other Italian. I have a father who looks French. I have a mother who looks Indian.

Every morning when I look in the mirror, I realize that—no matter how much I am an American I—the We of Mexico has left its mark on my face. I am *mestizo*.

* * *

In 1971, President Richard Nixon looked out the White House window and saw that America was changing. Changing immigration laws had transformed America into a global society. The old black and white description of America was no longer apt. So Nixon asked government bureaucrats to come up with a new scheme for describing America.

After a year spent in dreary federal offices under fluorescent lamps, rummaging through phone books, the bureaucrats came back with the notion that an American could be one of five options. These five have become the major categories we now use in bureaucratic transactions and in self-descriptions: First, whites. Next, blacks. Next, Asians, which includes "Pacific Islanders." Next, American Indians, which includes Eskimos. Finally, Hispanics.

According to government surveys, there are nearly 40 million Hispanics in the United States—I read that somewhere. I am, I suppose, one of these million, I mark "Hispanic," insofar as I am related to Latin America.

But there is a slight problem in saying that I am Hispanic because of my tie to Latin America. People in Latin America do not speak of themselves as Hispanic. If you go to Colombia, people there call themselves Colombians. People in Peru call themselves Peruvians. It is only in the United States that people speak of being Hispanic. In other words, the next time you hear someone call herself Hispanic, it means that she lives in America, not in Latin America.

Hispanic or Latino? A lot of the energy we should spend on real issues—like getting streetlights near bus-stops and better health care and reducing high-school dropout rates—we spend arguing about which word to use to describe ourselves.

The politically correct will tell you that "Hispanic" is too colonial a word because it gives too much of our identity to Spain. Hated Spain. Father Spain. Colonial Spain. These are the same people, by the way, who cling to the Spanish language, the same people who will tell you that the word "Latino" is preferable to Hispanic (the English word).

I say: Where do you think the word Latino comes from? It refers to southern Europe.

They say that I am a "coconut"—white on the inside, brown on the outside. They say I am a "self-hating" Mexican.

There are times when I tell people I am Chinese, just to be done with all the argument about whether or not I am Hispanic or Latino or Chicano or Mexican American.

Soy Chino, I say. I wish I knew how to say it in Mandarin.

* * *

What makes you an American is the land—a remarkable notion. If you are born on American soil, you become an American. And yet, America is also a country obsessed with blood. For a long time you were not fully an American if you had the wrong kind of blood. I refer to the tragic division between White Blood and Black Blood. In white-and-black America you could only be one or the other. The racist had come up with something called the "one-drop" theory. If you had one drop of African blood, you were "black," no matter how light your skin or straight your hair. Slave owners used this logic to keep people enslaved. To this day, even many of the liberal-hearted can't quite overcome this old American prejudice; they call Barack Obama "black," even though his mother was white.

Because we are a nation preoccupied by blood, the common assumption now is that Hispanics have brown blood. In fact, however, there is no such thing as a Hispanic race. Though you often will see Hispanics perched on government surveys between White and Black, we are not a racial group.

Latin America, like North America, is home to every race of the world. So Hispanics come in all colors and shades. We are blond. We are black. We look like the Indians in the cowboy movies. We are Japanese. We are Lebanese. And many of us are, like me, mixed.

In college, I first read a government prediction that Hispanics were destined "to replace" African Americans as America's largest minority group. The prediction was absolute nonsense since Hispanics are an ethnic group (clustered by culture) and African Americans constitute a racial group (organized by a supposed blood link). To compare one to the other is not linguistically possible.

And what's more: many of us who call ourselves Hispanic are also black or carry some measure of African blood. After all, Africans have lived in Latin America at least as long as Europeans.

So the next time you hear it said that Hispanics "outnumber" blacks, you might remember the more interesting thing about Hispanics in the United States is that we—most of us—are of mixed blood. For example, the majority of Mexicans, which is to say seventy percent of the entire Hispanic population, is *mestizo*, a mix of Indian and European.

Growing up, I was so familiar with the variety of cultures and races in my own family that I took it for granted. My Mexican aunt married a man—my favorite uncle—from India. My father was employed making false teeth for Chinese dentists. I was taught by Irish immigrant women, Catholic nuns; it was the Irish, in fact, who taught me English. India, China, Ireland—these countries had a share in my American life.

In those growing-up years I was also obsessed with African Americans. On our small black-and-white television, every night on the news, I could watch the "Negro Civil Rights movement"—men and women, determined to live free, marching through segregated towns in the South—Selma, Little Rock, Birmingham—singing "We Shall Overcome." I was so moved by the determination and bravery of the procession. I recognized that the story of the African in America was the central story that described the meaning of America. Their story defined mine.

But now there is a terrible Hispanic-black struggle across America, particularly at the bottom, for the lowest-paying jobs, and the cheapest apartments. Hispanics, the newcomers, want "in." African Americans want to protect what they have so long, and so bravely, struggled to hold.

In Los Angeles, the largest Latin American city in the United States, the great black neighborhoods are becoming Hispanic. Compton. South Central. Watts. It's one group against the other—the American way. So who bothers to say: What happens to a single Hispanic child also happens to a black child. One group cannot truly advance without the other advancing.

If we Hispanics forget this, and allow ourselves to make our way in America by separating ourselves from African Americans, as other immigrant groups have done for the last two centuries, we will lose our souls.

* * *

Elvis Presley went into my ear. Many years later, I learned that Elvis Presley had been deeply influenced in his singing by the black blues singer, B.B. King. Lives intersect in America. That's the truth of it. People influence one another. We end up overhearing each other's music. We end up using each other's slang. The burrito becomes as American as pizza.

I hear lots of Americans, these days, complaining about how Latinized the United States is becoming. There is suddenly so much Spanish heard and seen everywhere. California's Governor Arnold Schwarzenegger recently urged Hispanic teenagers to turn off Spanish-language television and learn English. Good advice, I thought. Though the most famous line from any Schwarzenegger movie was a hybrid: "*Hasta la vista,* baby."

Here is a great irony of our immigrant nation. The children of immigrant parents grow up haunted by how much America changes them and makes them unlike their parents. At the same time, America is constantly being changed by the immigrants who are changed by America. Native-born Americans are haunted by how much of the culture they knew as children has changed.

So one changes the other. Assimilation is reciprocal, though never equally. (The advantage goes to the older, the more settled, the wealthier.) Nonetheless, even while I was becoming Americanized, families like mine were Latinizing America.

One example: Traditionally, America has been an east-west country. We begin our history books on the east coast, with the Thirteen Original Colonies, with Pocohontas. We begin with Plymouth Rock and a group of Pilgrims dressed like Indians, throwing tea into Boston Harbor. Then the U.S. history book moves across the Great Plains, fulfilling Manifest Destiny—following the traditional narrative line all the way to the Pacific coast.

Today, however, there are 40 million Hispanics who live in the United States and speak of this country as "*el norte*." They (we) are forcing America to recognize itself as a north–south country, existing within the Americas—something we don't like to do. Suddenly, Americans are worried about our northern and southern borders, because of terrorism, because of the illegal flow of workers from Latin America, but also because America always saw itself distinct from the Americas.

America builds a wall against the peasants of Latin America. We wish that the Mexicans would stop illegally coming across. But at the very same time we are hungry for a burrito. It will make us gain weight. We will regret the burrito in the morning. But why, oh why, this yearning to burn our heart with *salsa picante*?

Joining in the Conversation

1. Rodriguez elaborates in his article on the subtle ways in which one becomes "Americanized" throughout his or her life. Review the article and then in a short paragraph describe Rodriguez's example of the process of Americanization and give two examples of your own. Also address Rodriguez's explanation of Huck Finn.
2. Rodriguez approaches the topics of cultural and racial interaction from a personal, first-person perspective shown through his use of the "I" when discussing his own personal experiences. But his argument often subtly shifts to the plural "we," thereby drawing in the reader almost as a coauthor of the text. Look at the article again to determine what areas or points Rodriguez chooses to consider from the singular "I" and which from the plural "we." Then determine for yourself what his strategy was in structuring his argument as such and how effective such a shift in point of view is. Compare your views with those of the others in the class. Finally, based on the article, answer the question, "What is a Hispanic?"
3. As with any of life's experiences, different generations view processes such as immigration and cultural identification in varying perspectives. When the issue of varying national cultures is considered, the views and lifestyles of generations becomes even more complex. Consider Rodriguez's own cultural complexities as Hispanic and American, for example, the "American I" and the "*mestizo*" origins of Latin America, and then consider your own cultural and national views. Which culture(s) do you identify with, in comparison of those of your parents or guardians?

What's the Problem with "Hispanic"? Just Ask a "Latino"

DAVID GONZALEZ

David Gonzalez is a well-established writer for The New York Times, *writing from the Metropolitan as well as the National Desk. His articles usually involve immigration, city crime, and health and living conditions of the poor. He wrote the following article for the November 15, 1992 issue of* The New York Times.

✦

HISPANIC Heritage Month ended recently. But someday—if some "Hispanics" are to be made happy—it may be Latino Heritage Month. Or perhaps Colombian-Dominican-Cuban-Mexican-Puerto Rican-and-Other Heritage Month.

The month dedicated to celebrating the contributions of those nationalities to the United States—and coinciding with the anniversary of Columbus's voyage—sparked anew the debate about just what to call the 22.4 million American residents who said they were of "Spanish/Hispanic Origin" on the 1990 Census.

Some feel the Census Bureau imposed the word "Hispanic," and prefer "Latino." Younger people in some cities, especially, find Hispanic archaic, if not downright offensive, much as "Negro" displeased a previous generation of blacks or African-Americans. They say it recalls the colonization by Spain and Portugal and ignores the Indian and African roots of many people it describes. Yet others, including business and political leaders, dismiss "Latino" as a fad. Still others use the terms Hispanic and Latino interchangeably.

Among those who grew up hearing "Latino" or "Latina" used often in their neighborhoods and homes, especially in the Southwest, it rolls off the tongue with a Spanish tinge (lah-TEEN-oh), its very pronunciation an affirmation of identity. By comparison, the word closest to Hispanic that exists in the Spanish language is *hispano* (ees-PAN-oh), or Spanish-speaker, its initial consonant silent in current Spanish pronunciation.

Source: David Gonzalez, "What's the Problem with 'Hispanic'? Just Ask a 'Latino'," *New York Times*, November 15, 1992, p. A6.

"To say Latino is to say you come to my culture in a manner of respect," said Sandra Cisneros, the author of *Woman Hollering Creek: And Other Stories,* who refuses to have her writings included in any anthology that uses the word Hispanic. "To say Hispanic means you're so colonized you don't even know for yourself or someone who named you never bothered to ask what you call yourself. It's a repulsive slave name."

Not so, insists Enrique Fernandez, the editor of *Mas,* a Spanish language entertainment magazine. In fact, he says, Latino taken to its roots refers to "an even older empire. That's the one that took over Spain." What, he asks, does Latino have to do with "Hispanics, Africans and native Americans"?

Ana Celia Zentella, a linguistics professor at the Graduate Center of the City University of New York, traced the origins of the word Hispanic to *"Hispania,"* a Phoenician word for "land of rabbits" that was used by the Romans during their conquest of the area that includes modern-day Spain. She uses Latino among others like herself, and Hispanic on grant proposals, but has found a growing push for Latino, which sometimes, she says, smacks of political correctness.

"Language is a smokescreen for other fundamental underlying problems," she said. Wave away the smoke and there remains, in her view, an issue at once simple and complex. And, yes, political. Ms. Cisneros, who grew up in Chicago using the word Latino at home, says the choice of words is a rapid sign of "what side of the line" a person stands on. In this analysis, "Hispanic" connotes social striving, a desire to be accepted at any cost, even by using an "English" word.

For Ricardo Salinas, a member of the comedy theater troupe Culture Clash, the argument over terminology is fodder for a skit in which an Americanized Hispanic picks a fight with a "Latino" by calling him an Hispanic. "It's the ultimate assimilation, with that word," he said.

According to Jorge del Pinal, the chief of ethnic and Hispanic statistics at the Bureau of the Census, the bureau began grappling during the 1970s with how best to describe the diverse groups which had been called "Spanish-speaking" or "Spanish-surnamed."

"Not all the people we considered Hispanic spoke Spanish," Mr. del Pinal said. "Not everybody had a Spanish surname." As a result, he said, the final category came to be designated "Spanish/Hispanic Origin," preferably used in tandem. "It was just really a way to come up with a term to fit this amorphous group," he said. "It really came right out of the dictionary."

Herman Badillo, at the time a Congressman from New York—and a founding member of the Congressional Hispanic Caucus—said the move was cheered among the nation's various Hispanic communities, who stood to gain more political representation and government services as a result of the designation.

Raul Yzaguirre, the president of the National Council of *La Raza*, a national civil rights organization, said he also pressed for "Hispanic." He chafes at the criticisms of those who deride it as politically incorrect. "The last thing in the world I want to do is fight over what we call ourselves," he said. "We really need to get beyond that."

In a recent national survey of Hispanic political attitudes, researchers may have found a key to the issue: Most Hispanics/Latinos prefer to identify themselves as Puerto Rican, Colombian, Dominican or just plain American.

"The intelligentsia engaged in a political debate that had no resonance among the people," said Rodolfo de la Garza, co-author of the study and a professor in the department of political science and government at the University of Texas at Austin. The larger question suggested by the study was whether a label for the larger group is useful at all in characterizing a population that is not monolithic.

Indeed, in Miami there are bumper stickers that proclaim *"No soy hispano, soy Cubano"* (I am not Hispanic, I am Cuban), a sentiment echoed among other groups loath to see their achievements and struggles vanish in the swirl of the melting pot.

"It's expected in a city of immigrants," said Lisandro Perez, the director of the Cuban Research Center at Florida International University. "They find out they're Hispanic when they get here. The mega-label is widely used in the United States, but people have an identity of where they migrate from."

For years, John Leguizamo, the part-Colombian, part-Puerto Rican writer and actor now starring in his one-man off-Broadway show, "Spic-O-Rama," simply called himself Spanish, a word whose noble connotations glossed over mainstream society's discomfort over the influx of new arrivals.

As someone whose show's title takes a slur and transforms it into the root of a slew of positive words, he does not find "Hispanic" offensive.

"I don't consider it a negative term. Now 'wetback, greasy spic'—*that's* derogatory," he said.

But he prefers Latino, saying its warmer feel unites him with his contemporaries from his Queens childhood who hailed from Puerto Rico, Colombia and the Dominican Republic. "When you're together and in your groove, I don't feel the difference," he said.

If anything, he said, he rejoices and identifies with the successes of his counterparts, whether they be Colombian, Mexican, Cuban or Puerto Rican. "I feel an intense pride well up," he said, revealing his New York roots in a way that is truly pan-ethnic: "I kvell."[1]

Endnote

1. "kvell" is a Yiddish term meaning to show great pride or to boast.

Joining in the Conversation

1. What identities does Gonzalez see as conflicting? What underlying beliefs create the conflict? Does his use of the Yiddish term "kvell" at the end support or detract from his main idea?
2. Identify Gonzalez's thesis. How does Gonzalez employ appeals to emotion to support his argument? Identify one other strategy Gonzalez uses to make him seem credible. Is it effective? Explain.
3. Create a short questionnaire of two to three questions. Interview students and nonstudents about their understanding of the terms "Hispanic" and "Latino" and about which they prefer. After the interview, ask for their ethnicity. Interview at least ten individuals and take your findings to class to discuss.

"New Urbanism" Embraces Latinos

HAYA EL NASSER

Haya El Nasser is an established staff writer for USA Today. *Nasser writes about Latin American issues, urbanization, environmental issues, immigration, and other topics of interest. Also, many of Nasser's articles can be found on the Internet. The following article was published in the February 16, 2005 issue of* USA Today.

✦

Source: Haya El Nasser, "'New Urbanism' Embraces Latinos: Communities Find Cultural Preferences Can Aid Efforts to Limit Sprawl," *USA Today,* February 16, 2005, p. 3A. Reprinted with permission.

COMMUNITIES FIND CULTURAL PREFERENCES CAN AID EFFORTS TO LIMIT SPRAWL

This is a slice of Orange County you won't see on TV's *The OC*. Bridal shops and corner grocery stores. Families strolling downtown. Workers walking to lunch. Store signs in Spanish next to the ubiquitous Starbucks shops. Street vendors. Professionals living in artists' lofts a block from Main Street.

Amid a suburban county's gated communities, three-car garages and megamalls, Santa Ana is a fledgling hub of "new urbanism," an increasingly popular antidote to sprawl that promotes dense, walkable neighborhoods where people live, work and play.

But it's new urbanism with a twist: Latino new urbanism.

Advocates of this budding movement suggest that places where Hispanics are fast becoming the majority could help rein in sprawl by capitalizing on Latino cultural preferences for compact neighborhoods, large public places and a sense of community.

"I grew up in Mexico. We had a traditional urban square and plaza where everything is happening," says Mario Chavez-Marquez, 31, who lives in one of downtown Santa Ana's new loft apartments. "To me, it made sense to move back to the center, closer to my job. Now I can walk to a supermarket."

Builders and planners have largely ignored the cultural identity of this new wave of home buyers, says planner Michael Mendez, who coined the term "Latino new urbanism."

As a result, many Hispanics moving up the economic ladder choose typical suburbs far from work, mass transit and shopping because it's usually the only path to home ownership, Mendez says. "They have to assimilate into what's available."

Hispanics are the largest minority in the USA and are projected to become the majority in California by 2040. How and where they live will shape neighborhoods, cities and suburbs for generations.

California expects to gain 21 million people from 2000 to 2050—18 million of them Hispanic. Housing the booming population without putting more stress on land and water resources and a congested highway system is a big challenge. The nation as a whole faces similar demands: The Census Bureau projects the U.S. population growing 49% to 420 million by 2050.

Latino new urbanism is taking hold in California and Texas, the nation's two most populous states and the ones with the largest numbers of Hispanics. And it's starting to garner national attention among growth-control advocates and developers eager to tap the Hispanic housing market. The National Association of Home Builders, for example, plans to publish a book on designing for the Latino market.

Almost a third of California homebuyers had Hispanic surnames in June 2004, according to DataQuick information Systems. That's up from less than a fifth in 2002. The top surnames of buyers: Garcia, Hernandez, Lopez and Rodriguez.

Latinos are comfortable living near stores and businesses and riding buses and trains, says Katherine Perez, executive director of the Transportation and Land Use Collaborative of Southern California.

"There is a natural group of folks ready to embrace these ideas," she says. "(But) what happens to the Latino that has 'assimilated' and moves into the single-family, detached home in the suburbs with the SUV in the driveway? What does that mean in air quality, land consumption and pure economics?"

Latinos already are reshaping old urban neighborhoods. In East Los Angeles, Mexican-Americans live in small wooden houses that were built more than 50 years ago by Anglos. They've added paint and stucco, put in large front porches, fountains and wrought iron, and turned neighborhood parks into the main social place outside the home.

In most communities, zoning and building codes prevent such ethnic touches. Now developers and civic leaders are trying to create these neighborhoods from scratch:

- San Diego approved five "Pilot Villages" last year. One of them, *Mi Pueblo* in San Ysidro near the Mexican border, is pure Latino new urbanism. Facades of new homes are vibrant red, blue, yellow and green. *Mi Pueblo* eventually will have 1,143 residential units, about a quarter of them moderately priced. Three-bedroom, two-bath homes built so far are selling for $270,000, about half the local median price.
- San Fernando, a small Los Angeles suburb that is 90% Hispanic, is working to attract housing, retail and services so residents don't have to go to Pasadena or Glendale for shopping and entertainment.
- There are plans for a mall and apartments, homes and condos downtown. About 15% of new housing will sell below the city's single-family home median price of $367,000 ($295,000 for condos).

Latino new urbanism has gotten the attention of Henry Cisneros, former secretary of Housing and Urban Development and now the chairman of American CityVista in San Antonio. The company develops homes in city neighborhoods that haven't seen new housing in decades. Moderately priced developments in Austin and San Antonio are built near established Latino communities.

Cisneros advocates designs that fit the needs of Hispanic families—from big kitchens with gas stoves for grilling tortillas to courtyards for social gatherings, multiple bedrooms for large and extended families, and driveways that accommodate numerous cars.

So far, new urbanism has chiefly targeted white and higher-income populations in suburbs, he says.

"I think Latinos can be the ideal audience for a new urbanist conversation," Cisneros says.

Developments tailored to such lifestyles account for only 5–10% of new construction, says Pasadena architect Stefanos Polyzoides, co-founder of the Congress for New Urbanism, a non-profit group.

Differences in what Hispanics, blacks, whites or Asians want are subtle, says Gopal Ahluwalia, who tracks buyers' preferences for the home builders group. "I have my doubts about this Latino new urbanism thing," he says. "It's more socioeconomics and demographics that drive this marketplace than ethnicity and race."

Santa Ana, whose population of 342,510 is about 80% Hispanic, embraced Latino new urbanism before there was even a name for it.

In the early 1990s, Santa Ana's downtown was dying. People came because they either worked in the county government center or had to serve on a jury.

Then Hispanic immigrants arrived in large numbers. But many left as soon as they could afford to, City Councilman Mike Garcia says. Now the city is trying to keep them. It refurbished historic facades, built brick sidewalks with benches and replaced a methadone clinic and bus depot with artists' lofts.

Mario Chavez-Marquez and his wife, Karyn Mendoza, 29, were lured by the changes. He works as a planner for the city of Irvine, a 10-minute drive from Santa Ana. Mendoza, who grew up in a mostly white suburb of Chicago, walks two blocks to her job as a social worker for a non-profit organization. They also exhibit works by Latino artists in their diseno ART Gallery, on the street level of the loft they own.

"Who's to say Latino new urbanism should be just for Latinos?" says Dowell Myers, a demographer at the University of Southern California. "Maybe it's a general model for the whole region."

Joining in the Conversation

1. Haya El Nasser distinguishes between the identities of Latinos who are part of the "new urbanism" and those who move to the suburbs. Explain the differences pointed out in the article. What is the difference between "new" Latino urbanism and old Latino *barrios*?
2. Is the development of new Latino urban spaces a way to accommodate the rapidly rising Latino population or a way to encourage segregation? Select a position and support it from the article.
3. Investigate the demographics of your downtown area and your suburbs. If you have a rural area around your town, include demographics for it as well. How are the different ethnic groups distributed? What conclusions can you draw? Create a chart to display your findings. Be sure to use various ways to represent the statistics. How could this information be used by the following: Realtors? Commercial developers? School districts? City planners? Grocery stores, small businesses, and fast food establishments?

"But Can She Cook?" Family Expectations Weigh Heavily on Latina Students

Ines Pinto Alicea

Ines Pinto Alicea has been writing for The Hispanic Outlook in Higher Education *since 1994, concentrating on politics in her "Outlook on Washington" column, and on education, especially the education of Latinos. She wrote the following article for the February 26, 2001 issue of* The Hispanic Outlook in Higher Education.

✦

Rebekah Rosas remembers family members telling her when she was ready to enter college that she should work on finding a good man who was rich and who could take care of her.

"I told them I didn't need that because I could take care of myself," said the sophomore from Bryn Mawr College, in Bryn Mawr, PA.

Dr. Lois Méndez-Catlin, assistant dean of the undergraduate dean's office, said Rosas' experience with gender expectations is encountered by many college-bound Latinas. In her study of Latina students at the private, predominantly white Bryn Mawr and at a public Hispanic Serving Institution, New Mexico Highlands University (NMHU) in Las Vegas, New Mexico, Méndez-Catlin found that while family members encouraged the Latinas to pursue their higher education dreams, often the young women were expected to assume the role of homemaker or family caretaker after graduation, even while pursuing a career.

The mothers weren't telling their daughters that their degrees were useless, but they were saying that in addition to having a job and a career, you still have to take on the traditional roles, said Méndez-Catlin. "You can't give up anything. It means taking on more work." Even though the Latino community is getting more educated, it is still of the mindset, she said, that women take care of the household. The Latina women's rights movement, she said, has not progressed as much as that of white women.

Méndez-Catlin's study, "Are We There Yet? The Impact of Higher Education on Hispanic Gender Roles," showed that while Hispanic females have made great strides in participating in higher education and in receiving baccalaureate degrees, "the basic assumptions of the Hispanic culture about the male's dominant role are very strong and a dominant force in women's educational experiences."

"Latinas feel a lot of pressure from a lot of places," said Rosas. "When we feel we did badly, it's multiplied. We carry a lot. Latinas are always told, 'You still have this and this to do.'"

The study was based on the responses of 318 undergraduate NMHU students and 16 Bryn Mawr students who answered a self-administered questionnaire and participated in focus groups. Students on both campuses shared some similarities—both groups had GPAs of 3.0 or higher, about half of each group's mothers had earned bachelor's degrees, most in each group attended full time, and both schools suffered from a lack of Latina role models in upper-level positions. There were differences, too.

At New Mexico, only seven percent of the respondents' mothers had earned a graduate or professional degree compared to 13 percent of their fathers. At Bryn Mawr, an equal number had earned a graduate or professional degree. Half the PA. mothers held professional positions compared to seven percent at NMHU. At Bryn Mawr only 20 percent of the mothers were homemakers compared to 40 percent at NMHU, said Méndez-Catlin.

"The NMHU Latinas expressed concern about the usefulness of their degree while the Bryn Mawr women felt no restraints: 100 percent of them had plans for graduate or professional school," said Méndez-Catlin. The New Mexico girls, she said, were encouraged to go to college but then had to return home and eventually assume the traditional role of wife, mother, and homemaker. "The degree was a fail-safe device in case her future husband lost his job or left the family."

Still, Méndez-Catlin said, the Pa. women did note that there are distinct gender roles.

The Bryn Mawr women reported that some of their mothers, though pursuing nontraditional gender roles and encouraging their daughters to do the same, "still catered to the notion of the woman as ensuring that the family and the men were comfortable and satisfied," wrote Méndez-Catlin in the study.

Méndez-Catlin recalls how upset her own family members were when she decided to go back to work and place her child in day care.

"My grandmother pushed me to be all I could be—but she was asking me, 'How can you leave your child to be cared for by someone else? You should take care of your child,'" said Méndez Catlin. Anglo women in the U.S., she said, "can now make a choice—stay home or hire a babysitter or do both. We can't as easily make that choice. In our culture, that is still an expected role."

Karen Moreno, a law student at Rutgers University (N.J.) who graduated with a bachelor's degree from Bryn Mawr, said she often feels as if she is leading a double life, taking on a typical Latina role of catering to the men at family gatherings and then another life in which she is a professional woman trying to complete her studies.

"My parents want me to become a professional and become a lawyer," said Moreno, who is of Dominican ancestry. "But then they start, 'Oh, I want to be a grandmother.'"

Marisa Rivera, assistant to the vice president for student affairs at Marquette University in Milwaukee, Wis., said she has had a similar experience. When she told her parents she wanted to pursue a master's degree in the Midwest, her mother asked her if she were crazy.

"'What man is waiting for you there? No woman in her right mind leaves the security of her family to move to a place that she knows nothing about and where she knows no one! Who will take care of you?'" quoted Rivera, recalling her mother's comments.

Méndez-Catlin said that geographic location influences the challenging of traditional gender roles. Since Bryn Mawr was located 20 minutes from a large metropolitan city, many of the students had already taken steps to move away from the family in pursuit of their career goals. New Mexico Highlands is located in a small community that offers few career opportunities. College graduates from NMHU would have to move from the area after college to advance their careers, something that family members were reluctant to have them do.

"When Latinas get a job that takes them away from their families, that's when the real problems start," said Méndez-Catlin.

Rosas said that since she was raised by a single mother, she did not feel the same gender stereotyping in her household as did other friends. But she does feel a responsibility to excel—for a variety of reasons.

"Few people in my family have gone to college, and I want to show them that you can go to college and beyond," Rosas said. "As a Latina and a part of a small minority group on campus, I have a responsibility to show other students that we can do well."

Rosas said she was a little intimidated initially in the classroom because the students seemed to speak so eloquently, but she soon overcame her fears and began to speak up in her classes.

Méndez-Catlin said her study found that Latina students tended to be "more reserved and compromising . . . not because they did not know the material . . . but because they were taught to be silent." But she added that as more entered higher education, the women became more independent, more self-confident, and their self-esteem rose. Many students became more assertive and vocal with this newfound confidence, particularly by the time they entered graduate school, she said. But at times, the Latina students who became vocal encountered sexism, as exemplified by a comment from a male faculty member in her study— ". . . these new women no longer just shut up and sit back."

Guadalupe Corona, assistant director of student activities and staff member to the United Front Multicultural Center at the University of San Diego in California, said that even though more Latinas than Latinos are entering colleges nationwide, many Latinas are still pursuing careers in traditional areas such as education and social work. The Latino community needs to encourage more Latinas to pursue degrees in engineering, science, and math, she said.

In her work as a mentor to minority students on her campus, Corona said she regularly finds herself helping Latinas deal with some of the pressures they face in the higher education environment. For example, one being pressured by a boyfriend to quit her college pursuit and come home to him eventually broke off the relationship.

"It seems as if the more education you get, the fewer men there are to date," Corona said, reflecting upon conversations she has had with many Latinas about the social challenges of college.

Rosas said she has felt some of the male backlash from pursuing an education. At home in Idaho, she said, some Latino males don't even talk to her and act as though to say, "Who do you think you are with your nose up in the air?"—which she finds hurtful. And once, while visiting a cousin, a male friend told her to get into the kitchen where she belonged.

"I don't enjoy that kind of work," she said. "I wanted to find something to use my brain, not my back."

Moreno said family members tease her that she will never find a husband if she does not learn how to cook.

"They always ask, 'Can you cook?'" Moreno said. "My grandmother is convinced I'm an old maid . . . and I'm only 24."

Méndez-Catlin said her study participants echoed Coronas and Rosas' statements, finding that their pursuit of higher education often threatened relationships and resulted in their "not being in a strong, permanent relationship and missing out on that part of life."

"We need to be as equal as non-Latina women," said Méndez-Catlin, adding that because she demands equality, "some people say I'm diluting the culture—but I'd like to think I'm enhancing it and making it stronger and better because I am contributing more equally."

Méndez-Catlin said her study showed that New Mexico Highlands University was doing a good job at retaining Latina students and that other higher education officials could learn from its approach. Méndez-Catlin said only one in 10 Latinos/as who enter college in the United States gets a degree.

"That attrition rate indicates a crisis for higher education," she said. "It is important to conduct research that identifies the characteristics of the Hispanic college experience and offers suggestions to enhance persistence and ultimately increase retention and graduation rates. More research will create a more defined and all-encompassing picture of Latinas' status in higher education and the effect on their relationship with traditional gender roles. Hispanics have been on the higher education agenda for at least 30 years and are still not understood nor their experiences well documented."

Rivera said not only was her family unsupportive as she pursued a master's degree and doctorate but also that many people she encountered in higher education at Midwest institutions [sic] "did not understand and had many stereotypes about what All Puerto Ricans were like." She recalls getting numerous comments that because she was Puerto Rican, she was probably lazy, on welfare, or had no goals or aspirations.

"I can recall visiting with my advisor to pick up my registration materials and inquiring about a post-it note on my file. He responded that people like me usually take more time to complete a Ph.D. than the majority students," Rivera said. "I was required to take three undergraduate classes prior to being fully admitted as a doctoral student—this was after having obtained my master's! I can go on and on with similar and more devastating examples. My experience in graduate school was extremely devastating to my self-esteem and confidence."

Méndez-Catlin said colleges and universities can take proactive steps other than conducting research on Latinas to improve their retention and graduation rates. More Latina role models should be recruited to colleges and universities and encouraged to serve as mentors for students. Colleges and universities can sponsor outreach programs to high school students to better prepare them for the college environment and address the gender-defined roles. Schools can also ensure that families are actively courted when recruiting students.

"The family is the core of our foundation and brings a sense of centrality and belonging," she said. "These are but a few of the strategies that could be used to nurture and retain college students."

She remembers the importance of her family in her own decision to go to college. Her grandmother visited every campus she was interested in attending.

"If she had felt uncomfortable at a school, I would not have gone there," she said. "At colleges here, they feel that once students get to college, the umbilical cord is cut. They just want to deal with the students, not with the families. With the Hispanic culture, that is the wrong thing to do."

At Bryn Mawr, Méndez-Catlin started a program called On Target to better meet the needs of Latinas on campus and improve their retention. On Target is a mentoring program that pairs students with faculty members, staff, and administrators as well as fellow students of color.

"We do a lot of talking in higher education rather than enacting our goals," she said. "I was willing to take the risk and start this program."

Rivera said a mentor does not necessarily have to be Hispanic. She said there are many people who "can be encouraging and supportive and be truly empathetic to the plight of a minority student." Her mentor was a Hispanic woman.

"She became someone I regularly communicated with and a strong champion of mine," she said. "Whenever I wrote her and told her how difficult the journey was becoming, she would write back and remind me that I was not alone, and that as a Puerto Rican woman, single parent, this degree was not just about me but rather it would reflect the entire female Hispanic community. Because there are so few, just one person's quitting would make a world of difference."

Joining in the Conversation

1. Identify the traditional expectations of the Latina and then describe how Latina identity is changing. List several ways educators are attempting to help Latinas stay in school, graduate, and go on to graduate school.
2. What expectations did you have about this article after reading the title? Is the initial question one you would expect about mainstream American young women? Explain. How do strategies such as emotional appeal, credible sources, testimonies, and so forth support/develop Alicea's position?
3. How does acculturation (replacing select cultural values, traditions, beliefs, etc. with those of mainstream culture) have an impact on how Latinas construct their female identity? Which characteristics of mainstream Anglo women seem attractive to Latinas? Choose two opposing characteristics—one traditionally mainstream and one traditionally Latina—and project what would happen if a Latina fully embraced the mainstream characteristic.

Creating the New Macho Man

Jennifer Delson

This article appeared in the Los Angeles Times *Home Edition on December 12, 2000. Jennifer Delson is an award-winning reporter for the* Los Angeles Times, *who received the Columbia School of*

Journalism Let's Do It Better Award for Immigration Re 2004, the National Association of Hispanic Journalists 2004, and the Orange County Press Association Award for Be in 2001, among others. She has also worked for other newspapers, including the San Jose Mercury News *and the* Fort Worth Star-Telegram. *She has traveled extensively in immigrant-sending regions of Mexico. She holds a master's degree in Latin American Studies from New York University and a bachelor's degree in the same discipline from Wesleyan University in Middletown, Connecticut.*

✦

TO THE MEN IN THESE LATINO DISCUSSION GROUPS, *MACHISMO* IS ABOUT STRENGTH, LOVE, FAMILY AND RESPECT

Eight men, some unshaven, are sitting around the table in a Santa Ana kitchen. Nobody's handing out beers to go with the talk circling the table. Instead, they are moving a pot of burning incense from one to another. And the talk? It's nothing to do with who bested whom in what sport. Each man, each *hombre*, offers a little prayer for something less tangible: better relationships with wives, children and parents.

The gathering, based on Aztec traditions, is part of a small but growing national Latino men's movement trying to unravel the age-old concept of *machismo*. The idea is to turn the word on its head—make it not about being a tough guy, but about being a good guy. Known in Spanish as *circulos de hombres*, the men's circles in places such as Orange County, Los Angeles, San Francisco, Albuquerque and San Antonio seek to redefine "*macho* man." There are between 2,000 and 3,000 men in formal *circulos* in the United States, organizers say.

Men's support groups have multiplied in recent years as the belief has grown that addressing some of society's toughest issues—including domestic abuse and kids growing up without fathers—won't be resolved without men's involvement. But few of the groups are for Spanish speakers, and none address the specific nuances of *machismo*.

"'*Macho*' is not a dirty word," said Angel Martinez, a health educator who is involved in a *circulo* in San Francisco. "In Spanish, a *macho* is a man, and there are a lot of positive concepts to that."

Although members of the *circulos* do not believe Latino men are different than those of any other ethnicity, *machismo* has been a topic of study in Latin America and beyond since the Spanish conquest. Most researchers see *machismo* as a unique Latino social phenomenon that affects families, how boys and girls are raised and how men and women are treated within the family. At its best, *machismo* is seen as a force creating powerful men. At its worst, *machismo* is viewed as making men arrogant while demeaning women.

Confronting *machismo* is no simple task, but that has not dissuaded the leader of the newest chapter in Orange County: social worker Alejandro Moreno, a hulking 6-foot-7 man, a native of Mexico with soft mannerisms and a baritone voice. He began the *circulo* nine months ago.

"A *macho* man can be someone who is strong, but he should be a person who wants to be the backbone of his family, support his wife, help his children and be sensitive to their needs and his own," Moreno says. But becoming this quintessential *macho* is not easy, in part because men of all ethnicities are often conditioned to be rough and even uncaring, Moreno says. He hopes the meetings will help men unravel this conditioned behavior and "reconstruct manhood."

Brown University anthropology professor Matthew Gutmann, author of the book *The Meanings of* Macho (University of California Press), said the task of changing attitudes is formidable.

"You find *machos* . . . sexists . . . in every culture in the world today. For complicated reasons, the word '*macho*' and the word '*machismo*' have come to be associated with Latin Americans and Mexico in particular," Gutmann said.

Jerry Tello, who runs one of three *circulos* in Los Angeles, said the word "*macho*" has been twisted so that it has become unnecessarily negative. "The true *machismo* is being a man of *palabra,* of honoring women, men, children. The false *machismo* is the man who rules, dominates and drinks. There is a role men should take. We do not want to eliminate the part that will stand up and protect the family," Tello said.

Members of the Orange County group—the number at a meeting ranges from eight to 15—bring their own chairs to the monthly gatherings at Moreno's home. Then they talk, in Spanish and English, about their *cargas* (responsibilities) and *regalos* (gifts or blessings).

They offer a prayer to the "four directions"—elders, children, women and men. They say the names of family members, particularly those struggling with problems. The spiritual opening to the meeting helps the members talk about things they usually keep inside. By talking, they say, they find solutions to dealing with troublesome pasts or the rocky present.

Venancio Chavez, 38, met Moreno in his work as a member of the Site Council for Garfield Elementary School. Chavez was grappling with a rocky marriage, extramarital affairs and an inability to communicate with his children.

"I'm finding out what a *macho* really is. . . . We are very confused about the word and about what we are supposed to be," Chavez says. When Chavez, a disabled factory worker, is passed the pot of incense, he says, "*Señor Dios*, let this day fortify me and my knowledge; let me gain clarity before the problems that face me."

Chavez said the group has shown him that men should take an active role in the family instead of leaving women with all the responsibilities. Furthermore, he has sought to redefine his manhood.

"Before I went to this group, I thought *macho* was having two or three women at a time. Now I think it's about having one and sharing love with her," he said. Chavez's wife, Lourdes, speaking at their home, says he has changed. "He used to yell all the time. He was impossible." Now, instead of yelling, she says, he tries to negotiate. Instead of feeling macho from being with many women, he tries to nurture his relationship with her, bringing flowers and babying a dozen plants that sit outside the couple's modest Santa Ana apartment. Lourdes says she appreciates that her husband put himself in the uncomfortable position of revealing personal matters so that he could become a better family man.

Moreno, Tello and a dozen other social workers from around the Southwest developed the *circulo* concept in 1987 and since then have worked to refine it when they meet personally or at professional conferences.

They also formed a nonprofit organization, the National *Compadres* Network, to act on their ideas. One campaign targets domestic violence. Another promotes literacy, storytelling and parental involvement in children's education.

The social workers who formed these groups were trying to respond to what they felt was a lack of social services for men. "It really concerned us what was going on in terms of the spirit of the

Latino men all around us," said Tello, whose *circulo* attracts eight to 30 attendees each month. The men have usually heard about the group through friends or acquaintances.

Tello said the founders decided they would operate in the tradition of indigenous peoples such as Maya, Apache, Lakota, Purepecha, Mexica and Azteca. All decision-making in such tribes came after meetings during which men brought their thoughts before the group.

Moreno said many of the men in the Orange County group "don't want to be like their fathers. They don't want to drink a lot, to treat their wives badly," he said. "There may even be internalized *machismo* that they are not aware that's there until they start talking."

Tello said the hope is that the message from *circulos* goes beyond the few thousand people who formally attend meetings. Even the youngest members leave meetings with new ways of thinking, organizers said. "I have seen a growth of young men who see a different way of seeing themselves. We want to engage young men with themselves, with each other and with older men," said Martinez.

Daniel Ochoa is a 17-year-old high school senior in Santa Ana who attended a *circulo*. "It's really different than anything I've ever experienced," he said. "It's not something too typical for Latinos. We're supposed to be very tough. When you talk about something, something comes back at you, and that makes you feel good."

Joining in the Conversation

1. The identity of *machismo* is being reconstructed, that is, redefined with a different perspective about its qualities. Explain the way men in the *circulo de hombres* want others to define the "new" *macho* identity. List ways in which traditional *machismo* is perpetuated.
2. How does Delson support the need for *"circulos de hombres"?* What does the number of men in these groups indicate about the need for change? How does Delson's use of Spanish enhance or detract from the article?
3. Some researchers find that *machismo* is the equivalent of sexism in American males. Define sexism denotatively (from a dictionary) and connotatively (from a social or cultural view) and determine if *machismo* for Latinos is the same as American male sexism. Find examples in the text that support your position. How do women contribute to the perpetuation of *machismo* and/or sexism.

Family Pictures Shape Memory

LINDA RADER OVERMAN

Linda Rader Overman holds a Master of Fine Arts in Creative Writing from California State University, Chico. Her work has appeared in Pacific Coast Philology, Willa: Journal of the Women in Literature and Life Assembly, Voices, *and* onthebus, *among others. "Family Pictures" first appeared in* Talking River *(2004) in a slightly different form. Currently, she teaches English at California State University, Northridge.*

Photographs of my intersection with self and history are images that have a profound impact on the way I remember my past. These images exist thankfully because of the photographs taken by my father (who made a career out of snapping the lives of others on film), and by photographers whose identities have long been erased from the memory of my family members: my elderly mother or my aunts and other uncles, repositories of my family history, some of whom are now frail, in their eighties, early nineties, or dead. Collected and stored by my mother (a woman who never throws anything away) thousands of pictures stuffed in albums, in envelopes, in dressers, and in boxes are now in my possession. The best I could gather over the past two decades line the walls of my home. These images of family members and friends, some long dead, some still alive, intrigue me. I wonder just who all these people and images I grew up with really were and what they were actually doing when the photographs were taken? Often there are no captions to inform the viewer of anything, so I wondered what had occurred just prior to the click of the shutter or just after. Why are the subjects in the snapshots positioned just so? What directions were the subjects receiving from the photographer? What responses were being directed back at the photographer? Were the subjects told to look just off-camera, put on lipstick, smooth a misplaced hair, or simply just told after a 1-2-3 count to "Smile"? What did the photographs so masterfully composed not show or tell about the people or events captured? Was the attention centered on the picture's real subject? What kind of statement was being made as a result? Was the photographer taking a kind of revenge on a particular subject or offering forgiveness?

During this looking and recalling, I had many discussions with my mother about the treasure trove of photographs she so lovingly and caringly saved along with her idealized and/or perceived memories. Mother's descriptions often suffered from an occasional fuzzy memory exacerbated by poor eyesight. It was then that I would discuss these photographs with aunts and uncles who often affirmed or contradicted Mother's (re)memories of the very same images. Within the contradictions, misconceptions about memory arise, and although photographs evoke memories, those memories do not simply spring out of the images themselves; they generate meaning-making, traces, suggestions of something else—disagreements within family culture. Moreover, any references to my parent's ultimately unhappy marriage, lasting only eight years and ending in divorce, were also cause for conflicting narratives and, at times, distorting the topography of remembrance. Looking back on realities and ideals shared between us, fueled by countless 8 × 10 glossies, Mother (without realizing it) ended up assisting me in producing narrative complements or imagetexts, which allowed me to fill in what the pictures left out.

Photography, and the role of my father as photographer and my mother as subject, play a large part in this act of looking back. All over my home I have photographs displayed in which Mother is neither the only subject in the photographs, nor is Dad the only photographer of record. I am the subject in many of the photographs, but those are not so important as the images that preceded my coming into being. A year following Dad's death, on a rainy Tuesday morning as I walked down one of the longest hallways in our home, I suddenly realized that living within these images, nailed upon the wall in black, brown, brass and silver frames, are the journals/diaries of my parents. My father's diaries are his photographs so passionately composed and printed; my mother, who makes no formal record of her life, nonetheless narrated it to me from the photographs she has shared by describing, discussing, recalling, storytelling, and reinventing her past, their past and my own. The memory of this narrative constitutes a journal of sorts.

Photo, Circa 1948 Perfect Couple

"I could have married the son of the Mexican ambassador to France, you know," Mother says. I've heard this off and on most of my life. "His family owned the biggest newspaper in Mexico. They were extremely wealthy. My God, you could dive into their pool from the glassed-in dining room, swim underneath the glass walls and end up outside swimming laps." Mom loves to tell me this part.

I have heard it hundreds of times. She also reminds me for the thousandth time that "We are not Mexican *Dios mío, mija,* remember don't say you're Mexican. You're French descent, Spanish, Holland Dutch, and"—"So why didn't you marry him, Mom?" I ask this question every time she tells this story, interjecting anything to interrupt her denial rant over being a *Mexicana.* I know it irritates her. "I couldn't. I had my father, my mother, my sisters and my brother to take care of. And the business. I could never leave my family! What's the matter with you? What kind of question is that?" The photograph begins to slip out of her hands.

I still, on occasion, toy with tormenting her as she tormented me when I was little with her insistent pronouncements: *"No eres Mexicana,* always say you're Spanish!" Mom would fly into a rage if, while growing up, I ever announced I was Mexican within earshot. After all, I thought, Mom was born in Mexico, so were all her siblings, so was my grandmother, whom I grew up speaking Spanish with at home. In fact, my *abuelita's* mother, Petra Rios, was an Indian. *"Era una India"* is how my mother described her grandmother. But when Mother spoke this word, *india,* it was always in low hushed tones, her eyes looking around in case someone might hear. I never guessed exactly just who might hear, but Mother always treated this information as damning. Petra married into an upper class family of Spaniards in Mexico. Her husband was a private secretary to one of the interim presidents of Mexico in the late 1800's. Antonio Morales, my great grandfather, was a stately, elegant man with a handlebar mustache and curly beard. In his old age, Mother said, he resembled Henry Edwards Huntington. When I was eight, we visited the Huntington Library, and when we came upon a large photograph of Huntington, Aunt Terri, Mom's sister, pointed and said, *"Ya vez, se ve como Papá Tonio."* Papá Tonio was his nickname. Papá Tonio's family never really accepted Petra although she was beautiful enough at fourteen to catch Antonio's eye. However, Petra was ignored, dismissed and denied by his family and by the same token any association with being indigenous in my family was also ignored. *La india* meant that my *abuela* was part indigenous, and, that means that Mother too, is part indigenous. Shortly before dementia blew a fog into her brain, *Abuelita* used to teach me words in Nahuatl when I was around nine or ten, words I no longer remember. But at the time—I thought—who cares what I am, I'm just a kid. Mother's paranoia made me care. I slowly stopped speaking Spanish outside of our home while in junior high school because if I did my friends would gawk at me and ask, "How come you speak Spanish?" I never knew what the right answer was. If Mother even spoke Spanish to me in front of my girlfriends, I wanted to die. They were Caucasians and so am I, at least half of me is. I would pretend I did not understand a word of Spanish, but my face burned red. I scolded Mother for humiliating me. Speaking Spanish, labeling myself as Mexican separated me from my paternal-Caucasian-teenaged half, and that was the half my thirteen year-old self aligned herself with in the early sixties. So, I identified myself as Spanish, French, English and German, all of them.

It was not until graduate school, about thirty years later, that I was able to come to terms with the label Mexican, or even what the word Chicana meant. As for Mother, Chicana was and is always a pejorative term meaning uneducated, lower class.

And Mother still cannot help herself on this subject of ethnic identity, and so her tapes play on. "Your grandfather was French Basque. He was descended from aristocracy . . . and remember he used to say, just because a dog is born in a barn—"

"*Sí, sí,* does that make him a horse? I know, Mom." I've heard this refrain a million times.

"Well, what's wrong with that? When we came here, Mexicans were treated like dogs, like dogs," she yells. "Mom, *cállate, hombre.* Will you just stop?" She does, for a moment. I take a breath. This is an old battle with no winners. Mother's Latin temper fluctuates between familial history, fantasy, wishes unfulfilled, and a fighting stance in zero to sixty seconds. I've always gained a sick sort of pleasure at this achievement, seeing how fast I can piss her off. Pushing her buttons used to be my favorite pastime as a kid; now, it's a less frequent one, especially since my twenty-something son and daughter enjoy doing it to me in a similar manner. Sometimes I just can't help myself, but I have learned through the years to read my cue to move on. It's time. I catch the photograph before it falls to the floor. "Mom, is the silk dress you're wearing sitting next to Dad in this photo one you made or bought?" "Which one, ah . . . I think I made that one. Yes that's the green one. I made most of my dresses then. We had just gotten married. That was taken in Las Vegas. It's early yet." The wedding ring is prominently displayed on her third finger, left hand balled into a fist on top of Dad's thigh. "They bought it at a five and ten store," she says. I'm never sure if she means Woolworth's or a store called Five and Ten, because sometimes she calls it a five and dime store. Anyway, the ring is fake, not real gold, but it works, for the moment. "All together both rings were $3.50. At least it had a stone in it. So I called it my diamond ring." Dad wears a fake gold band on his third finger, left hand, but it's obscured behind Mother's dress. "What month of the year is it?" Mom stares at me at a loss. "I'm trying to remember." Years ago I asked my father the same question. He couldn't tell me either.

"Dad looks like a gangster in that pin striped suit," I remark. His salt and pepper hair is accented by the fabric's white stripes on black. "We were just beginning to have a lot of good times." I notice that Mom has a full set of straight white teeth in her smile, a toothy smile that costs her almost $4,000.00 fifty-three years later. Mom and Dad are in full lustful newlywed mode. They will be doing the rounds at parties, traveling up the California coast to Big Sur and San Francisco to see friends. Running off to Vegas is a quick, cheap way to sanctify such a social life of "good times." The perfect couple sits on the love seat in their Las Vegas hotel room; Mom snuggled against Dad's chest. The "green print" on her dress shows grapes. "Purple ones," she says, "sprouting from vines," abundant, rich, and ready to be picked. "Yes, that is another dress I made," she repeats herself. Something she does often. Something I have inherited. Repetition. If it's worth saying at all, in my family, it bears repeating, again and again. Her nail polish ("red," she says) looks worn around the tips of her fingers, which rest gently and un-hesitantly on top of Dad's right hand. Her left hand is poised to show off that wedding ring, the official seal of the marital bond. She will never get a real gold ring.

"He couldn't afford it. I never went to a jewelry shop. I wore the wedding-night ring until it fell off, maybe two or three years, maybe four. Real wealthy, huh! The truth is we left for Vegas rather quickly," she explains. She drops the photograph again. It lands on the floor this time. As I retrieve it, I notice Dad's left hand, with the hidden wedding band, resting upon Mom's left thigh. Plenty of good times await. But not for long.

Within this photograph, my identity remains invisible, unknown, nowhere, a not-yet. I still hover left and right just out of frame. I wait my turn. Many of my cousins will come before me, but no siblings, and if I could refocus the attention of these photographic subjects, redirect their gaze, my turn might never come at all. But by entering the photographs and stepping through the windows they provide into the essence of things, I construe deeper meanings, create imagetextual space, and subsequently affirm the past's existence and my own.

Joining in the Conversation

1. What does Overman say about her attitude toward her heritage when she was a youngster of 14 years? How does she feel by the end of the narrative? Explain.
2. Overman uses photographs to help her tell her story about her identity. Choose one or two of the photographs she describes and explain how photography helps enhance the development of an essay.
3. Go through old pictures you might have of your parents or of yourself when you were growing up. Use them as Overman did, as a starting point to discuss how you feel about your heritage. Take one more step and include the pictures in the appropriate place in a project to help the reader get a clear idea about who you or others are.

Changing Names and Making Connections: *¿Cómo te llamas?*

ROSAMARIA CHACON

RosaMaria Chacon received her Ph.D. from the University of Wisconsin-Milwaukee in August 2001, and teaches Chicano and African American literature in the Department of English at California State University, Northridge, as an assistant professor. She currently has two articles under submission: "Generating Liminal Contexts and Alternative Spaces: La Abuelita*" and "Mapping the Teaching Body." She wrote the following article for this book.*

✦

Several years ago, when I still worked in the courts, a man came into Los Angeles Superior Court and changed his name to Santa Claus. Or perhaps, he came into our court and claimed his name. Name change hearings were always my favorite. One could forget, for a short while, all the divorces, personal injury lawsuits, and fights over property (the entire range of cars, businesses, animals, children in custody suits, creative rights to screenplays, and of course land). One could forget judgment debtor hearings when usually the poor come to confess they had nothing to pay their debts with. Even adoptions, which are rather pleasant legal affirmations of new families, are a bit too solemn for me despite the smiles, hugs, and tears of joy. Name changes are infinitely better—light, quirky, and celebratory with little solemnity. You can almost see people dance directly out the courtroom door.

Although we weren't quite sure what to expect when we learned of his petition for name change, it was truly Santa Claus who came to Department 1A on June 4, 1982. If we might have expected him to come to court in December, it is clear that he had to conduct his legal business during the off season. Winfred Eugene Holley arrived a bit early (as he is generally known for his timeliness). He was wearing a bright red, long sleeved flannel shirt and sported a full white beard. Just about the right age (63), he handed out candy canes to everyone present and freely dispensed good cheer. There was no objection to the name change inasmuch as Holley's petition asserted that "the proposed name is in keeping with petitioner's special desire and activity" (quoted in Oliver 124). As our Court Commissioner Bertrand D. Mouron, Jr., said, "But he looks just like Santa Claus. He absolutely radiates Santa Clausness. You like him instantly when you see him" (I24). Although we had anticipated someone who was not in full control of his mental faculties, Santa left us with smiles and a bit humbled. Holley's name change was, indeed, entirely appropriate.

Another name change that was not quite as quirky but still provided us with a bit of pleasure and delight was Buzz Aldrin's. Despite the fact that the courthouse was centrally located, we could not imagine that the second man to walk on the moon was scheduled to appear in our courtroom. Inasmuch as almost anyone can legally change his or her name unless they are trying to avoid debts, dodge the legal system, or commit identity theft, we were expecting someone who was obsessed with space flight, moon landings or even Aldrin himself. A Fresno man chose, for example, to be called "God" in 1981 and a Los Angeles couple chose the names "R. U. Kidding?" and "Whooya Kidding?" in 1983. Who could conceive that the real Edwin Eugene Aldrin, Jr., would seek a name change to Buzz Aldrin 13 years after walking on the moon with Neil Armstrong (Apollo 11, July 1969)? There was nothing in the petition, furthermore, that specifically linked the case to the astronaut though a tiny bit of research or a call to his lawyer would have revealed the identity of the petitioner. When the court commissioner asked, I could only respond that I didn't think it was the real Buzz Aldrin who would appear on July 16, 1982.

On the day of the hearing, the commissioner asked the standard question, inadvertently giving us away. "Are you seeking this name change in order to pass yourself off as the real Buzz Aldrin?" To which he could only reply, "I am the real Buzz Aldrin." To say that we had embarrassed ourselves (and perhaps the astronaut) is an understatement. It was, fortunately, a small courtroom with an audience of nothing but fellow petitioners. Although it was a difficult moment to live down, it was, nonetheless, a thrill to have Buzz in our courtroom. One can only hope that we did not spoil the process for the astronaut. Originally called Buzzer by his sister, and later Buzz by everyone else, he simply wanted to officially change his name.

The desire to change one's name occurs for a wide range of reasons. Some people have a preference for a favorite name or a nickname while others passionately desire to leave behind an embarrassing name. This motive is comically immortalized in Shel Silverstein's song "A Boy Named Sue" (recorded by Johnny Cash, February 24, 1969). Characterizing the naming as "the meanest thing that he [the speaker's father] ever did," something worthy of "kicking and a' gouging in the mud and the blood and the beer," Silverstein clearly explains why some people rush to court to change their given name. Others use their name changes to align themselves with different elements. Working in Department 1A, I witnessed a number of changes based, for example, on the desire to fully assimilate into American culture and society. Often immigrants, these petitioners wanted names that sounded All American as opposed to their different countries of origin. For them the process might have been like shedding their skin to grow a new one. Thus, Eichermueller becomes Smith and Zanbakyan, Jones.

Another category of alignment or affiliation was based on love interest. Seeking to reach beyond homophobia and the current laws of California, same-sex couples, filled with romance and a desire to legally unite themselves, would occasionally come to court. Taking the same last name, they would be, in a sense, married; at minimum, they shared the same last name. Usually it was a sweet, young, male couple. I don't know what the commissioner thought. As a gay woman, I always smiled knowingly and was especially attentive to their paperwork. And then of course, one of the most interesting reasons for taking a new name to align with a particularly personal aspect of life was based on sex change operations—usually postoperative but sometimes preoperative. Although it is totally logical and reasonable that Paul must now be called Paulina, I wanted to ask and still I wonder: Why were these petitioners always men—tall men, generally six feet or more? And why were they always blondes? Were there no women who wanted to become men and change their names? Were there no short men who wanted to be both a brunette and a woman?

If some petitioners wanted to affiliate themselves with their new country, many others wanted to make a symbolic return to their culture or homeland. They wanted to shuck off their American names and reconnect with home cultures. A court reporter I worked with wanted to realign herself with Thailand. I still remember her clear pronunciation and spelling to attorneys who wanted transcripts: Chia Mei Jui, C-H-I-A, another word M-E-I, and last name J-U-I. Aiming for clarity and accuracy in the transcript orders, she spoke clearly and slowly. But I also distinctly heard pride. Little did I know, after leaving Department 1A, that I, too, would return to name-change court some 17 years later, not as a court manager (superior court clerk) but as a petitioner.

Like others who come to identity issues relatively late, I was mobilized by my experiences in graduate school. Leaving California, I was not searching for any particular cultural connection. Rather than a cultural quest, I wanted, quite simply, to obtain professional certification for university teaching; I went to Milwaukee to acquire the Ph.D. and required tools for scholarship and teaching. I did not know that I would also become more myself. Although I was not strictly cautioned as Laura Elisa Pérez was "to [not] get mixed up in all that Chicano stuff," it was precisely what happened (268). "It is ironic," she asserts, "that the hierarchically differentiated process of my education 'politicized' me" (270). In other words, Perez became political as a direct result of her university experience and the ranking system that marks some students as different and sets them apart from other students. "There was," she notes, and still is I might add "good reason [for the university] to worry" about her and others marked with the sign "minority identity." How then did the university drive me, almost against its will, incongruously toward "that Chicano stuff"?

From Feminist Critical Theory to seemingly more innocent courses such as American Women Regionalists (literature), I absorbed the methods of scholarship—probing, interrogating, and challenging. Transferring these skills from literature to my place and space in graduate school was almost intuitive. I was drawn to the way the university, the graduate program, and the Department of English positioned me. This attraction can be attributed to several factors. Coming from Los Angeles with a large and rather diverse population, I was initially stunned by the racial makeup of Milwaukee and, especially, its segregation. It is worth noting that "the term 'hypersegregation' is often applied to the Milwaukee metropolitan area" (Peterson 3). It was a completely new experience for me to walk on the east side, near the campus, and be stared at while doing absolutely nothing in particular. This odd experience was abundantly reflected on campus. With a minimal amount of diversity at the undergraduate level, the air became even thinner beyond the bachelor's degree. Out of 200 students in the English graduate program, people of color made up less than 5 percent of the total at the time I entered in 1994; there were six of us. No longer in Kansas, I did not know my place. "It becomes," Perez asserts, "a commonplace that one [the student or professor marked as minority] is guilty of some kind of intellectual inadequacy or incompetence until one proves otherwise, or until one successfully deploys a politics of assuagement" (272). One must, as Perez indicates, either demonstrate academic ability or employ strategies of appeasement to receive a portion of the status automatically granted to others. Before, in fact, I could even attend my first class, one professor went out of his way to let me know that I did not belong. Completely erased in another situation by a graduate student who claimed there were no students of color in our class, my insistence on my presence was met by the professor's question: "So, what are you then?" One might have expected a more subtle response from a tenured professor given the fact that she taught feminist theory and Toni Morrison.

Stimulated thus, I was forced to stop and reflect on my identity in ways that I had not done for years. Identity is constructed around a wide range of classifications including ethnicity, language, class, and sexuality. Focusing on place and space more recently, Chican@s often use a critical perspective of regional location, the search for home, land, or even a specific house like Esperanza's house on Mango Street (Sandra Cisneros). This focus has expanded to embrace multiple elements as defined by Gloria Anzaldúa in *Borderlands/La Frontera: The New Mestiza* and by Tey Diana Rebolledo and Eliana S. Rivero in *Infinite Divisions: An Anthology of Chicana Literature.* Although I find, like others impacted by border issues, that a number of these elements cut across my personal identity, I feel especially summoned by language, and most specifically by naming.

The significance of examining and decoding names and naming is found in history, literature, theory, and personal experience. Discussing Chicana identity from the perspective of a historian, for example, Deena J. González suggests, "for us, teaching a class in Western American history, then, makes no sense. We ask, why not call it a history of the Mexican North? Why not call it a history of many names . . ." (124). Hidden in these questions is the radical, sudden reshaping of national boundaries between the United States and Mexico—constituting the loss of a million square miles of Mexican land or 50 percent of its national territory—and the

1848 Treaty of Guadalupe Hidalgo, which was blatantly disregarded. Hidden still further is the much earlier Native American residence on this land and perhaps even further, Pierre J. Proudhon's assertion that "property is theft." I firmly believe that part of the reason students sign up for a class in Western American history "is the power to be able to define. The definers want the power to name" (Morrison 74). As several critics have noted, Toni Morrison explores the nature of this power in her fiction, particularly in her novel *Song of Solomon.* Analyzing this novel, Christian Moraru cites Nietzsche's "definition of naming as an expression of power relations: *Die Mächtigen sind es, welche die Namen geben,* 'it is the powerful people who name'" (191). Using a different critical perspective, John Carlos Rowe focuses on Gertrude Stein's assertion in "Poetry and Grammar" that "people's 'names' do 'not go on doing anything to them'" after they have been assigned. In a translation of Stein's subsequent challenge "so why write in nouns," Rowe explains, "she means that poetic writing should use 'names' differently and more in the manner of verbs, as if they were capable of producing new results, rather than commodifying existing meanings [or converting them into something that can be exchanged or exploited]." If names are much more than nouns as Stein suggests, if they can function like verbs and become active agents, and if they carry a tremendous amount of personal and political power as reflected in the literature of Morrison, Cisneros ("My Name"), and others,[1] then they are most certainly potent markers of identity.

My own identity was generated, to some extent, by a deep connection to my Mexican family, especially my grandmother. Although I am part Scottish, and apparently also part Puerto Rican (a more recent discovery), I do not focus on these aspects of my makeup because the cultural elements that have defined me have never been Scottish or Puerto Rican. I remember, instead, women making *menudo* (spicy Mexican soup) and crushing chiles in the *molcajete* (Mexican mortar or bowl for grinding spices); I remember laughter in Mexican Spanish. This closeness was, unfortunately, fractured. First, I was denied access to the language. My mother married a white man who did not allow her to teach us Spanish. Although she tried to do so anyway, we were too young to understand the artificial language barrier that separated his working hours from his home hours; she had to stop. After my parents' divorce, and after eagerly picking up a few words in sixth-grade Spanish, I was forced to enroll in French in junior high school. While no rationale was ever provided, this practice was, in fact, quite common; Mexican students were often prevented from taking Spanish. Compounding this linguistic distance, my mother pulled away from her family in one of those quarrels that families sometimes have.

Growing up, partially separated from my family, and intensely aware of our definitive lack of money, I was beckoned by the American narrative of assimilation. Like many who are located in the confined spaces between cultures, I could not see that the promise of assimilation conceals the permanent position of the subordinate and requires letting go of the past. As I was drawn gradually into assimilation, my cultural core began to slip further away from me. At the same time, ironically, that my cultural identity was fragmented, other aspects such as sexuality began to occupy center stage.

Coming to Wisconsin years later, confident in multiple aspects of my identity, including my identity as a lesbian, I was compelled by the place and space that was created for me in graduate school to reconsider my cultural identity. Restricted by the boundaries erected for those marked as minority, I reached beyond these limits to reshape the ways in which I was being positioned, and ultimately to return more properly to my initial cultural grounding. An integral part of the Chacon family, I was named after my grandfather Rosario and my grandmother Maria. Named in an Americanized style, I was first called Rosemary as a child, and then Rose for years and years. Although this Americanized name served to pull me even farther away from the language that I was already distanced from, in its shortened, more convenient form, it also seemed more than vaguely disrespectful to my grandmother. As I immersed myself deeper into my work in identity issues, continuing to eliminate Maria was not possible; on June 7, 2001, I filed a petition to change my name to RosaMaria Chacon, with a capital "M," to honor my grandparents, and more specifically my *abuelita* (grandmother). In doing so I have (re)discovered my Mexican identity. Although it is "radical . . . [to] refuse to be completely contained by that homogeneous, devouring word American," it is also immensely satisfying to move away from the illusion of assimilation (Sáenz 79). Inasmuch as the "capacity to name your place and your being, is a marker of self-determination and naming yourself means defining yourself and ultimately 'owning' yourself," it is no small matter to change your name (Moraru 192). It is, in fact, "placing ourselves by name within the long and intimate heritage of our mothers, our grandmothers, and great-grandmothers [and grandfathers]"—it is a matter of finding name, finding self, finding voice (Rebolledo 106). If I nearly wince thinking about the long road to my name, I remember how Gloria Anzaldúa used the Banyan tree as a metaphor for women like me who are finding themselves (again) at age 20, 30, or 40 . . . by putting down roots from the top, and I shuck off the shame that does not belong to me.[2] Instead I feel the active agency in my name. I feel the way it functions as a verb. I do not miss the other name—the one I carried for 47 years. I feel, rather, stronger in those times when things are difficult—those times when I must reach back for courage; it is easier somehow to tap the fortitude of my Mexican family, particularly my grandmother Maria Medajilda Valenzuela Bracamonte Chacon. RosaMaria Chacon: I like the sound, and I carry its power now.

Endnotes

1. For an interesting treatment of the complex signification of names, see, in addition to Morrison's text, Américo Paredes's novel *George Washington Gómez.*
2. She used this figure of speech at a talk at the University of Wisconsin, Milwaukee, Spring 1996.

Bibliography

Dreifus, Claudia. "Chloe Wofford Talks about Toni Morrison." *The New York Times Magazine* 11 Sept. 1994:73–75.

González, Deena J. "Chicana Identity Matters." *Aztlán* 22.2 (1997): 123–38.

Moraru, Christian. "Reading the Onomastic Text: 'The Politics of the Proper Name' in Toni Morrison's *Song of Solomon.*" *Names* 44.3 (1996): 189–204.

Oliver, Myrna. "A Typecast Santa Gets the Title Role." *Los Angeles Times* 5 June 1982:124.

Pérez, Laura Elisa. "Opposition and the Education of Chicana/os." *Race, Identity and Representation in Education.* Ed. Cameron McCarthy and Warren Crichlow. New York: Routledge, 1993. 268–79.

Peterson, Bob. "Neighborhood Schools, Busing, and the Struggle for Equality." *Rethinking Schools Online* 12:3 (1998): 1–8. 4 Aug. 2005 <http://www.rethinkingschools.org/archive/12_03/busl23.shtml>.

Rebolledo, Tey Diana. "Infinite Divisions: Constructing Identities and Dis-Identities." *Women Singing in the Snow: A Cultural Analysis of Chicana Literature.* Tucson: U of Arizona P, 1995. 95–116.

Rowe, John Carlos. "Naming What Is Inside: Gertrude Stein's Use of Names in *Three Lives.*" *Novel: A Forum on Fiction* 36.2 (2003): 219–. *Academic Search Elite.* EBSCO. California State University Lib. 25 July 2005. <http://search.epnet.com/>.

Sáenz, Benjamin Alire. "In the Borderlands of Chicano Identity, There Are Only Fragments." *Border Theory: The Limits of Cultural Politics.* Ed. Scott Michaelson and David E. Johnson. Minneapolis: U of Minnesota P, 1997. 68–96.

Silverstein, Shel. "A Boy Named Sue." *Song Lyrics.* 21 July, 2005. <http://www.toptown.com/hp/66/sue.htm>.

Joining in the Conversation

1. Chacon's article presents several reasons individuals legally change their names and describes such legal changes as happy occurrences for the individuals. Review the article and then list the various reasons for changing names. Consider if you would want to change your name. If you do, what would your reason(s) and your new name be; if not, why?
2. In Chacon's essay, she indicates that one's name can either distance one from or tie one closer to a former "culture or homeland." Interview individuals with names representing four different cultures, asking them about their relationship to the United States and to the culture(s) represented by their family names. Share your findings with the rest of your class members and create a chart that displays your results. Draw conclusions from the evidence based on this single study. Do you have a big-enough sampling to make major assertions about each group?
3. One's name is generally considered a "noun" in the English language; however, Chacon considers the word(s) in a different light, seeing a name as having the power of a "verb," the most forceful of the grammar components in the English language. Consider your own name in relation to the two basic functions of a verb, that is, as an action and as a state of being. If there are students in your class who share your name, make a group presentation.

A New Minority Makes Itself Known: Hispanic Muslims

Evelyn Nieves

This article appeared in the December 17, 2001 issue of The New York Times. *Evelyn Nieves has written for the* Washington Post *and currently writes for* The New York Times. *In her article, Nieves*

Source: Evelyn Nieves, "A New Minority Makes Itself Known: Hispanic Muslims," *New York Times*, December 17, 2001.

discusses the rising number of Latina conversions to Islam from Catholicism.

CHANGING FAITHS BUT NOT CULTURES

They file into the mosque when Sunday school is over and the conference rooms are cleared, staking a small piece of turf in the main hall. For many, Spanish is their only language, and this is a whole new world. They are new immigrants, new to the big city and new to Islam.

Over the last year, the Islamic Center of Southern California has been conducting these weekly 90-minute Spanish-speaking sessions for new Muslims by popular demand. Marta Galedary, who converted after immigrating here from Mexico two decades ago, has helped lead them. She finds that the group, which can include 20 to 50 people in any given week, is intensely interested and a little nervous.

"Something in these Latino meetings that we keep telling people," Ms. Galedary said, "is that you don't leave your culture because you convert to Islam. You have to continue to be proud of whatever part of Latin America you are from."

They come from all over. Each week, immigrants from Mexico, El Salvador, Nicaragua, Peru and Costa Rica—just a handful of the countries represented—come to the Islamic Center, relieved to find that they are not alone. Far from it. In recent years, Latino Muslim groups have formed in most large cities in the United States, stretching from New York to Los Angeles. Latino Muslim groups have also formed in smaller cities with large Spanish-speaking populations, including Fresno, Calif.; Plantation, Fla.; and Somerville, N J. Though exact figures are hard to come by, since people tend to drop in at mosques and may not appear on any membership rolls, the American Muslim Council, an advocacy group in Washington, estimates that 25,000 Hispanics in the United States are Muslims.

It is a small fraction of the nation's Muslims—estimates of the total number range from 4 million to 6 million—but a figure that appears to be growing by the year. (Several Latino Muslim organizations say the number is closer to 40,000, with the largest Hispanic Muslim communities in New York City, Southern California and Chicago, where Hispanics and Muslims are plentiful.) Indeed, Spanish-speaking immigrants, the nation's fastest-growing minority, are converting to Islam to such an extent that a national organization, the Latino American Dawah Organization, founded in 1997 by a handful of converts in New York, now claims thousands of members in 10 states.

Why Islam, a religion cloaked in mystery in Latin America—as it was in this country before Sept. 11—is attracting so many Latino converts has several answers. For many women who attend the Islamic Center of Southern California here, the path is a relationship with a Muslim man. Many others say they chose Islam because they preferred a religion without the trappings of a vast hierarchy or the complicated dogma that they saw in the Catholic Church.

For new immigrants, Latino Muslim leaders say, the close-knit Hispanic Muslim community is also an attraction, helping Latinos understand the society as the Latinos help Muslims become more mainstream.

Religion scholars say that Islam also attracts those who prefer a more rigorous way to worship than what they find here in the modern Catholic Church.

"There are those in the Roman Catholic tradition who are somewhat discontent with the modernizing trends of the Catholic Church," said Wade Clark Roof, chairman of the religious studies department at the University of California at Santa Barbara. "To those people," Mr. Roof said, "a religious tradition such as Islam, that attempts to maintain a fairly strict set of patterns and practices, becomes attractive."

For Nicole Ballivian, 27, an aspiring film producer from Falls Church, Va., whose mother is Bolivian and father Armenian, Islam was a natural progression from Catholicism.

"I loved religion," said Ms. Ballivian, who converted to Islam eight years ago in Virginia and now practices in Los Angeles. "I was very religious in Catholic high school. I told myself that I would study philosophy and religion. I remember getting in trouble in Catholic school for debating things like the concept of original sin at a really young age. When I actually studied Islam, it made it all simple."

Ms. Ballivian, who has been working on a documentary on Latino Muslims, sees two distinct groups of converts. One is composed of new immigrants, poor and usually with little education, who come to Islam out of an emotional connection. The second, she said, is made up of young, usually first-generation, middle-class, college-educated Americans of Hispanic descent who make a deliberate, well-researched conversion. "We actually have a lot of women who convert because they're married to a Muslim," said Ms. Ballivian, who married a Palestinian Muslim two years ago.

Like Ms. Ballivian, Juan Galvan, 26, a senior at the University of Texas at Austin, came to Islam in a deliberate way. One of eight children born and raised in a strict Catholic household, he remembers never being truly comfortable with some of the church's tenets and hierarchy.

"When I was growing up in the Texas Panhandle, I read a lot, and even then I had a lot of questions," Mr. Galvan said.

"I was a very strong Catholic," he said. "I did all my sacraments and I lectured as a Eucharistic minister. But even when I was young I had a lot of problems with the Bible, ideas like original sin. So coming to Islam solved a lot of problems for me."

Three years ago, as he began seriously questioning some Catholic doctrines, he came across a man praying on campus. "I asked him his name and I could not believe it when he said his name was Armando. What was this Hispanic guy doing praying to Allah? He told me some things about Islam—how Spain had been Muslim for 700 years, how so many Spanish words had come from Arabic."

Mr. Galvan, president of the Texas chapter of the Latino American Dawah Organization—dawah, he said, means education in Arabic—has found that it is sometimes lonely being a Muslim. He connects with other Latino Muslims, including Ms. Ballivian, through e-mail and Web sites like www.latinodawah.org. "Sometimes it feels like I am in the wilderness," he said.

For many Latino Muslims, the hardest part of converting is handling the reaction of relatives. Ms. Galedary, 45, a nurse from a particularly religious Catholic family—one of her sisters is a nun—had to convince her mother that she had not joined a cult. "I told her to ask her priest about Muslims," she said, "and she did, and he told her that it was a good religion. That's what I recommend to people—to ask their family to ask their priest, because they know since they've studied comparative religions."

Latino Muslims—before and after Sept. 11—said they have been confronted by peers who ask how they could trade in their culture for another. "I've been asked why I adopted an Arab culture," Ms. Ballivian said. "That's just a lack of knowledge about Islam."

Even for longtime Muslims, there are challenges. Vita Abdelmohty of Miami, who goes by her Muslim name, Sister Khadija Rivera, converted to Islam in 1983 in New York City. She helped found a Latino Muslim women's organization and is preparing a radio program that will help people understand that

Islam is a religion, not an ethnicity. It is to be broadcast on a Spanish-language station in Miami.

"Islam is still a mystery to most people, and we want to reach out so people understand, especially that it is an Abrahamic religion," said Ms. Rivera, who wears the traditional Muslim head scarf. She said that like other Muslims, she has been harassed since Sept. 11. "I was insulted in the supermarket, on the street. I would be waiting for a bus and people would see me and just yell obscenities. I have had dirty looks from Latino people, too."

Ms. Rivera, like many others who came to Islam from a Catholic background, said that as a girl she was not always comfortable with the teachings of the church.

"I always wanted to read the Bible and learn more, but it was all about the catechism," she said. "You just have to believe it, not understand it. For me, Islam gave me answers, made sense."

Joining in the Conversation

1. Nieves indicates several times in the article that "Islam is a mystery" to many people. What did you learn in this article that gave you more information about Islam? What are the reasons Latinos give for converting to Islam? What reasons are given for the converts' preference of Islam over Catholicism?
2. Visit a mosque or the Islam center on your campus if you have one and speak with Muslim students on campus. Find out more information about Islam without giving the impression that you are converting, simply that you are conducting research about it for your English class. During this process, do not argue or criticize. Simply gather information. Then visit the Catholic student center or attend a Catholic mass and talk with Catholic students on campus for the same fact-gathering purpose as you had with the Muslims. Write a comparison and contrast essay in which you describe what you have learned about each religion. Draw conclusions at the end.
3. Religion is a very personal matter. Many people follow the religion their family followed when they were children. Others make different choices. Examine your choice of religion and in a personal narrative explain why you maintain or do not maintain the religious beliefs that your family followed when you were growing up. This is not intended to be an argumentative, persuasive, or convincing essay.

Additional Topics of Conversation

1. Select one or two articles that particularly appealed to you and from which you learned something new about yourself or about the Chican@

community. Using the topic of identity, develop a thesis that asserts what you have learned and that allows you to develop a project using personal experience, and adding information from the articles to help you develop and support your ideas.

2. Every culture has certain expectations for its young men and young women as they grow into adulthood. Consider your own gender identity and determine whether it is consistent with the expectations of your culture. Consider who your same-sex role models are in your culture. They might be part of your family or members of society or your religious community who are especially important. Consider also how members of the opposite sex in your culture contribute to who you are and who you will become. Construct a visual project in which you use pictures, objects, and/or other representations of individuals who have been important in your life and who may or may not be in your life today. Give an oral presentation that describes your identity contextualized within your culture, defining your culture and its expectations for your gender as well as the role models you are expected to emulate and why. Evaluate how well you are or are not conforming to those expectations and explain your feelings. Conclude by offering advice to other young women or men growing up in your culture based on your experiences.
3. In Chapter 4, Anzaldúa and Hinojosa write specifically about locations and traditions, but they tie the topic of identity to their setting. Choose one or two of the articles and analyze each for the way identity helps to support and/or develop their thesis.
4. Select one of the following pairs and in a group discuss how the authors write by identifying and selecting specific examples of the following:
   - appeals to emotion
   - personal experiences
   - appeals to logic
   - supporting material

As a group decide which of the two articles was more effective to you as readers and defend your decision in a class discussion.

"We Owe History" and "What Is a Hispanic?"

"What Is a Hispanic?" and "What's the Problem with 'Hispanic'? Just Ask a 'Latino'"

"'But Can She Cook?' Family Expectations Weigh Heavily on Latina Students" and "Creating the New *Macho* Man."

Pop Culture

Spend a loud, dusty Saturday afternoon at a local *charreada* (Mexican rodeo) or cruise your favorite boulevard in a decked-out '56 Chevy lowrider, and you'll have some idea of how vibrant and close to home the concept of Popular (Pop) Culture is to the people of a Chicano community. From the artistic murals on public walls and underpasses to the latest Tejano dance steps, Pop Culture exists within the culture of a community and spreads outward into the overall population, thus offering the observer an insight into the visible cultural forces at work. The representations of art, whether through religious icons or art displays on cars and in tattoos, become living symbols of the changes going on within that culture, changes that are often met with praise by some and with disdain or outright public demonstration by others. Whatever the event or activity, Pop Culture reflects the artistic and cultural representations close to the soul of its people and is a living, breathing part their everyday life. It is not so much studied as experienced. Often the use of such terms as "Hispanic" or "Mexican-American" gives the impression that there is one solid, unified culture behind such terms when in fact cultures as diverse as the Chican@ culture have a vast pool of traditional and new styles and beliefs from which to choose one's own lifestyle. For example, an individual may not like *nopalitos* for dinner but recognizes the prickly pear cactus dish as part of his/her culture.

Because Pop Culture involves more of the personal or "grass-roots" elements of culture, one can quickly see how the interaction of two major cultures affects each other and how one's culture responds to the forces of mainstream America. In the United States, soccer is gradually gaining a foothold in American sports long dominated by such games as football and baseball. Within the Chican@

communities, consider how the artistic representations of Tejano music have changed over the previous decades from a more grass-roots level to the commercialized styles of today. One could also look at the gradual introduction of Latino actors and actresses into American television and film, a far cry from the representations years ago when such roles were very often played by non-Latino actors/actresses with heavy, dark makeup and speaking in very clumsy dialects. How the Chican@ is represented in independent films is just as important as the Chican@ actresses and actors who break into mainstream film and music, radio, TV, and the news broadcasts. When reading the following articles on Pop Culture, keep in mind the alterations that had to occur within that culture for those changes not only to happen but to succeed. Such changes and the resistance they encounter reflect the efforts involved in keeping a culture alive and growing.

Prime-time Soaps Sizzle in Spanish, but Fall Flat in English

GLENN GARVIN

This article came from the February 11, 2007 issue of The Miami Herald *newspaper. In it, Glenn Garvin exposes the problems inherent in producing television programing intended specifically for one cultural audience and translating it for a different cultural group. Garvin writes about television for* The Miami Herald *and is the author of* Everybody Had His Own Gringo: The CIA and the Contras *(1992).*

✦

The contrast couldn't be more stark: Last week, a new television network with a schedule of all English-language *telenovelas* admitted defeat, abandoning the format in the face of devastatingly low ratings. And Monday night, the Spanish-language network Telemundo rolls out a new big-budget *telenovela* version of *Zorro*, shot

---

Source: Glenn Garvin, "Prime-time Soaps Sizzle – if They're Made in Spanish," *Miami Herald,* February 11, 2007, p. 1A.

in high-definition and festooned with pricey bells and whistles like a theme song by Beyonce and Mexican pop star Alejandro Fernandez.

"It's one of the big questions of television, why Spanish-language viewers love *telenovelas* so much, and English-language viewers won't watch them at all," said Derena Allen, an executive with a Hispanic marketing company. "Everybody's trying to figure it out."

Novelas, the serialized dramas long a staple of Latin television, are essentially soap operas with an important difference: They run for only a few months and are plotted with a beginning, middle and end, unlike their American counterparts that roll along for years and even decades.

Between six and eight of them are running during prime-time hours 52 weeks a year on *Univision* and *Telemundo*, America's two biggest Spanish-language networks, and they've never been more successful. *Univision's* most popular novela, *La fea mas bella* (*The Prettiest Ugly Girl*) in January attracted 6.2 million viewers, the biggest prime-time audience in the network's history. *La fea mas bella*, itself a remake of the hit novela *Betty La Fea*, was virtually the only program on television on Tuesday and Wednesday nights that didn't lose viewers when Fox's ratings juggernaut *American Idol* returned to the air last month.

Telemundo is expecting similar numbers for *Zorro: la espada y la rosa* (*Zorro: The Sword and the Rose*), which debuts for a 24-week run at 9 p.m. Monday, the first episode in high-def. Adapted from a novel by Isabel Allende, this *Zorro* follows the familiar story of a wealthy landowner who by night dons a mask to defend the poor against cruel Spanish colonial rulers in early-19th-century California. But, in typical *telenovela* fashion, this *Zorro* will lock lips as often as swords.

"Don't worry, there's still a lot of sword-fighting and horseback chases," said Mexican heartthrob Erick Elias, who plays Renzo the Gypsy, Zorro's main rival. "Zorro is still the only Hispanic superhero. But there's a romantic angle, too—a big one."

Zorro will be shown with closed captions available for English speakers who want to watch, but if the recent fate of MyNetworkTV is any guide, there won't be many. Launched in September with an all-novela lineup featuring established stars like Morgan Fairchild, Bo Derek and Tatum O'Neal, MyNetwork foundered badly, barely drawing a million viewers most nights.

That's chump change in the English-language television universe, where *Grey's Anatomy*, *House* and other successful dramas routinely pull in more than 20 million sets of eyeballs. MyNetwork announced last week that it will cut *novelas* back to two nights a week and fill the rest of its schedule with movies and martial-arts tournaments. Meanwhile, chatter about launching a prime-time *novela*, once persistent among executives of the big four broadcasting networks—CBS, ABC, NBC and Fox—has died away.

"There are a lot of people in television trying to figure out why it is that Spanish-speaking Hispanics are so loyal to novelas, and in English they don't seem to have the same cachet," said Allen, the managing partner of the California-based Santiago Solutions Group, which devises strategies for reaching the Hispanic market.

Network executives, academics who study television and other broadcast analysts say everything from immigration patterns to program content to cultural values has affected the relative success of *novelas*. But, they say, there may be fewer differences in viewing tastes than the audiences themselves think—and that *novelas* may still have a future on English-language television.

"The fact is, several of our top shows in English-language television are following a *novela* format," Allen argued. "*Desperate Housewives, Grey's Anatomy, Ugly Betty*—which of course was adapted from a Spanish-language *novela, Betty la fea*—and even reality shows like *Survivor* and *Dancing with the Stars*, these are all programs with continuing storylines and distinctive characters who inspire a very emotional type of loyalty."

Robert Thompson of Syracuse University's Center for the Study of Popular Culture and Television, says that English-language television has been creeping steadily toward the *novela* model ever since *Dallas*, the first big nighttime soap opera, debuted to monster ratings nearly three decades ago.

"Until *Dallas* came along, the general theory of prime-time television was that people had no memory," he said. "Every episode of a show was 100 percent independent of every other episode, to the point it was maddening. I mean, how many times did Archie Bunker learn a lesson about the evil of bigotry on *All In The Family*? But at the end of every episode, the 'clear' button was pushed and he had to start all over."

"Now, though, some of the most successful dramas on television are some of the most heavily serialized, like *Lost* and *24,* and even the sitcoms have serial elements."

But there's an important difference: However soapy and serialized English-language programs get, they still air just once a week, unlike the Monday-through-Friday *telenovelas* on Spanish-language television.

Kristin Moran, who teaches communications studies at the University of San Diego and has written a book on *novelas*, believes that airing its *novelas* every night was what killed MyNetworkTV.

English-language viewers, she says, have too many television options to commit to a single show five or six nights a week.

"They aren't going to want to miss the water-cooler shows, the ones everybody talks about like *Lost* and *Grey's Anatomy* and *American Idol*," Moran said. "That's why *Ugly Betty* has been so successful. It's just as campy and fun as *Betty la fea*, but it's not every night."

Spanish-speaking viewers, with far less television to choose from—fewer than 20 channels, compared to 300 or so in English—are more willing to sign on to a program that airs every night, agrees Vivian Rojas, a communications professor at the University of Texas-San Antonio. But she also believes there are significant differences in the audiences that will keep Hispanic viewers loyal to *novelas* even as Spanish-language TV grows.

"Hispanic immigrants don't necessarily assimilate fast," Rojas said. "It's an individual process. Some people are more in transition than others, some are still negotiating with elements of their traditional culture. The novelas, which they know from Mexico or Guatemala or wherever they came from, are a way of staying in touch with that."

Even as new generations are born and grow in the United States, she adds, the *novela* habit continues. "In almost every Hispanic household, there's at least a grandpa who doesn't speak English, so the family sits and watches *novelas* together because it's something they can all enjoy," she said. "Look, I teach at a school that's about 65 percent Hispanic. Many of them don't even speak Spanish, but they're all pretty familiar with the *novelas*. That's because somebody's watching them at home."

Eventually, English-speakers will be watching too, predicts Telemundo President Don Browne. He says the digital revolution that's allowing viewers to watch TV shows on their computers, cellphones and iPods, at times they, rather than network programmers, choose, will make novelas more practical. And as television continues its shift to original programming around the clock 365 days a year, economics will make the low-cost novelas necessary.

"You watch," Browne said. "One of the big networks will try this again soon, maybe during the summer, and this time it will work. The *novela* is the model of the future."

Joining in the Conversation

1. List the effects that *novelas* have on families. What are the effects they have for different television stations, both English-speaking and Spanish-speaking? What are the causes that produce these effects?

2. Translations from Spanish to English or from any language to another tend to lose meaning from a connotational perspective. For example, the suffix "*-ita*" in Spanish is a diminutive. Thus, to add it to a word would logically indicate that the speaker is making the word smaller; however, it also has a connotative meaning of love. Therefore, to add "*-ita*" to daughter, "*hijita,*" does not only mean little daughter, but it also connotes a sense of love and affection to or for that person. That connotative meaning could possibly be lost when Spanish is translated into English. Garvin lists several reasons why *novelas* do not work with English-speaking audiences. Watch a *telenovela* for one week and compare and contrast it with a popular English-speaking drama and draw your own conclusions. Write a comparison and contrast essay that describes the programs you watched and that explains your feelings and offers solutions beyond those in this article.
3. In a group activity, watch an English-speaking drama of the group's choice and then watch a Spanish-speaking *telenovela*. Among the members of the group and with the help of anyone in the class who speaks Spanish, translate as much as possible one episode of the English-speaking drama into Spanish. Remember that there are customs and expectations the audience will be looking for that might or might not be present in the English-speaking version. Those are elements that the group will have to make decisions about when "translating" the drama into a Spanish version.

Josefina Lopez: A Writer's Life

Regina R. Robertson

Regina R. Robertson is a freelance journalist whose work includes human-interest stories, personal essays, and arts and entertainment coverage. To date, her byline has appeared in O, the Oprah Magazine, Essence, *the Associated Press newswire,* AOL's Africana.com *and* BlackVoices.com, *and* Honey *and* Savoy. *She is also a contributing writer for the Los Angeles-based monthly,* Venice, *which originally published "Josefina Lopez: A Writer's Life" in July 2004. The article was later reprinted in their sister publication,* Latin Style (2004). *In addition to her editorial writing, Robertson is currently working on her first book project, an anthology of stories about fatherless daughters. A native New Yorker, she currently splits her time between the East and West Coasts.*

✦

While popular opinion suggests the art of writing to be a solitary exercise, what if the vibrant characters created actually keep a writer company during her process? Such seems the case for poet, screenwriter, filmmaker, and playwright, Josefina Lopez, who crafts charming, heartfelt tales for television, film, and the stage.

Lopez, an alumna of UCLA's esteemed Film & Television School, began her life's journey in Mexico—San Luis Potosi, to be exact. At the age of five, she relocated to East L. A. with her family where she lived undocumented for over a decade and nurtured her on-going love affair with the arts. Formerly a member of the Young Playwrights Lab at the Los Angeles Theatre Center, her written work began taking shape in the form of stage plays. In fact, Lopez wrote her first play, *Simply Maria or the American Dream,* when she was just 17 and earned an Emmy Award for her efforts.

Along with her stage writing, which includes *Confessions of Women from East L. A., Food for the Dead,* and *Unconquered Spirits,* Lopez has shared her magic with television and film audiences. For CBS, she penned *And Baby Makes Three* as well as *MacArthur Park* for Showtime and *Blame It on Ria* for the Disney Channel. Oh, and lest we not forget to mention *Real Women Have Curves* (2002), the screenplay she co-wrote based on one of her plays. After garnering both the Audience and Special Jury Awards at Sundance, the film became a must-see among women who "take chances, have flaws, embrace life."

In July, Josefina Lopez unveils her latest stage play, *Lola Goes to Roma.* The story, which chronicles the intercontinental exploits of a mother and daughter, is laden with life lessons about passion, freedom, and awakening . . . but that's all we can say as she doesn't want to give away *too* much.

Latin Style caught up with Lopez one day prior to attending a rehearsal at Casa 0101, a quaint and colorful storefront theater in the barrio. Not one to hold her tongue, she shared with us her inspiration for writing her current work, a prescription for living an authentic life, and why her eye is keenly focused on the director's chair.

Latin Style: Let's talk about your new production, *Lola Goes to Roma.* What was your motivation for crafting the play?

Josefina Lopez: Well, I actually wrote it as a screenplay first. The play is also very cinematic, so it's going to be fast-faced. Lupe Ontiveros, who played Carmen in *Real Women Have Curves,* is a friend of mine who's been my muse for many years. I wrote this screenplay for *her* because I want her talent to shine. Lupe is so charismatic and refuses to be discarded as an old woman. She is a very sensual person who is just full of fun and charm and is very much in touch with her goddess self. She's my role model and I wanted to write a piece that celebrated older women.

This story is about a mother and daughter, but this time, it's the *mother* who's getting laid. [*laughs*] The daughter is actually kind of embarrassed because her mother refuses to be a widow and grow old. It's an odd couple/buddy play about these two women who go on a two-month trip to Europe, but it's really a journey of self-discovery, passion, and sexual awakening.

What was your casting process?

Well, I was very ambitious with casting. I could have just made it a two-person play, but instead I have them going through many scenarios with different characters throughout the piece.

We work with a lot of local talent, so we sent out an e-mail to our list and also went to BackStage West. We held auditions and it was just a matter of finding the best people for the roles, which was quite easy. And of course, it's non-union, so . . . [*laughs*]

What do you want audiences to walk away with after experiencing the piece?

I want them to see that living without passion is to invite a division of your soul, your heart, *and* your body.

I was listening to Dr. Wayne Dyer who says that we all need to understand that an inauthentic life really costs us *a lot* in terms of illness. When we live life without integrity and don't do what we feel, we create disease, which can catch up to us.

Living authentically is really a journey into ourselves. It's a risky thing, but it's worth it because there's no such thing as living in security or comfort—that's choosing death.

I applaud you for your efforts to nurture artistry in downtown L. A. What was your impetus for creating Casa 0101?

We're actually in Boyle Heights, which is just minutes from downtown, yet it seems like it's worlds away. It's a Mexican, immigrant neighborhood and although there's bilingualism, it is mostly Spanish-speaking.

When I was growing up, everyone wanted to get out of the *barrio*—they wanted to come, pay their dues, and then leave to go to live in the suburbs. I never thought that was right. The people who come *back* to the *barrio* are those who've come out of prison, so there are a lot of [young] people in this neighborhood who grow up without role models. When I was living here, I never felt that *my* reality was reflected on film or television. There were gang movies like *Colors* and even *American Me* which portrayed my neighborhood with a thread of fear that just wasn't my experience. Maybe it's because I had an intact family, but it never occurred to me that I should join a gang.

I knew that when *I* left the *barrio,* it was to get an education and learn as many skills as I could so that I could come back and do something to inspire people. I opened Casa 0101 in 2000 and we've been doing theater consistently for two years.

It seems as though you're a poet and playwright, first, and all of the rest of your work is an extension of that craft.

Well, if I could be so arrogant, I'd like to think of myself as a renaissance woman. [*laughs*] I have ADD and bore very easily, so I take on many things and my mind is constantly working—I write poetry, I paint, I do production and costume design. Part of that comes from the fact that we don't have a budget and the other part is that I love to do anything and everything just to get the job done. I must live life to the fullest, otherwise, I'll fall asleep.

I've discovered that I *am* a poet. It became obvious to me after I'd written all of those poems and I thought, "Wait a minute, I have a whole collection here." So I decided to publish them.

I actually started out an as actress when I was 18. I went to the High School for the Arts where I had a wonderful teacher who told me the truth about the realities of the business. She told me from her own experience about how much sexism there is. She also said that I needed to lose weight or I wouldn't have much of a career as an actress. That really opened my eyes because I knew that if I wanted to work, I'd have to lose weight, get a tan, dye my hair blonde, and change my name. All of these characteristics of who I am are what I was born with, and I wanted to embrace that, so I decided that I would start writing roles for women like me. I do many things and luckily, I've had success with writing.

From where do you derive the ideas for your written work?

My mother is one of my muses and, also, Lupe. I would say that the ideas come from my family, of course, and a lot of the people that I meet. Also, a lot of the ideas just come to me.

I teach screenwriting at Casa 0101 and I tell my students that the best stories usually come from something that you're angry about. The stories can come out of rage or even the way our society mistreats women and minorities. I'm outraged when I see Latinos portrayed as being lazy or uneducated and it makes me want to turn those assumptions around and shock people.

As a writer who works in several mediums, which offers you the most fulfillment?

I would say playwriting. You can write a play, get it produced, and get immediate feedback from the audience, whether they laugh or cry.

I've written many television pilots and movies and so far, only one of my movies has been made. It's kind of sad sometimes because you don't know whether it's because of you or your writing but, then again, getting a movie made is so political. [The process] can leave you feeling really unsatisfied if you take it personally.

Doing theater feeds my soul; it makes me feel like we can tell these stories. At the end of the night, at least we get a response, a reaction, and even some applause. So what I try to do now is write [my work] as a movie first and then adapt it into a novel or a play which gives it a life of its own even if the movie doesn't get made.

So, how would you like to continue writing your *own* story?

The next chapter of my story is Josefina Lopez: The Film Director. I'm ready to make my directorial debut, so that's where my attention is now. I have so many ideas and would like to direct a piece that I've written—it takes so much time and effort, you know? For instance, there's a movie that I want to direct, *ADD Me to the Party,* which is about three Latinas who are addicted to adrenaline. Having grown up with ADD, I feel that it would take someone like me to explain the kind of world you live in [when you suffer from the disorder].

I know that some writers who wish to direct fall so in love with their writing that they can't be objective. Of course, I would direct a piece [by another writer] if it meant that I could contribute to a movie rather than getting in the way of it. I know I can't go on living if I don't direct. [*laughs*]

Joining in the Conversation

1. Josefina Lopez uses her enormous talents in a variety of ways. Identify the various types of personal careers she discusses in her interview and some of her major works noted in the article.

2. Lopez indicates in the article that her ideas take on a life of their own that she then transforms into varying genre forms: for example, play to novel or novel to movie. Choose a favorite form of entertainment, such as a movie, and determine the ways it can be transformed into a new format, such as a wall mural.
3. Lopez discusses how her theater, Casa 0101, is a positive force within her community. Investigate the positive elements in your own community keeping in mind that Pop Culture covers many aspects of a culture including its food, music, shops, yard decorations, styles of home, and public art. Present your findings to your class using several methods, such as listening to music, providing pictures or drawings of the public art, and giving descriptions of the homes and businesses in the area.

Victory to the Low and Slow

DAN NEIL

Dan Neil is the automobile columnist for the Los Angeles Times *newspaper. This article appeared in* The New York Times *on May 21, 2000. Neil, an experienced magazine and newspaper writer, graduated from North Carolina University in 1986 and from East Carolina University in 1982. He has won awards from the Detroit Press Club Foundation (1992), the International Motor Press Association (2001), and he was selected for the Houghton Mifflin's Best American Sports Writing Award (2002). In the following article, Neil provides a brief sketch of the interest that many have acquired in lowriders.*

✦

The crowd parts in front of Lonnie Lopez's golf cart, faces beaming with hope that the editor of *Lowrider* magazine—the bible of the Latino-centered customizing movement—will stop to take a picture. Mr. Lopez, 39, is looking for new talent in the parking lot of the Florida State Fairgrounds, a weekend stop last month on the 15-city Lowrider Boulevard Tour 2000.

"Yo, yo, Lowrider man!" a young man in baggy shorts and basketball jersey calls after him. "What about my ride?" The youth

---

Source: Dan Neil, "Victory to the Low and Slow," *New York Times,* May 21, 2000.

has a buzz cut and a beard that looks as if it were penciled onto his jaw. He and Mr. Lopez exchange a complicated handshake and a few words in English and Spanish.

The car is a late 1980s Cadillac Sedan de Ville, painted in an ice-blue metallic—"metal flake"—with snowy tuck-and-roll upholstery, golden-spoke wheels and a sound system with the power of a public-address system. Outfitted with a hydraulics system in its suspension, the car holds its right front wheel a foot off the ground, like a dog favoring a wounded paw.

The Cadillac does not quite make the cut. "Keep working on it, bro," Mr. Lopez says "I'll be back next year."

Lowriding emerged in the 1950s in California, as Mexican-American youths—in what may have been a reaction to the hotrod culture dominated by whites—transformed their cars into fantastical, ground-hugging showboats. "Go low and go slow" were the watchwords. From the beginning, lowriding was as much about ethnic identity as about machinery. "It was a way for the Chicano people to feel pride in who they were, in their way of life," Mr. Lopez said.

In the 1980s, lowriding began to break out of its traditionally Latino stronghold, a trend fueled by Mr. Lopez's magazine itself. *Lowrider*'s provocative covers, featuring buxom models in the scantiest of bikinis, had undeniable shelf appeal to young men of all ethnic backgrounds. *Lowrider* magazine became a multicultural crossover hit.

Today, Latinos account for only 58 percent of *Lowrider*'s audience, Mr. Lopez said. Fully a quarter of the magazine's readers are white, he said, and the balance are African-American and Asian. While its circulation of 216,000 is low compared with mainstream auto magazines that rely heavily on mail subscriptions, like *Motor Trend* and *Road & Track*. It perennially leads the car enthusiast segment in rack sales. Once confined to the West Coast, lowriding, like "slamming"—the high-performance modification of small cars, usually Japanese imports—has spread east.

As a measure of mainstream acceptance, when the Petersen Automotive Museum in Los Angeles recently staged a lowriders exhibit, museum attendance doubled.

Whatever gang-life origins the hobby once had have long since disappeared. Mr. Lopez said, leaving only a mildly menacing patina, including the occasional flaming skull or smoking gun motif on the elaborate murals that adorn many of the cars. "It's a bad-boy image, but it's not a bad-boy sport," he said. "A guy spends $30,000 on a lowrider, the last thing he's going to do is a drive-by."

Danny Cortinaz, a member of the Low Lyfe Car Club in Plant City, Fla., said lowriding was actually an alternative to gang life. "It keeps kids off the streets, gives them something to do," said Mr. Cortinaz, 26, festooned with gold chains to match his gold-plated Chevy pickup. His attention strays when two teenagers in miniskirts and halter tops walk by. "Mostly we do it for the females."

* * *

While the prototypical lowrider remains a Chevrolet from the early 1960s, hobbyists have surprisingly ecumenical tastes. There are "oldies" and "bombs," cars and trucks built before 1955; "traditionals," American cars built from the 1960's through the 1980's, trucks and mini-trucks; and "euros," which, despite that label, are typically compact Japanese cars with oversize wheels and elaborate plastic body cladding that mimics the look of European sports coupes.

"A lot of young people get into it with newer cars," Mr. Lopez said. "It's a lot more affordable to do a used Honda than a classic car."

What is striking—and poignant—about the lowriding movement is the tender devotion lavished on what would otherwise be the throwaways of consumer car culture. The clunky detritus of the 1970s and 1980s—these Monte Carlos, Regals, LeBarons and Bonnevilles—seem to have won some sort of karmic lottery. Instead of being crushed and forgotten, these cars will live forever in a glitzy state of perpetual recycling.

The luckiest lowriders become show cars, dramatically ornate and customized vehicles that are all but undrivable. In Tampa, the show cars—whose owners are often paid to appear at lowrider events—took up residence inside the fairgrounds arena. Each car was mounted in its own tableau of crushed velvet, mirrors, lights, fog machines and other Vegas-style stagecraft.

Appearing was Manuel and Carta Corbala's 1979 Cutlass Supreme, "Strictly Business," three-time winner of the "Lowrider of the Year" award and a project that cost Mr. Corbala about $80,000. A fantasy in deep purple and fuchsia, the car has had what is known as a frame-off customizing job. All the suspension and undercarriage components have been gold plated, from the control arms to the wheel hubs. All of this work is visible since "Strictly Business," like most of the show cars, sits on gold-plated jack stands over a mirrored floor, its wire wheels removed and arrayed around the car.

The car's body has been transformed. The roof has been cut out like a targa-top Porsche, known in the hobby as the "Hollywood" treatment. The hinges on the doors have been reversed so that they open "suicide" style. Both the hood and trunk lid now open to the side, though the hood is removed during shows to give visitors a better view of the engine. The engine block and exhaust headers have been painted in lavender, the valve covers have been gold-plated and engraved with spectacular filigree.

The original interior of the car is only a memory, replaced by purple velour upholstery and matching swivel chairs, accented with hundreds of mirror tiles. In addition to the exotic hydraulic setup nested in the fully upholstered trunk, Mr. Corbala's lowrider also has the requisite sound system, a 5,000-watt Rockford Fosgate stereo to supply that notorious boulevard "bump."

For many cars in Mr. Corbala's class—radical custom—the pièce de résistance is mural art. This is an intriguing style of painting: Aztec priests carrying swooning maidens toward a sacrificial altar; dream-scapes with Indian shamans, succubi and coiling serpents; Cortez and Quetzalcoatl.

Yet many of the murals are very intimate and plainly sincere, such as the artwork on Romero Bautista's "Just a Dream." Once an ordinary 1982 Pontiac Grand Prix, the car has metamorphosed into a shrine devoted to the memory of both Selena, the Mexican pop star who was murdered in 1995, and Our Lady of Guadalupe.

* * *

The featured event of lowrider gatherings is the car-hopping contest, where hydraulic-equipped cars compete to see how high they can bounce their wheels off the ground. The contestants stand beside the vehicles, operating the hydraulics with a switch box connected to the car through a cable. Jorge Guzman's 1987 Toyota pickup truck set a world record in the truck hop, with a wheelie 62 inches high, before the truck's gas tank ruptured and the vehicle burst into flame, sending judges and contestants scampering for the fire extinguishers.

Without exception, each of the cars suffers heavy damage in the course of the competition. Because the hydraulics overheat, fire is a common occurrence. Wheels fall off, hubs shatter and suspensions collapse. As each car disassembles itself in noise and fire, the crowd gets to its feet and cheers.

"We reinforce them a lot," says Armendo Nunez, the leader of the hopping team sponsored by Hilow Hydraulics. "But they don't last too long."

And then, a freak accident during the truck dance competition, a tire explodes, firing a portion of the fractured wheel rim like an artillery shell. It hits the truck's owner Glen Strickland of Jacksonville, Fla., in the face, dropping him to the concrete floor.

His jaw is shattered and he loses some teeth. It takes 15 minutes to summon an ambulance to the arena floor. The festive mood sobers quickly and further competition is canceled.

An R-rated rap concert ends the show. But the kids themselves don't seem to notice the performers. Many are interested instead in the lowrider bikes and trikes, Schwinns and Huffys given the full lowrider treatment, including custom frames, elaborate gold-plated scrollwork, even hydraulics, TV's, stereos and PlayStations. In time, the kids who own these bikes will trade them in for something faster, and lower.

Joining in the Conversation

1. Explain the evolution of lowrider participants. Who initially participated in the activity, and how have those individuals changed? Who reads *Lowrider* magazine and why does that seem to surprise people?
2. Assume that you have decided that you want to enter your car into the annual Art Car Parade that is sponsored by some major cities. On the entry form, you must describe your car so the sponsors can decide if your car qualifies. Write a descriptive paragraph of your car's make, model, year, and how it has been decorated for the parade. Go to Google and enter the words "art car parade" for pictures of winning entries in the parades. The Houston Art Car Parade web site has a form that you can download to see what they require in their description.
3. Write a research paper that documents the history of lowriders since the 1950s. Be sure to include pictures of the "classic" lowriders, as well as those of the more contemporary cars. Also include in your research information from *Lowrider* magazine and other magazines that are devoted to lowriders. Be sure to include the competitions and the individuals who have made a name for themselves in lowrider circles.

Muralism

Charles M. Tatum

Although a native of Texas, Charles M. Tatum spent much of his life in Parral, Chihuahua, Mexico, before returning to the United States. He is currently the dean of the College of Humanities at the University of Arizona and a professor of Spanish. His professional career has focused not only on exploring the literature and popular culture of the Chican@ community but also on recovering much of the Chican@

literature that has been lost. His publication efforts include Chicano Literature *(1982),* Not Just for Children: The Mexican Comic Book in the Late 1960s and 1970s *(1992) that he coauthored with Harold E. Hinds, Jr., coediting the scholarly journal* Studies in Latin American Popular Culture, *and* Chicano Popular Culture *(2001) from which the following report is taken. In addition to his writings and teaching, Tatum is currently a member of the advisory board for the Recovering the U.S. Hispanic Literary Heritage Project.*

✦

Perhaps the most dynamic form of secular art is Chicano muralism: large paintings on the outside or inside walls of public buildings, schools, storefronts, community and cultural centers, drainage channel walls, and just about any other space where art can be made available to the masses. By definition, this art is not hidden away in museums or in private collections. Mural art surged from the mid-1960s to the mid-1970s throughout the Southwest and particularly in California. It is still practiced today but in a less energetic way.

The name of this art form comes from the Spanish word for wall, *muro,* and its adjective form, *mural,* which is a cognate to the English adjective *mural.* Many cultures throughout history have practiced mural art, but Chicano muralism takes its inspiration from post-revolutionary Mexican muralism that, in turn, drew on the ancient artistic traditions of the Aztecs and other Mexican Indian civilizations.

MEXICAN MURALISM

The 1910–1920 Mexican Revolution was marked by a strong nationalist current that tended to reject European traditions in areas such as painting. Many of the young Mexican painters had historically gone to France and other European countries to receive their artistic training, aspiring to incorporate into their own work the latest European trends. During and shortly after the revolution, they began returning to Mexico to join a nationalist wave that emphasized Mexico's indigenous cultures. Classically trained painters such as Diego Rivera, José Clemente Orozco, and David Alfaro Siqueiros—often referred to as *Los tres grandes* (The Three Great Ones)—joined the ranks of Mexican revolutionary cultural workers to resurrect the ancient muralist traditions. These and other painters rejected European gallery art in favor of public art. With the enthusiastic financial support and patronage of the new revolutionary government and under the leadership of José Vasconcelos, its Minister of Education, they were encouraged to cover the exterior and interior walls of government buildings in and around Mexico City with paintings. Their murals emphasized revolutionary themes, including the exaltation of Mexico's indigenous cultures and the history of oppression that these cultures had suffered under the yoke of the Spanish (European) conquerors. The Mexican government has taken great care over the past eighty years to preserve these original murals as well as those painted later by Rivera, Orozco, Siqueiros, and many other muralists. The Mexican public today may view these paintings on the walls and staircases of several government ministries as well as on museums and schools in and around Mexico City.

All three Mexican muralists came to the United states [sic] at some point in their respective careers. Rivera was in the United States from 1930 to 1934. In 1931, he was contracted to paint several murals of the San Francisco Bay Area, including one on the wall of the San Francisco Stock Exchange Luncheon Club. He also painted a commissioned mural in the lobby of the Rockefeller Center in New York City in 1933. The mural was so controversial, in part because it contained the figure of Vladimir Lenin, that the Rockefeller family ordered it whitewashed just days after he unveiled it. (Rivera later re-created this mural at the Palace of Fine Arts in Mexico City.) Orozco spent the late 1920s and early 1930s in exile in the United States. In 1930 he accepted an art commission at Pomona College, where he painted Prometheus and other heroic figures. Siqueiros went into exile in 1930 and lived for a time in Los Angeles, where he taught mural painting at the Chouinard School of Art. He painted some controversial murals including one, *Meeting in the Street,* with a strong pro-union theme that caused an uproar in a city that was at the time strongly antiunion. His most famous Los Angeles mural, located in a *barrio* called Sonoratown, was called *Tropical America.* His depiction of a near-naked Indian boy on a cross surrounded by signs of the sixteenth-century Spanish conquest of Mexican Indians led to such a public outcry that local Los Angeles officials had the artist deported and the mural whitewashed.

THE INFLUENCE OF MEXICAN MURALISM ON CHICANO ARTISTS

More than thirty years passed between these mural projects by Mexico's three master muralists and the Chicano art movement that began in the late 1960s. Some Chicano artists of the 1930s were, or course, familiar with Mexican muralism and at times studied under Rivera, Orozco, Siqueiros, and other muralists in Mexico and the United States. Most of the Chicano artists that were active during the 1960s and 1970s had not yet been born, however, and muralism had not continued as an unbroken artistic tradition in the United States in the intervening decades. Nonetheless, for reasons rooted deeply in the cultural nationalist ideology of the Chicano Movement, Chicano artists looked back on Mexican muralism in general and on its three masters for inspiration. The Marxist revolutionary themes of many of the works by Orozco, Rivera, and Siqueiros also resonated with the social activism of the Chicano Movement.

Young Chicano painters, energized by the political ferment of the 1960s, were encouraged to explore artistic traditions that supported their cultural nationalist philosophy, and Mexican muralism with its strong pro-Indian and social protest character provided a logical and compelling model. Artists began studying Mexican muralist painters and their brief but important presence in the United States in the 1930s. . . .

I should emphasize, however, that murals, at least most of those painted in the late 1960s and 1970s, were produced as collective works of art. A project typically would have an artistic director or consultant who would work with a small team of artists and/or community residents to produce a mural. . . .

One of the earliest murals, painted by Antonio Bernal, covered the walls of the United Farm Workers union headquarters and paid tribute to César Chávez and his struggle to win better working conditions and a living wage for Chicano, Mexican, Filipino, and other migrant workers. In 1974, Mexican-born muralists painted a mural on the inside walls of the United Farm Workers union hall in San Juan, deep in the Lower Rio Grande Valley of Texas. It depicts the difficult life of farm workers laboring under the watchful eye of the feared Texas Rangers, who are portrayed in the mural as overseers in complicity with the local growers. One side of the mural focuses on struggle while the other side celebrates victory as a Catholic priest witnesses the signing of a labor contract. Because the union hall functions as a social center for the farm workers, the mural attempts to make a strong connection with their plight by including them within the painting itself.

Murals figured early in the political struggles of urban *barrios* against established authority on any number of issues. One of the first known urban *barrio* murals was completed in 1970 in East Los Angeles by students at the UCLA Chicano Studies Center. This led to the formation in 1971 of the Mechicano Arts Center, made up of *barrio* artists who painted many murals throughout the area. One notable mural produced through the center is Willie Herrón's Ramona Gardens mural, which portrays through vivid colors the rage, anger, and frustration of youthful victims of drugs and police violence. . . . Muralism continues to be a vibrant art form among Chicano artists and artistic communities today. Perhaps its best-known and most vigorous proponent is Judith Baca, who . . . created the *Great Wall of Los Angeles* mural project. The giant mural, which narrates the multiethnic history of Los Angeles and the surrounding area from prehistoric times through about the 1950s, took around nine years to complete during the 1970s and 1980s. Painted on the concrete wall of the Tujunga Wash flood control channel in the San Fernando Valley, the mural is certainly about as distant as an artist could get from gallery or museum art. In addition to its subject matter, its venue, and its stunning colors, its collective nature—Baca supervised thirty artists who in turn worked with more than one hundred youths—was solidly in the tradition of both Mexican and Chicano muralism. In 1984, Baca and other muralists such as Willie Herrón and Frank Romero were commissioned to paint murals on freeway retaining walls, underpasses, and overpasses in honor of the 1984 Olympic Games in Los Angeles. The Social and Public Art Resource Center, which Baca founded in 1976, has continued to play an active role in training and sponsoring young mural artists and their projects throughout the city of Los Angeles and elsewhere in California. Two of these outstanding young artists are Yreina Cervántez and Juana Alicia, the latter a resident of San Francisco.

Joining in the Conversation

1. Tatum brings out several aspects of mural art: the three main influences of mural art in Mexico and America, the fact that the art form is public in nature, and that mural art is a group project that often has a social or political theme. Look through the article to find examples of each of these aspects of mural art that Tatum points out.
2. Tatum mentions the Social and Public Art Resource Center that still fosters new talent in the art world. Investigate the center's web site to see the opportunities it offers. Or, you may want to contact the center to find out what projects are being planned for the future. If your own area has a cultural

or art center, contact the same to find out what events and training they offer. Prepare a list of questions before you contact the center and prepare a report on your findings.

3. The idea of art as a *public* art form is not new to either Mexican or American art. Think about the *reliefs,* the figures carved on buildings, in both countries or even such art forms as billboards and neon signs in your own community. What types of art forms are most visible today and what purpose do they serve? Be prepared to present your finding to the class in a variety of formats, including pictures and writing.

Whether or Not Selena Changed Tejano's Status Quo, She Certainly Changed the Genre

EYDER PERALTA

Eyder Peralta is currently the film critic for the Houston Chronicle; *she has also written and contributed articles ranging in topics from religion to pop culture in the Houston area. Tejano music star, Selena, was killed in 1995, and various newspaper, magazine, and journal articles were written celebrating her contributions to the field. Peralta's article is from the* Houston Chronicle *(March 25, 2005).*

✦

NO MATTER WHERE YOU ARE IN CORPUS CHRISTI, THERE ARE REMINDERS OF SELENA

"Dreaming of You" was to be the final piece of a crossover that would solidify Selena's place in mainstream music.

Source: Eyder Peralta, "Whether or not Selena Changed Tejano's Status Quo, She Certainly Changed the Genre," *Houston Chronicle,* March 25, 2005.

A tourist map lists her grave site, the Selena Museum and a memorial that was erected in 1995. Selena, in many ways, has become this region's miracle—the subject of a heralded story about life and death with themes similar to the hurricane that wrecked the city in 1919.

Like that storm, she came and went and left a difference in her wake—in her case a new Tejano-music scene. Despite a modest upbringing in Corpus Christi, Selena went on to dominate a patriarchal music business.

Selena, you could say, was an unintentional feminist.

"For a long time, Tejano music was a male area," said Maria González, a professor of Mexican-American literature and feminist philosophy at the University of Houston. "Selena was one of those musicians who entered a musical field that was completely dominated by *macho* Tejano musicians." And she did it within the strong patriarchal framework of her family and her religion.

FAMILY PORTRAIT

Her father, Abraham Quintanilla, was the indisputable head of the family. He was Selena's manager and handled business affairs for her and her band. His wife, Marcela, was always in the background. Even after Selena's death, Abraham was the family's spokesman, while his wife mourned privately.

Selena also grew up a Jehovah's Witness, a member of a group that considers a woman as a weaker vessel (1 Peter 3:7) and the biblical teaching that a wife should submit to her husband.

Selena didn't submit, at least not professionally. Instead, she headed a mostly male band, and her husband, Chris Perez, backed her up on guitar.

"She came in and celebrated her femininity," González said. "And not just her femininity, her sexuality as a female person."

Houston's Lydia Mendoza is considered the first woman to make it in Tejano.

"Women in Tejano were usually seen as a side thing, and read as objects. Selena turned around and said, 'This is my subjectivity. I am projecting this position. It's not being projected onto me'. In that sense she was taking a fairly (typical) patriarchal stance."

EXPLOITING SELENA

Manuel Peña, a professor of music at California State University at Fresno and the author of two books on Tejano music, disagrees. He points to the early '90s when Selena and Emilio Navaira were at the top of their games. "He and Selena were the male and female icons of Tejano music," he said. "But Selena was always portrayed as this sultry temptress who nonetheless was seen as the girl next door, whereas Emilio projected this virile, in-charge, masculine dominance with his form-fitting clothes. He was the man, and she was still the woman, just shy of being the sex kitten. . . . She was very much exploited by a very much male-dominated industry."

Selena is always set apart from the other two female icons in Tejano music: Chelo Silva and Lydia Mendoza. Silva was seen as an incendiary and standoffish figure, the queen of the bolero and the torch song, who took flak from no one.

Houston's Mendoza is considered the first woman to make it in the Tejano world, during the late '20s. Her signature song became "*Mal Hombre,*" a diatribe against a bad man. In the chorus she sings with the style of Edith Piaf: "Bad man," goes the song (translated from Spanish), "your soul's so damaged it hasn't got a name."

Musicologist Chris Strachwitz, who founded Arhoolie Records, notable for its extensive catalog of classic Tejano music, wrote a book about Mendoza. He points to the different eras in which these women lived. While Selena was an urban Tejana, Mendoza and Silva grew up when a lot of Mexican-Americans were part of the migrant-worker community. Silva's father struggled with alcoholism, so the hard times about which she sang weren't a put-on.

"(Selena) didn't impress me," Strachwitz said, "except she was obviously a young chick who said, 'Listen, I'm a young modern Chicana. I'm going to flaunt what I got if that's what the people want, if that's what MTV loves. I don't care what the old folks said'"

HER TORCH SONGS

At a glance, Selena's catalog doesn't seem to have the same grit as Silva's. Selena's hits, like the lovelorn "*Como la Flor,*" the soap-operaish "*Amor Prohibido*" or the posthumous "I Could Fall in Love," are clean pop offerings. But deeper into the albums you find that all her recordings (minus the posthumous "Dreaming of You") contain at least one scathing torch song in the spirit of Silva.

ARHOOLIE RECORDS

Singer Chelo Silva was the no-nonsense queen of the bolero and the torch song.

"*Mentiras*" (off her major-label debut *Selena*) is basically the same song as Silva's "*Mentirosa,*" except Silva sang it from the perspective of a wronged man, and Selena sings it from the perspective of a wronged woman.

On "*¿Qué Creías?*" from her third release, *Entre a Mi Mundo,* she sings, "You thought you'd find me happy to take you back / But as you can see, it's not that way. / I want nothing to do with you, / So just pick up and go."

Her most scathing song is on her landmark *Amor Prohibido.*

"You're nothing but a coward," she sings on "*Cobarde.*" "You lack the bravery to speak to me / But sooner rather than later, you'll remember me good."

In simple terms, González said, feminism is about challenging a socially acceptable patriarchy and offering an alternative.

And while some argue that Selena was used by the male society as an object, González points out that escaping patriarchy is nearly impossible, because it's so deeply ingrained in many parts of society.

What most agree on, though, is that Selena did cross boundaries.

"I think (she) gave the women a tremendous liberation charge, yeah," Strachwitz said.

Selena was able to walk the fine line between being a sex symbol and a musician, between being a goddess and a peasant. She was married and—like Mendoza and Silva—kept working, a rarity for Tejano-music singers.

And for that she's been canonized. She fooled society into thinking she was playing by the rules, while she was really gently breaking them.

Joining in the Conversation

1. Peralta writes about Selena and her impact on Tejano music, asserting at the end that Selena "play[ed] by the rules, while she was really gently breaking them." Explain how Selena did this.
2. This is a newspaper article that appeared in the March 25, 2005 edition of the *Houston Chronicle*. Therefore, it has to follow the journalistic style of answering the questions: Who? What? When? Where? How? and Why? Analyze the article and find the answers to each of these questions by highlighting the answers to the questions or underlining them. If you have information that is left over, what is it there for? How does the material not highlighted or underlined work to support the thesis of the article? While the article is basically about Tejano music and Selena's contribution to it, how does feminism fit into the article to support the thesis?

3. Peralta did not write an article that follows the format of the profile like the interview format of "Josefina Lopez: a Writer's Life" in this chapter. She included information that she received from experts in the fields of music and feminism. Write a newspaper article that answers all the required journalistic questions and that also gives some academic information about a subject you choose to discuss. Include interviews from at least two different academic areas to include in your article.

Hispanic Girls in Sports Held Back by Tradition

MaryJo Sylwester

MaryJo Sylwester wrote this article while working for the USA Today *sports department projects team. She is currently the computer-assisted reporting editor for the* St. Paul Pioneer Press *in St. Paul, Minnesota. She has also worked at the Center for Public Integrity, Investigative Reporters and Editors, and various newspapers in Minnesota and Wisconsin. A native of Minnesota, Sylwester has an undergraduate degree in journalism from the University of Wisconsin-River Falls and a master's degree in journalism from the University of Missouri-Columbia. Her article included here was published in* USA Today *on March 29, 2005.*

✦

Korina Hernandez is one of only two Hispanics on the varsity girls basketball team at Greeley Central High School, where half the students are Hispanic. That's not unusual for girls teams here. Just 20% of Greeley Central's Hispanic girls play a sport, compared with 60% of non-Hispanic girls, according to the athletics director.

Nationwide, this disparity is only slightly smaller. It worries school officials and others because girls who don't play sports miss a wide range of benefits for their health and academic success. They

---

Source: MaryJo Sylwester, "Hispanic Girls in Sports Held Back by Tradition: Family Duties Keep Many from Playing High School Sports," *USA Today,* March 29, 2005, p. 1A. Reprinted with permission.

are also in more danger of feeling left out of their school. Experts say promoting sports to prevent these problems is crucial for Hispanic girls because they are at greater risk for problems such as teen pregnancy and obesity and are more likely to drop out of school than non-Hispanics.

The number of girls involved is substantial. Hispanics have surpassed African-Americans as the nation's largest minority group. In October 2002, the Census reported there were 1.8 million Hispanic females ages 14 to 19, slightly less than African-American males in the same age group.

Hernandez, 16, is an example of a growing number of Hispanic girls who are closing the athletic gap by casting aside cultural tradition and convincing reluctant parents that sports can be an avenue for staying out of trouble and getting better grades—and perhaps a ticket to a college education.

Many are the first females in their families to play sports, unbound by a custom that dictates girls help with the family after school; boys often have more freedom. Some families maintain this practice simply because everyone needs to help to survive financially.

For the Hernandez family, it was a difficult decision to let Korina play: Her parents were both working, and her mother needed someone to help care for younger daughter Ashley. "But it was something I really wanted to do," Korina says. "I kind of convinced her to let me play." Her parents found an after-school program for Ashley instead.

This type of situation is key to why Hispanic girls have a lower sports participation rate than non-Hispanic peers, according to numerous athletes, parents, athletics directors, coaches, and researchers. Practical problems, such as lack of money or transportation, also are factors but are common for other girls, too.

Rosa Perez knows about this firsthand. She defied her parents' wishes and played softball in high school and at Stanford, where she graduated in 1971. Now she frequently meets with Hispanic parents who are reluctant to let their daughters play sports at Canada College, a Redwood City, Calif., community college.

"The issue of participation in athletics first and foremost has to do with the responsibilities (Hispanic) girls still have in traditional households," says Perez, 55, who is president of the college. "A lot of our Latino families are still either first- or second-generation immigrants. . . . But it is changing, and especially with those people who were raised in the United States."

IT'S NOT JUST ABOUT MONEY

Nationally, about 36% of Hispanic sophomore girls played interscholastic sports, compared with 52% of non-Hispanics for the 2001–02 school year, according to a *USA TODAY* analysis of the most recent U.S. Department of Education survey data.

The data show the low participation rate isn't just about money. Hispanic girls from high-income homes also lag behind non-Hispanic peers, while the gap between boys of different ethnicities is much less pronounced. The participation rate for Hispanic boys is 50%, compared with 57% for non-Hispanics.

High school sports participation data, collected by state high school associations, do not include race or ethnicity. As a result, the education survey is the only available snapshot to quantify such participation.

Coaches and athletics directors across the country say they have had difficulty encouraging Hispanic girls to play sports, often because of parental reluctance.

"Most of these girls are athletically inclined," says Raul Hodgers, athletics director at Tucson's Desert View High School, which is 80% Hispanic. "But it's difficult to acclimate parents to the idea of kids staying after school."

Schools in Mexico, where the majority of Hispanic-Americans come from, don't have after-school activities, Hodgers says. That time is reserved for family obligations. When Mexican families arrive in the USA, the idea of after-school activities is even more problematic because they often don't have the money or time to shuttle kids to practice or to attend games.

STRUGGLING TO MAKE IT POSSIBLE

This has been a struggle for Korina Hernandez's parents, Anita, 38, and Guadalupe, 39. "At first it was hard because I was working, and there were times when I couldn't be there," says her mother, who recently was laid off from a Wal-Mart distribution center and is studying at a local college to be a radiology technician. "It wasn't that I didn't support her."

Supporting Korina's wishes is important to Anita Hernandez because she had been denied that as a child. The daughter of migrant workers who spent the school year in Texas, Anita joined the band to play saxophone but her parents never came to performances. When she asked to become a cheerleader, her parents refused. They didn't have time, she says, but also "they didn't think it was important for me."

"I didn't want to do the same thing to my girls," she says. Her oldest, Ruby, now 21, was a cheerleader. Korina wants to play basketball in college. And now, Ashley, 11, plays basketball, too.

Ultimately, the deciding factor for the Hernandez family was the benefits after-school activities could provide. They made a deal: Their daughters could participate as long as they help when their parents work overtime and they keep their grades up.

"My husband and I . . . thought it was something good for (Korina), and we knew that she was there practicing and not in the streets or hanging around with bad influences," Anita Hernandez says.

Greeley Central officials have stepped up their efforts in recent years to encourage more Hispanics, especially girls, to participate in school activities. This includes parent meetings for incoming freshmen in their own neighborhoods, instead of at the high school, and efforts by coaches to reach out to potential players, athletics director John Bettolo says.

Girls basketball coach John Steckel says talented girls play pickup basketball regularly in many Hispanic neighborhoods but don't join the school team.

"If we don't overcome this, I don't know if we'll ever recover from not making them a part of their school," says Steckel, who just finished his first season as head coach. "If you don't feel a part of your school, you're not going to have a very enjoyable high school career and possibly even postsecondary school. If they don't buy into it, we may never get them back."

SCHOOLS SELL PARENTS ON BENEFITS

School officials in Greeley and at other schools across the country are focusing their efforts on telling Hispanic parents about the academic and other long-term benefits that sports can provide.

Bert Otero, who has coached Softball at Tucson's Desert View High for 20 years, says, "It used to be that after high school you went to work. A lot of that was the old-school way of thinking. Now it's really being made the forefront that education is a path to further your goals in life."

The well-respected 1989 Women's Sports Foundation report "Minorities in Sports" found Hispanic female athletes are at least twice as likely as non-athletes to attend and stay in college. This report remains the only research linking minority involvement in sports with academic success. More recent studies also have found sports can reduce numerous health problems—such as obesity and diabetes—and reduce the likelihood of teen pregnancy, alcohol and drug use or eating disorders for all girls.

"The racial/ethnic sub-group to benefit the most from sports participation is Latina girls," Women's Sports Foundation executive director Donna Lopiano says. "There's no question that if we can solve the problem of parental support . . . and create a more nurturing, motivating environment . . . that we can make some great contributions to Hispanic girls in terms of their future health and well-being."

Crystl Bustos, a two-time Olympic gold medalist with the U.S. softball team, says lack of money shouldn't be an obstacle. Bustos, 27, says her family didn't always have the money to buy good equipment. When she speaks to Hispanic kids across the nation, Bustos talks of how she and her siblings made bats from broomsticks and balls from duct tape and stuffing while growing up in Granada Hills, Calif.

"I want them to understand it's hard, but there are ways," Bustos says. "You don't have to have the best equipment or the newest equipment. If you want it, you can do it." That's the mantra her father drilled into her.

"I was fortunate," Bustos says. "My parents, all my uncles and cousins were behind me since I was little. It took a whole family effort to get where I'm at right now."

Perez, gender equity committee chair for the Commission on Athletics for California Community Colleges, says hurdles remain in involving more Hispanic girls. Perez informally asked athletics directors at some of the community colleges with large Hispanic enrollments what they have done to attract Latinas. Responses ranged from "not aware of anything" to some who had worked with high school parents to raise awareness of scholarship opportunities, Perez says.

At Kennedy High in Granada Hills, which is about 80% Hispanic, athletics director Rae Brittain says it's still common for girls to drop out because they need to stay home to babysit. But a push to encourage athletics as a positive step toward college is bringing more Hispanic girls to sports. "The tides are definitely changing," Brittain says. "In the past you didn't see that many Hispanic women (athletes). You will in the coming years start to see multitudes of them."

Joining in the Conversation

1. Sylwester mainly presents two sides to the issue of Hispanic girls in sports, the needs of the family and the benefits to the young Hispanic students. Review the article to find the viewpoints for each side and then decide which side you favor.
2. Sylwester quotes girls basketball coach John Steckel as stating that "If you don't feel a part of your school, you're not going to have a very enjoyable high school career and possibly even postsecondary school." Do you feel that coach Steckel is correct in his statement? Find out if others in your school share your viewpoint and why. Then evaluate your own school as to the opportunities it offers in after-school activities to foster a feeling of belonging to a school.
3. Assume you have been elected superintendent of a new school district and have to create a series of programs for students to encourage a sense of belonging on campus. Decide if you want to work at the elementary, middle, or high school level and then create a series of programs and clubs aimed at student participation. Remember to keep in mind the various difficulties many students face, such as work, family obligations, and transportation, just to name a few, plus the costs to the school and the need of faculty sponsors to maintain such programs.

Spanglish: Pop Culture's Lingua Franca

Teresa Wiltz

Theresa Wiltz is a staff writer for The Washington Post *who covers both arts and culture for the publication. Her articles range in topic from media and television commentaries to insights on contemporary musicians. The following article appeared in* The Washington Post *on January 26, 2003.*

✦

Source: Teresa Wiltz, "Spanglish: Pop Culture's Lingua Franca," *Washington Post,* January 26, 2003, p. G1. © 2003, The Washington Post, reprinted with permission.

It's a moment of high drama, the kind of drama of which Tony Soprano would heartily approve. Except that in this instance, the players are brown, the mob is Mexican, and the moment of truth gets played out with a radically different *sabor:*

It's showtime. As in show-me-and-then-I'll-give-you-the-money time.

"Enseñame la carga," a mobboss orders his flunky, rubbing his hands with anticipation. *"Enseñamela"*

He's an excitable sort, and the very idea of *la carga* has him so geeked, he's literally jumping up and down.

"A ver . . . A ver que tienes! A ver que tienes!"

The flunky obeys, and opens up his SUV. And out conies tumbling *la carga:* the bloody and bullet-ridden body of a DEA agent.

Even if you don't *habla español,* it doesn't take a linguist to figure out what's going on in "Kingpin," NBC's upcoming drama about a Mexican drug lord. Which is exactly the point these days, as increasingly, snippets of Spanish, sometimes translated but often not, crop up on the big and little screen.

As the U.S. Latino population expands to 37 million, on-screen life is gradually changing to depict *la vida latina.* And that means that Spanglish—the mixing of Spanish and English—is the featured act these days in mainstream Hollywood fare, from *Traffic,* where a substantial part of the dialogue was in subtitled Spanish, to John Sayles's almost-all-Spanish *Men With Guns,* to both *Spy Kids,* where Spanish words were tossed about, to Spike Lee's *25th Hour,* where untranslated dialogue floats around like background noise, to John Leguizamo's *Empire,* to *Real Women Have Curves,* in which the Latina protagonist is fluent in both California-ese and her parents' native tongue.

On the smaller screen, there was the mournful—and controversial—chihuahua who crooned, *"Yo quiero* Taco Bell" But now, there is "The George Lopez Show," where the Chicano comic peppers his speech with *"orale,"* while on PBS's "American Family," starring Edward James Olmos and Raquel Welch, Spanish is an integral part of the family's Mexican American culture. For preschoolers, there's Nickelodeon's bilingual *Dora the Explorer,* aka *Dora la Exploradora.* On *CSI: Miami,* the hip forensic crew will throw in a word or two while questioning witnesses, just to let everyone know they're down. (Or maybe it's just to cue in viewers lest they confuse *CSI: Miami* with the other *CSI* set in Las Vegas.)

The linguistic revolution isn't limited to the screen: Lalo Alcaraz's comic strip, *"La Cucaracha,"* uses Spanglish to poke political fun at both Anglos and Chicanos. In literature, there was Chicano poet Alurista and the Nuyorican Poets Cafe out of New York, who set the stage for other bilingual writers such as today's Junot Diaz. His highly acclaimed short-story collection *Drown* incorporated elements of Spanish, as does Sandra Cisneros's *Caramelo*. Then there's Puerto Rican poet Giannina Braschi, who recently published her all-Spanglish novel, *Yo-Yo Boing! (Discoveries)*.

Music groups such as the Los Angeles-based Ozomatli frequently sing in Spanish and rap in English, while rapper N.O.R.E. boasts in his latest hit about being "half Spanish, all day *arroz con pollo*."

Spanish is hip, a flavoring, a punctuation, a way to express cultural pride—and an awareness of the rapidly changing U.S. landscape.

"Latino culture is moving from the periphery to center stage," says Ilan Stavans, author of *Spanglish: the Making of a New American Language*, and professor of Latin American and Latino culture at Amherst College.

"Mainstream Americans are absorbing this and thinking that it's hot. I've even seen Spanglish Hallmark cards. . . . This Spanglish thing is very cool, even if you don't speak it. It makes you attractive to younger people, to a particular audience that's out there and that corporations want to address."

Which means that, at times, the use of Spanglish is nothing more than a marketing move, a wink-wink, nod-nod way to acknowledge the nation's new reality without doing a whole lot more. There are many examples, after all, of resistance to issues such as bilingual education—never mind that the vast majority of the Americas' population, North, South and Central, is Spanish-speaking. Tossing a few Spanish words into the mix becomes a shorthand, a quick way to indicate other. There's a fine line between celebrating a culture and pimping it.

"I find it just interesting that certain elements of me are fit for consumption but certain aspects of my culture are not," says the Dominican-born Diaz, who is now working on his first novel. "I see the language more than I see the people, the complicated space we inhabit in the culture. . . . I'm not sure the appearance of Spanish means much for the masses of Latinos who are struggling for social justice or . . . just trying to have better lives."

In Hollywood, there are few Latinos who have the power to greenlight a project—and therefore the power to control Latino images. The few who do have tried to increase representation.

Showtime's *Resurrection Boulevard,* one of the first TV dramas to be written, produced by and star Latinos, put some 500 Hispanic actors to work during its three-season run—more than all four networks had done in the previous 10 years, according to Alex Nogales, president of the National Hispanic Media Coalition. (The show has since been canceled because of poor ratings.) Gregory Nava produces *American Family,* while Moctesuma Esparza, who produced *Selena,* is working on a project about activist Cesar Chavez. Director Richard Rodriguez is careful to cast his *Spy Kids* in a Latino milieu. *The George Lopez Show* made it to ABC, thanks in large part to the A-list pull of executive producer Sandra Bullock.

Alcaraz, the comic strip artist, recalls the time he was hired as a writer to work on the short-lived Fox comedy show *Culture Clash.* At first, he says, almost all the writers were Latinos. By the end, he says, there were only two: Alcaraz and Josefina Lopez, the playwright who wrote *Real Women Have Curves,* and co-wrote the screen version.

"In the end, I was just kind of translating things," Alcaraz says, adding that he wasn't too disturbed by it. "I was like, 'Ahh . . . that's showbiz.'"

When it came to his sitcom, stand-up comic Lopez had no illusions about showbiz: He wanted to create a mainstream sitcom about a family that just happened to be Latino. And he wanted it to be stereotype-free. So he cast Latinos who spoke unaccented English. He wanted no bad accents, no rapid-fire, hands-on-hips harangues, no "I'm so upset, and then go off into '*Que tal loca no sabes . . .*'"

So his first season, Lopez says, he dropped only one bit of Spanish into the mix: He called his TV grandmother a "crazy old *vieja.*"

"My plan," he says, "was to get renewed, and then start dropping my *orales.* Now I feel comfortable dropping it on the American people.

"We've been invisible for so many years. I want to bring what's really out there, culturally, with language. Latinos have infiltrated every aspect of the culture. It's a connection that we are making when TV is not as milquetoast as it's always been. It's like food—it adds flavor."

But sometimes the flavor can leave a bad aftertaste. Desi Arnaz, with his impeccable suits and rapid-fire Spanish, introduced much of Anglo America to Cuban culture on *I Love Lucy.* In the late '70s, U.S. audiences tuned in briefly to the bilingual

Que Pasa, USA?, a PBS sitcom about a Cuban American family. (And starring the actor Steven Bauer, back when he was known as "Rocky Echevarria.")

But now, critics say, things haven't progressed much beyond the stereotypes of Pepino in *The Real McCoys,* reducing the Spanish language and Latino culture to a caricature. Today, with our nation's endless fascination with cops and robbers, that caricature is the Latino as drug dealer, whether it's in *Traffic* or the remake of *Shaft,* in which the Dominican baddie is portrayed by African American actor Jeffrey Wright.

"If we're not maids, we're [expletive] drug dealers," Diaz says. "It's no accident you're going to find the first usage of Spanish" in drug films.

Which is why some Latinos are taking issue with the upcoming *Kingpin,* NBC's limited-run drama that debuts next Sunday. *Kingpin* tracks the life of Miguel Cadenas (Yancey Arias), a Stanford-educated Mexican drug lord, as he struggles to reconcile his troubled conscience with the grimy reality of the family business. Set in both Mexico and the States, it is written primarily in English but leans heavily on the use of untranslated Spanish phrases. (Two key scenes in the series are shot entirely in Spanish and use subtitles.)

"At a time when there's no balance of Latinos on television, for us, *Kingpin* is not so great," Nogales says. "It's got superb writing, superb acting and great, great direction—all the ingredients to be a great hit. But there will be a lot of problems with the Latino community."

The show's creator is David Mills, an African American (and former *Washington Post* staff writer) who cheerfully admits that he speaks "not a lick" of Spanish.

"That bothers me, absolutely," Lopez says. "It sends the wrong message. Would African American people love a show that depicts slavery in 2003? I don't think so. It's been seen, it's been done."

Says Mills: "I'm not writing this as a Mexican. How can I? I don't know anything about Mexican culture. But I know about the human condition. . . . The breakthrough here is, this is a story about the condition of a man's soul. . . . Often in TV, to get that deeply in the psyche of a character, that character is white. It's pretty rare that a nonwhite character [gets that kind of attention]. . . . It's not a victory to have every Latino character on television viewed as an emblem of his ethnicity. It's a burden the actors don't want, and that I don't want."

Except for Mills, all the show's writers are Latinos, but most of them don't speak fluent Spanish, either. Bilingual actors were cast;

still, since the actors' heritage ranges from all over Latin America, a vocal coach was hired to help them with their Mexican accents. After all, there's a world of difference between the nuances of North-Mexican Spanish and, say, the Caribbean rhythms of Cuba or Puerto Rico.

"I have a very good ear for dialogue," *Real Women's* Josefina Lopez says, and she's able to tell when the Spanish was written by a native speaker, or by someone who wrote it in English and then translated it into Spanish.

"There's a rhythm to Spanish, especially if it's Mexican or Puerto Rican. I hear it a lot on TV when they do it, and I say, 'No, they missed the beat'"

Still, she says, it doesn't bother her when non-Latino writers take on her language and culture.

"As long as they get the rhythm right, I'm happy that they're doing that. It shows a respect for our language and our culture."

Joining in the Conversation

1. Wiltz's article points out several stereotypes of Chican@s, both positive and negative. Search through the article and discover examples of ways the Chican@ culture has been represented in television and movies, adding any that you are familiar with. Then decide which ones are positive and which portray a limited or negative aspect of the Chican@ culture.
2. Portraying only a limited or narrow view of a culture on television or in movies is not limited to the Chican@ culture. All cultures are stereotyped in some way. Consider the stories and essays you read, the ads you see every day, and the programs and films you watch. Then determine how cultures other than Chican@ are portrayed in a limited or stereotyped manner.
3. In her article, Wiltz quotes writer Josefina Lopez as stating, "As long as they get the rhythm [of the language] right, I'm happy that they're doing that. It shows a respect for our language and our culture." Do you agree with Lopez's statement? What would be some of the difficulties involved in achieving such "respect" at school and work? Be prepared to present your ideas to the class.

Additional Topics of Conversation

1. The contemporary world of cultural art is a dynamic space with artists ranging from old-world potters to religious artists, each with his/her own views of cultural expression. Choose one area of artistic representation in graphic design or painting, such as religious or Lowrider artistic

expression, and prepare presentation, with images, illustrating the transition of artistic change for that type of art over at least the last ten years.

2. Pop Culture can take an aesthetic turn, similar to art, but it can also be more physical and active. Investigate the phenomenon of local rodeos, car designs, theater, or music artists whom you think belong to the Chican@ culture and elaborate your findings in a class presentation and explain the cultural elements of the participants or artists. Be sure to incorporate visual images whenever possible.
3. When cultures interact, as they do in the United States, many cultural artists "cross over" into mainstream avenues of cultural expression, such as movies, soap operas, directorships, and music producing. Many of these successful individuals manage to blend both cultures and, thus, enjoy the benefits of both worlds. Selecting an individual from the Chican@ culture whom you feel has successfully crossed over into mainstream entertainment or writing, research her/his life and then prepare a biographical report detailing the individual's life and accomplishments.
4. The issues of who is represented and how she/he is represented are always culturally sensitive aspects of public broadcasting and entertainment. Who is given the most prestigious parts in a news broadcast, which actor/actress plays what type of character, who is the "bad" guy/girl versus the "good" guy/girl, and how a community is represented all play an important role in representing a culture. Even within culturally specific forms of entertainment, such as the *novelas*, gender and other cultural types exist that may offend individuals. Select either a mainstream or a culturally specific form of entertainment that represents the Chican@ community in some manner and analyze such representation in relation to the concept of stereotyping. Then determine the best methods for presenting your information to the class and construct your project.

Language and Education

Whether a person is 2, 20, or even 80 years old, he or she is engaged in the lifelong process of learning. How one learns, the processes at work on TV, radio, videos, Internet, casual exchanges between friends, work, and, yes, even in the classroom, just to name a few, all contribute to how we learn about the world and how we respond. We are all students every day of our lives. One key in all learning processes and a foundational marker in any culture is language: the sounds one hears, the patterns, tones, inflections, and, most importantly, the privileging of one language system over another all contribute to how one learns about his/her world and one's place in the world. And since we live in a material, physical world, the process of learning often takes on political and social ramifications as well: who gets to attend the top colleges, who can go to college at all, whose children are in the "best" elementary schools, how far is the local library from home, and what programs are available for tutoring children in need? On a different note, the function of education in the United States has taken on political and social dimensions unheard of in earlier times; for example, often schools provide the only meals during the day that many low-income students will have, and high schools and colleges are now the recruiting grounds for the sports industry. When one considers the multitude of nationalities immigrating daily to the United States, the dynamics of American education become even more complex.

This chapter looks at the American educational system through multiple levels of learning. At the core of the educational debates in America today is the concern for language use in the classroom and how Spanish-speaking Mexican Americans relate to the dominant, American English-speaking culture. How Spanish-speaking students are introduced to English is every bit as debated as is the representation of the Mexican-American culture in the students' textbooks. The debate regarding bilingualism has not been resolved. On a different level, the presence of the affirmative action programs at all levels of education opens up the debate as to who now has access to the *few* college seats available in the country: does one's abilities or one's cultural heritage now set the criteria for admission? In short, who gets chosen and who does not? The results often provoke a storm of rage on the losing side. A final level of consideration concerns the very ugly side of politics and education, the issue of segregation, and how one must, at times, be his/her own champion in the struggle for educational equality. The process of education is not only a life-process but often a life-struggle as well.

Profession

Richard Rodriguez

The following selection is taken from Richard Rodriguez's award-winning autobiography Hunger of Memory: The Education of Richard Rodriguez *(1982). In the work he explains that he, like Maria González, was a recipient of affirmative action. And like her, he received numerous benefits from affirmative action in terms of access to higher education and graduate school, and even an offer of an important teaching position. Other publications by Rodriguez include* Mexico's Children *(1990),* Days of Obligation: An Argument with My Mexican Father *(1992), and* Brown: The Last Discovery of America *(2002).*

✦

Minority student—that was the label I bore in college at Stanford, then in graduate school at Columbia and Berkeley: a nonwhite reader of Spenser and Milton and Austen.

In the late 1960s nonwhite Americans clamored for access to higher education, and I became a principal beneficiary of the academy's response, its programs of affirmative action. My presence was noted each fall by the campus press office in its proud tally of Hispanic-American students enrolled; my progress was followed by HEW statisticians. One of the lucky ones. Rewarded. Advanced for belonging to a racial group "under-represented" in

American institutional life. When I sought admission to graduate schools, when I applied for fellowships and summer study grants, when I needed a teaching assistantship, my Spanish surname or the dark mark in the space indicating my race—'check one'—nearly always got me whatever I asked for. When the time came for me to look for a college teaching job (the end of my years as a scholarship boy), potential employers came looking for me—a minority student.

Fittingly, it falls to me, as someone who so awkwardly carried the label, to question it now, its juxtaposition of terms—minority, student. For me there is no way to say it with grace. I say it rather with irony sharpened by self-pity. I say it with anger. It is a term that should never have been foisted on me. One I was wrong to accept.

In college one day a professor of English returned my term paper with this comment penciled just under the grade: 'Maybe the reason you feel Dickens's sense of alienation so acutely is because you are a minority student.' *Minority student.* It was the first time I had seen the expression; I remember sensing that it somehow referred to my race. Never before had a teacher suggested that my academic performance was linked to my racial identity. After class I reread the remark several times. Around me other students were talking and leaving. The professor remained in front of the room, collecting his papers and books. I was about to go up and question his note. But I didn't. I let the comment pass; thus became implicated in the strange reform movement that followed.

* * *

The year was 1967. And what I did not realize was that my life would be radically changed by deceptively distant events. In 1967, their campaign against southern segregation laws successful at last, black civil rights leaders were turning their attention to the North, a North they no longer saw in contrast to the South. What they realized was that although no official restrictions denied blacks access to northern institutions of advancement and power, for most blacks this freedom was only theoretical. (The obstacle was 'institutional racism.') Activists made their case against institutions of higher education. Schools like Wisconsin and Princeton long had been open to blacks. But the tiny number of nonwhite students and faculty members at such schools suggested that there was more than the issue of access to consider. Most blacks simply couldn't afford tuition for higher education. And, because the primary and secondary schooling blacks received was usually poor, few qualified for admission. Many were so culturally alienated that they never thought to apply; they couldn't even imagine themselves going to college.

I think—as I thought in 1967—that the black civil rights leaders were correct: Higher education was not, nor is it yet, accessible to many black Americans. I think now, however, that the activists tragically limited the impact of their movement with the reforms they proposed. Seeing the problem solely in racial terms (as a case of *de facto* segregation), they pressured universities and colleges to admit more black students and hire more black faculty members. There were demands for financial aid programs. And tutoring help. And more aggressive student recruitment. But this was all. The aim was to integrate higher education in the North. So no one seemed troubled by the fact that those who were in the best position to benefit from such reforms were those blacks least victimized by racism or any other social oppression—those culturally, if not always economically, of the middle class.

The lead established, other civil rights groups followed. Soon Hispanic-American activists began to complain that there were too few Hispanics in college. They concluded that this was the result of racism. They offered racial solutions. They demanded that Hispanic-American professors be hired. And that students with Spanish surnames be admitted in greater numbers to colleges. Shortly after, I was 'recognized' on campus: an Hispanic-American, a 'Latino,' a Mexican-American, a 'Chicano.' No longer would people ask me, as I had been asked before, if I were a foreign student. (From India? Peru?) All of a sudden everyone seemed to know—as the professor of English had known—that I was a minority student.

I became a highly rewarded minority student. For campus officials came first to students like me with their numerous offers of aid. And why not? Administrators met their angriest critics' demands by promoting any plausible Hispanic on hand. They were able, moreover, to use the presence of conventionally qualified nonwhite students like me to prove that they were meeting the goal of their critics.

In 1969, the assassination of Dr. Martin Luther King, Jr., prompted many academic officials to commit themselves publicly to the goal of integrating their institutions. One day I watched the nationally televised funeral; a week later I received invitations to teach at community colleges. There were opportunities to travel to foreign countries with contingents of 'minority group scholars.' And I went to the financial aid office on campus and was handed special forms for minority student applicants. I was a minority student, wasn't I? the lady behind the counter asked me rhetorically. Yes, I said. Carelessly said. I completed the application. Was later awarded.

In a way, it was true. I was a minority. The word, as popularly used, did describe me. In the sixties, *minority* became a synonym for socially disadvantaged Americans—but it was primarily a numerical designation. The word referred to entire races and nationalities of Americans, those numerically underrepresented in institutional life. (Thus, without contradiction, one could speak of 'minority groups.') And who were they exactly? Blacks—all blacks—most obviously were minorities. And Hispanic-Americans. And American Indians. And some others. (It was left to federal statisticians, using elaborate surveys and charts, to determine which others precisely.)

I was a minority.

I believed it. For the first several years, I accepted the label. I certainly supported the racial civil rights movement; supported the goal of broadening access to higher education. But there was a problem: One day I listened approvingly to a government official defend affirmative action; the next day *I* realized the benefits of the program. I was the minority student the political activists shouted about at noontime rallies. Against their rhetoric, I stood out in relief, unrelieved. *Knowing:* I was not really more socially disadvantaged than the white graduate students in my class. *Knowing:* I was not disadvantaged like many of the new nonwhite students who were entering college, lacking good early schooling.

Nineteen sixty-nine. 1970. 1971. Slowly, slowly, the term *minority* became a source of unease. It would remind me of those boyhood years when I had felt myself alienated from public (majority) society—*los gringos. Minority. Minorities. Minority groups.* The terms sounded in public to remind me in private the truth: I was not—in a *cultural* sense—a minority, an alien from public life. (Not like *los pobres* I had encountered in my recent laboring summer.) The truth was summarized in the sense of irony I'd feel at hearing myself called a minority student: The reason I was no longer a minority was because I had become a student.

Minority student!

In conversations with faculty members I began to worry the issue, only to be told that my unease was unfounded. A dean said he was certain that after I graduated I would be able to work among 'my people.' A senior faculty member expressed his confidence that, though I was unrepresentative of lower-class Hispanics, I would serve as a role model for others of my race. Another faculty member was sure that I would be a valued counselor to incoming minority students. (He assumed that, because of my race, I retained a special capacity for communicating with nonwhite students.) I also heard academic officials say that minority students would someday form a leadership class in America. (From our probable positions of power, we would be able to lobby for reforms to benefit others of our race.)

In 1973 I wrote and had published two essays in which I said that I had been educated away from the culture of my mother and father. In 1974 I published an essay admitting unease over becoming the beneficiary of affirmative action. There was another article against affirmative action in 1977. One more soon after. At times I proposed contrary ideas; consistent always was the admission that I was no longer like socially disadvantaged Hispanic-Americans. But this admission, made in national magazines, only brought me a greater degree of success. A published minority student, I won a kind of celebrity. In my mail were admiring letters from right-wing politicians. There were also invitations to address conferences of college administrators or government officials.

My essays served as my 'authority' to speak at the Marriott Something or the Sheraton Somewhere. To stand at a ballroom podium and hear my surprised echo sound from a microphone. I spoke. I started getting angry letters from activists. One wrote to say that I was becoming the *gringos'* fawning pet. What 'they' want all Hispanics to be. I remembered the remark when I was introduced to an all-white audience and heard their applause so loud. I remembered the remark when I stood in a university auditorium and saw an audience of brown and black faces watching me. I publicly wondered whether a person like me should really be termed a minority. But some members of the audience thought I was denying racial pride, trying somehow to deny my racial identity. They rose to protest. One Mexican-American said I was a minority whether I wanted to be or not. And he said that the reason I was a beneficiary of affirmative action was simple: I was a Chicano. (Wasn't I?) It was only an issue of race. . . .

All Mexican-Americans certainly are not equally Mexican-Americans. The policy of affirmative action, however, was never able to distinguish someone like me (a graduate student of English, ambitious for a college teaching career) from a slightly educated Mexican-American who lived in a *barrio* and worked as a menial laborer, never expecting a future improved, Worse, affirmative action made me the beneficiary of his condition. Such was the foolish logic of this program of social reform: Because many Hispanics were absent from higher education, I became with my matriculation an exception, a numerical minority. Because I was not a cultural minority, I was extremely well placed to enjoy the advantages of affirmative action. I was groomed for a position in the multiversity's leadership class.

Remarkably, affirmative action passed as a program of the Left. In fact, its supporters ignored the most fundamental assumptions of the classical Left by disregarding the importance of class and by assuming that the disadvantages of the lower class would necessarily be ameliorated by the creation of an elite society. The movement that began so nobly in the South, in the North came to parody social reform. Those least disadvantaged were helped first, advanced because many others of their race were more disadvantaged. The strategy of affirmative action, finally, did not take seriously the educational dilemma of disadvantaged students. They need good early schooling! Activists pushed to get more nonwhite students into colleges. Meritocratic standards were dismissed as exclusionary. But activists should have asked why so many minority students could not meet those standards; why so many more would never be in a position to apply. The revolutionary demand would have called for a reform of primary and secondary schools. . . .

I wish as I write these things that I could be angry at those who mislabeled me. I wish I could enjoy the luxury of self-pity and cast myself as a kind of 'invisible man.' But guilt is not disposed of so easily. The fact is that I complied with affirmative action. I permitted myself to be prized. Even after publicly voicing objections to affirmative action, I accepted its benefits. I continued to indicate my race on applications for financial aid. (It didn't occur to me to leave the question unanswered.) I'd apply for prestigious national fellowships and tell friends that the reason I won was because I was a minority. (This by way of accepting the fellowship money.) I published essays admitting that I was not a minority—saw my by-line in magazines and journals which once had seemed very remote from my life. It was a scholarship boy's dream come true. I enjoyed being—not being—a minority student, the featured speaker. I was invited to lecture at schools that only a few years before would have rejected my application for graduate study. My life was unlike that of any other graduate student I knew. On weekends I flew across country to say—through a microphone—that I was not a minority.

Someone told me this: A senior faculty member in the English department at Berkeley smirked when my name came up in a conversation. Someone at the sherry party had wondered if the professor had seen my latest article on affirmative action. The professor replied with arch politeness, 'And what does Mr. Rodriguez have to complain about?'

You who read this act of contrition should know that by writing it I seek a kind of forgiveness—not yours. The forgiveness, rather of those many persons whose absence from higher education permitted me to be classed a minority student. I wish that they would read this. I doubt they ever will. . . .

* * *

In 1975, I was afraid of the success I knew I would have when I looked for a permanent teaching position. I accepted another one-year appointment at Berkeley in an attempt to postpone the good fortune awaiting me and the consequent issue it would finally force. But soon it came time: September, October, November—the traditional months of academic job-searching arrived. And passed. And I hadn't written to a single English department. When one of my professors happened to learn this, late in November, he was astonished. Then furious. He yelled at me over the phone. Did I think that just because I was a minority, the jobs would come looking for me? Didn't I realize that he and several other faculty members had already written letters on my behalf to various schools? Was I going to start acting like some other minority students he knew. They struggled for academic success and then, when they almost had it made, they chickened out. Was that it? Had I decided to fail?

I didn't want to respond to his questions. I didn't want to admit to him—thus to myself—the reason for my delay. I agreed to write to several schools. I wrote: 'I cannot claim to represent socially disadvantaged Mexican-Americans. The very fact that I am in a position to apply for this job should make that clear.' After two or three days, there were telegrams and phone calls inviting me to job interviews. There followed rapid excitement: a succession of airplane trips; a blur of faces and the murmur of soft questions; and, over somebody's shoulder, the sight of campus buildings shadowing pictures I had seen, years before, when as a scholarship boy I had leafed through Ivy League catalogues with great expectations. At the end of each visit interviewers would smile and wonder if I had any questions for *them*. I asked if they were concerned about the fact that I hadn't yet finished my dissertation.

Oh no, they said. 'We regularly hire junior faculty members who complete their dissertation during their first year or two here.' A few times I risked asking what advantage my race had given me over other applicants. But that was an impossible question for them to answer without embarrassing me. They rushed to assure me that my ethnic identity had given me no more than a foot inside the door, at most a slight edge. 'We just looked at your dossier with extra care, and, frankly, we liked what we saw. There was never any question of our having to alter our standards. You can be certain of that.'

In the first part of January their offers arrived on stiff, elegant stationery. Most schools promised terms appropriate for any new assistant professor of English. A few made matters worse by offering more: an unusually large starting salary; a reduced teaching schedule; free university housing. As their letters gathered on my desk, I delayed my decision. I started calling department chairmen to ask for another week, another ten days—'more time to reach a decision'—to avoid the decision I would have to make. . . .

At school, meanwhile, I knew graduate students who hadn't received a single job offer. One student, among the best in the department, did not get so much as a request for his dossier. He and I met outside a classroom one day, and he asked about my prospects, He seemed happy for me. Faculty members beamed at the news. They said they were not surprised. 'After all, not many schools are going to pass up the chance to get a Chicano with a Ph.D. in Renaissance literature.' Friends telephoned, wanting to know which of the offers I was going to take. But I wouldn't make up my mind. Couldn't do it. February came. I was running out of time and excuses. I had to promise a decision by the tenth of the month. The twelfth at the very latest . . .

Late afternoon: In the office at Berkeley I shared with several other lecturers and teaching assistants, I was grading some papers. Another graduate student was sitting across the room at his desk. At about five, when I got up to leave, he looked over to tell me in a weary voice that he had some very big news. . . . He had decided to accept a position at a faraway state university. It was not the job he especially wanted, he said. But he needed to take it because there hadn't been any other offers. He felt trapped and depressed, since the job would separate him from his young daughter, who would remain in California with her mother. . . .

He stared at me as I put on my jacket. And then stretching to yawn, but not yawning, he asked me if I knew that he too had written to Yale. In his case, however, no one had bothered to acknowledge his letter with even a postcard. What did I think of that?

He gave me no chance to reply.

'Damn?' he said, and his chair rasped the floor as he pushed himself back. Suddenly it was to *me* that he was complaining. 'It's just not right, Richard. None of this is fair. You've done some good work, but so have I. I'll bet our records are just about even. But when we go looking for jobs this year, it's a very different story. You're the one who gets all the breaks.' . . .

His words stung anger alive. In a voice deceptively calm, I replied that he oversimplified the whole issue. Phrases came quickly: the importance of cultural diversity; new blood; the goal of racial integration. They were all the old arguments I had proposed years before—long since abandoned. After a minute or two, as I heard myself talking, I felt self-disgust. The job offers I was receiving were indeed unjustified. I knew that. All I was saying amounted to a frantic self-defense. It all was a lie. I tried to find an end to my sentence; my voice faltered to a stop.

'Yeah, yeah, sure,' he said. 'I've heard all that stuff before. Nothing you say, though really changes the fact that affirmative action is unfair. You can see that, can't you? There isn't any way for me to compete with you. Once there were quotas to keep my parents out of schools like Yale. Now there are quotas to get you in. And the effect on me is the same as it was for them. . . .'

At the edge of hearing, I listened to every word he spoke. But behind my eyes my mind reared—spooked and turning—then broke toward a reckless idea: Leave the university. Leave. Immediately the idea sprang again in my bowels and began to climb. Rent money. I pictured myself having to borrow. Get a job as a waiter somewhere? I had come to depend on the intellectual companionship of students—bright students—to relieve the scholar's loneliness. I remembered the British Museum, a year in silence. I wanted to teach; I wanted to read; I wanted this life. But I had to protest. How? Disqualify myself from the profession as long as affirmative action continued? Romantic exile? But I had to. Yes, I found the horizon again. It was calm.

The graduate student across the room had stopped talking; he was staring out the window. I said nothing. My decision was final. No, I would say to them all. Finally, simply, no.

I wrote a note to all the chairmen of English departments who had offered me jobs. I left a note for the professor of my own department at Berkeley who was in charge of helping graduate students look for teaching positions. (The contradictions of affirmative action have finally caught up with me. Please remove my name from the list of teaching job applicants.)

I telephoned my mother and father. My mother did not seem to hear exactly what I was trying to tell her. She let the subject pass without comment. (Was I still planning on coming for dinner this Sunday?) My father, however, clearly understood. Silent for a moment, he seemed uncertain of what I expected to hear. Finally, troubled, he said hesitantly, 'I don't know why you feel this way. We have never had any of the chances before.'

We, he said. But he was wrong. It was *he* who had never had any chance before.

Joining in the Conversation

1. Rodriguez seems obsessed with the term "minority student" at the beginning of his article. Explain what feelings he expresses when he uses the term. Is it the same feeling every time? Explain and give examples. What is Rodriguez's turning point in this article? Explain what you think Rodriguez told his mother that she "did not seem to hear" and that his father heard but "seemed uncertain" about how to respond.
2. This is clearly an autobiographical article in which Rodriguez is in conflict with various entities. Analyze the article and trace each time he is clearly aware of a conflict and determine how he resolves it. Focus on several of the conflicts Rodriguez faces and attempts to resolve, including his last one, and express your feelings about his turmoil and how he handled it.
3. Write about a serious decision that you had to make and that caused you conflict. How did you handle it? Who helped you resolve it? Were you happy with the resolution? What did you learn from the experience?

Proud to Be a Product of Affirmative Action

Maria C. González

Maria C. González is an associate professor of English in the Department of English at the University of Houston. Her scholarly writings include work on Mexican-American writers, feminist writers, Chicana lesbian writers, and queer theory. Her published works include Contemporary Mexican-American Women Novelists: Toward a

Feminist Identity (1996). She received her B.A. and M.A. degrees in English from Our Lady of the Lake University in San Antonio, Texas, and her Ph.D. in English from The Ohio State University. González wrote this article for Chican@s in the Conversations.

Before 1972, most law schools, medical schools, and engineering programs had low quotas for women or did not allow women into their programs at all. These same schools practiced "separate but equal" restrictions that would not admit African Americans into all-white universities. We now have laws that prohibit discrimination against women and minorities in education and employment. Having diverse representation in the professions, courts, committees, and any entity that is a part of our public society has become a fundamental belief in many American institutions. This belief was formalized in specific programs, known as Affirmative Action Projects, to address the lack of diversity in education and employment along with formal nondiscrimination statements that public and private entities now have. Although the privileging of certain individuals over others seemed unfair, this was a reaction to the historic discrimination women and minorities endured in the past. To correct the "separate but equal" practice, the educational institutions addressed historical inequality through Affirmative Action, and I am a proud product of the institutional efforts to diversify our educational and public institutions. I had access that was not offered to many women and minorities before 1972. Furthermore, I had privileged access to a blue-chip education, privileged access to a research university position, and privileged access to specific opportunities in my career thanks in part to Affirmative Action.

Rarely does one declare that he or she is proud of being a product of Affirmative Action. I am! Too often, individuals who have had the privileged access to opportunity attempt to deny that privilege. A child of enormous wealth does not automatically acknowledge the opportunities and privileges received. But at no point is that child expected to be ashamed of that wealth. Hence, why do some people think one should be ashamed of being a product of Affirmative Action? I would have liked the additional privileges that wealth often offers, but I did not have wealth. I do, however, appreciate the additional opportunities that Affirmative Action offered me as a woman and a minority. I think it is important that my individual story be part of the history of the institutional system known as

Affirmative Action. By understanding my experience, others can understand why I am a proud product of Affirmative Action.

I was born to a working-class Mexican-American family in West Texas in 1959. During that period, we lived in a society that was clearly segregated by ethnic markers as well as one that was sexist. Our society had a basic apartheid mentality toward different cultures and a sense of male superiority over women. Mexicans knew they were not welcome in certain parts of the city or in certain schools. The so-called "races" did not mix. Mexican-American children attended predominately perceived "inferior" schools where student-to-teacher ratios were very high, and many teachers had no certification. The Anglo children had access to the perceived "better" schools, which had lower student-to-teacher ratios and teachers who were certified.

In the sixties, our society began to see real shifts and opportunities for the poor. In 1964, President Lyndon Johnson signed the Civil Rights Bill guaranteeing federal support for equal opportunities for all Americans. The Johnson administration began its "War on Poverty" programs that included making attempts to challenge poverty at its root, especially through education. The Head Start Program was created, and I was one of the first of many children to benefit from this program. Targeted for poor, working-class children, many of whom were minorities, access to early education and additional educational resources meant that my stuttering was addressed early by professionals. I had access to a language tutor who gave me one-on-one attention and instruction that included teaching me how to write my own name. My parents could not have afforded to get me an individual speech therapist.

I did well in school once many of my learning disabilities were diagnosed and addressed. Hence, when I was ready to go to college in 1979, many different kinds of schools were interested in my applying to them. I had scored fairly well on my SAT, had performed solidly in my college preparatory course work, and was decently ranked in my class. However, my parents were not ready to allow me to leave the protection of their home. They understood, in a way I did not, that once I left, I would probably not return. They wanted to delay that for as long as they could. So I went to the University of Texas, El Paso, and waited for the opportunity to escape El Paso. It came a year later when my brother showed interest in a school in San Antonio, Our Lady of the Lake University, a historically woman's college. I told my brother he had to attend for at least one semester because otherwise I would not get to go to college out of town. He acquiesced, and we went off to school together. While there, the administration encouraged me to sit on committees as the student representative. They liked the fact that my name showed the kind of diversity they were proud to foster at their university. I did not mind because it gave me an opportunity to have access to the decision-making process on campus.

In the early eighties, I was in search of a school where I could do my Ph.D. work. And although many suggested The University of Texas at Austin, I realized that the University was not offering much in terms of incentives. I needed a school that would help me defray the costs of my education. One of the schools high on my list was one that was actively working to diversify its graduate student body. The Ohio State University had made a strong commitment to Affirmative Action. They had a specific program that sought minority scholars to do their graduate work in Ohio. I am sure that much of that program no longer takes the form it had in 1984. The school aggressively sought me out, invited me to visit the campus at their expense, and then offered a minority-designated fellowship for graduate school. Much of that kind of targeting is no longer allowed. However, without their outreach and aggressive recruitment, I would never have considered The Ohio State University as a viable option for graduate work. I had the scores they were looking for, having done well on the Graduate Record Examination, and the background and preparation they were looking for, having done well in my undergraduate and master's work. What I did not have were the financial resources to go to a top-tier research university.

When I arrived at The Ohio State University, I realized how lucky I had been to get into the program. Some of the brightest and the best were at this university. They also had competed for the fellowship slots in the Ph.D. program. There was very little in our files that could distinguish us from one another. Everyone had top scores and grades along with excellent research skills as our sample essays displayed. How does one stand out in such a crowd? It helped to have a name that was distinctly a marker of diversity. My last name gave me that slight edge in getting noticed. Texas was not looking for Mexican-American students. They did not have to. However, The Ohio State University needed me because they did not have many Mexican-American students, as Ohio did not have a large Mexican-American population from which to draw.

My experiences at Ohio State as a minority student were probably not unique. The mass majority of students were white and middle class. At that time, I would say a small percentage of the student body was diverse, and at the graduate level even fewer students were not white or middle class. Once in a while in a fit of disdain, a person would say I was there only because of Affirmative Action. I would flippantly respond with, "I happen to be one of the brightest persons I know."

My education at the university was one of the best the country could offer because it was a top research institution. I had access to one of the top libraries in the country, and I also had opportunities few other graduate students had such as serving on university-wide committees. Always willing to accept positions of leadership, I found I was sought by many different parts of the university to participate in their governance and not just student government. Also, The Ohio State University needed a name like mine on their committee rosters to show that they did value diversity. I took advantage of such opportunities to understand how a university this large worked. It was nice to know that the president and the provost of the university actually knew my name and who I was. It was also a chance for them to meet someone who was a Mexican-American with a different kind of background from their own.

When I completed my studies, I began my search for an appointment as a professor of English. Once again, Affirmative Action helped. I had chosen to concentrate on Mexican-American literature, guaranteeing I would stand out in any job search. My name and my topic meant I was a unique candidate. People noticed my file among the hundreds they had seen. It is a crowded field when looking for an appointment, and any advantage to stand out is important. Ultimately, however, one's work has to speak for itself.

I do not deny that there are flaws in a system that uses diversity as one of the positive factors in making decisions and opportunities available to others. I have friends who sit on both sides of this issue: those who adamantly work very hard to continue an Affirmative Action policy and those who work very hard to create a so-called color-blind society. What both teams want is for our society to be able to give to individuals the opportunities they deserve based on merit. For millennia, women and minorities were kept out because of who they were. After 35 years of attempts at moving the system in the other direction so more women and minorities are part of the public sphere, there are times when decisions seem to be made only upon the one judgment of diversity and no other criteria seems to be used. I am proud of the fact that the Department of English at the University of Houston sees diversity as one of its many priorities in selecting its professors, thereby allowing a more diverse group of faculty to be hired.

When the best and the brightest are among the applicants, bringing diversity to the table is an asset, but there are no guarantees beyond that point. I, myself, have sat on committees making decisions on the hiring of others. I do notice whether there are women and minorities among whatever pool I look at, but these markers are not the only criteria I use. It is a small attempt at trying to diversify any endeavor. And I have to admit that some of my colleagues seem to use the diversity factor as their only criteria, guaranteeing a skewed decision.

Affirmative Action is not a free ride. It is an opportunity. What individuals do with the opportunities offered by Affirmative Action is their choice. Individuals helped by Affirmative Action can deny it, or they can say thank you for the opportunity. My mother and father were not offered a systematic Affirmative Action opportunity because it did not exist when they were young. I am here to make sure that the historically underrepresented get an opportunity. I hope to leave an important mark upon the academy and acknowledge the pride I have in being a product of Affirmative Action.

Joining in the Conversation

1. González outlines the various levels and types of education she experienced throughout her life, from elementary school through graduate school. Identify the different types and forms of education she experienced and compare them with your own experiences in terms of not only the general type of education you have received but also any personal experiences or advantages that you feel were of benefit to you and your success.
2. González presents a positive view of Affirmative Action through the genre of personal narrative. Consider what her cover letter to the University of Houston for her current position would have looked like, based on the information provided and compose the letter. You might research the different committees faculty members serve on that González might have been invited to join.
3. Using the Internet, investigate at least two educational districts to discover the different programs offered at the elementary and secondary levels to aid students in their education. Then look at the college-level entrance requirements for your campus and the level of learning needed to succeed. Based on your findings, determine whether the programs offered in the districts you investigated adequately prepare students for higher education. Find

another student in the class who holds an opposing position from yours and present both views to the class. Allow your peers to determine who is more convincing.

An Offering to the Power of Language

SANDRA CISNEROS

Sandra Cisneros was born in Chicago but currently lives in San Antonio, Texas. She is the recipient of numerous awards, including the prestigious MacArthur Fellowship for "show[ing] exceptional merit and promise for continued and enhanced creative work." Her first novel, The House on Mango Street *(1991) is a semi-autobiographical work, and her second novel* Caramelo *(2002) is a multigenerational story of a Mexican family. Cisneros also wrote a collection of short stories* Woman Hollering Creek and Other Stories *(1991) as well as several collections of poetry. The following article is one of many she has had published in magazines and newspapers. This one appeared in the October 26, 1997 issue of the* Los Angeles Times.

✦

"*Mi'ja,* it's me. Call me when you wake up." It was a message left on my phone machine from a friend. But when I heard that word *"mi'ja,"* a pain squeezed my heart. My father was the only one who ever called me this. Because his death is so recent, the word overwhelmed me and filled me with grief.

With my father's death, the thread that links me to my other self, to my other language, was severed. Spanish binds me to my ancestors, but especially to my father, a Mexican national by birth who became a U.S. citizen by serving in World War II. My mother, who is Mexican American, learned her Spanish through this man, as I did. Forever after, every word spoken in that language is linked indelibly to him.

I continue to analyze and reflect on the power a word has to produce such an effect on me. As always, I am fascinated by how those of us caught between worlds are held under the spell of words spoken in the language of our childhood. After a loved one dies, your senses become oversensitized. Maybe that's why I sometimes smell my father's cologne in a room when no one else does. And why words once taken for granted suddenly take on new meanings.

"Mi'ja" (MEE-ha) from *"mi hija"* (me EE-ha). The words translate as "my daughter." Daughter, my daughter, daughter of mine, they're all stiff and clumsy, and have nothing of the intimacy and warmth of the word *"mi'ja."* "Daughter of my heart," maybe. Perhaps a more accurate translation of *"mi'ja"* is, I love you.

When I wish to address a child, lover or one of my many small pets, I use Spanish, a language filled with affection and familiarity. I can only liken it to the fried-tortilla smell of my mother's house or the way my brothers' hair smells like Alberto VO5 when I hug them. It just about makes me want to cry.

The language of our *antepasados,* those who came before us, connects us to our center, to who we are and directs us to our life work. Some of us have been lost, cut off from the essential wisdom and power. Sometimes, our parents or grandparents were so harmed by a society that treated them ill for speaking their native language that they thought they could save us from that hate by teaching us to speak only English. Those of us, then, live like captives, lost from our culture, ungrounded, forever wandering like ghosts with a thorn in the heart.

When my father was sick, I watched him dissolve before my eyes. Each day the cancer that was eating him changed his face, as if he was crumbling from within and turning into a sugar skull, the kind placed on altars for Day of the Dead. Because I'm a light sleeper, my job was to sleep on the couch and be the night watch. Father always woke several times in the night choking on his own bile. I would rush to hold a kidney-shaped bowl under his lips, wait for him to finish throwing up, the body exhausted beyond belief. When he was through, I rinsed a towel with cold water and washed his face. —*Ya estoy cansado de vivir,* my father would gasp. —*Si, yo se,* I know. But the body takes its time dying. I have reasoned, since then, that the purpose of illness is to let go. For the living to let the dying go, and for the dying to let go of this life and travel to where they must.

Whenever anyone discusses death, they talk about the inevitable loss, but no one ever mentions the inevitable gain. How when you lose a loved one, you suddenly have a spirit ally, an energy on the other side that is with you always, that is with you just by calling their name. I know my father watches over me in a much more thorough way than he ever could when he was alive. When he was living, I had to telephone long distance to check up on him and, if he wasn't watching one of his endless *telenovelas,* he'd talk to me. Now I simply summon him in my thoughts. Papa. Instantly, I feel his presence surround and calm me.

I know this sounds like a lot of hokey new-age stuff, but really it's old age, so ancient and wonderful and filled with such wisdom that we have had to relearn it because our miseducation has taught us to name it "superstition." I have had to rediscover the spirituality of my ancestors, because my own mother was a cynic. So it came back to me a generation later, learned but not forgotten in some memory in my cells, in my DNA, in the palm of my hand that is made up of the same blood of my ancestors, in the transcripts I read from the great Mazatec visionary Maria Sabina Garcia of Oaxaca.

Sometimes a word can be translated into more than a meaning. In it is the translation of a world view, a way of looking at things and, yes, even a way of accepting what others might not perceive as beautiful. *"Urraca,"* for example, instead of "grackle." Two ways of looking at a black bird. One sings, the other cackles. Or, *"tocayola,"* your name-twin, and, therefore, your friend. Or, the beautiful *"estrenar"* which means to wear something for the first time. There is no word in English for the thrill and pride of wearing something new.

Spanish gives me a way of looking at myself and at the world in a new way. For those of us living between worlds, our job in the universe is to help others see with more than their eyes during this period of chaotic transition. Our work as bicultural citizens is to help others become visionary, to help us all examine our dilemmas in multiple ways and arrive at creative solutions; otherwise, we all will perish.

What does a skeleton mean to you? Satan worship? Heavy-metal music? Halloween? Or maybe it means—Death, you are a part of my life, and I recognize you, include you in mine, I even thumb my nose at you. Next Saturday, on the Day of the Dead, I honor and remember my *antepasados,* those who have died and gone on before me.

I think of those two brave women in Amarillo who lost their jobs for speaking Spanish, and I wonder at the fear in their employer. Did he think they were talking about him? What an egocentric! Doesn't he understand that speaking another language is another way of seeing, a way of being at home with one another, of saying to your listener, I know you, I honor you, you are my sister, my brother, my mother, my father, my family. If he learns Spanish, or any other language, he would be admitting I love and respect you, and I love to address you in the language of those you love.

This Day of the Dead I will make an offering, *una ofrenda,* to honor my father's life and to honor all immigrants everywhere who come to a new country filled with great hope and fear, dragging their beloved homeland with them in their language. My father appears to me now in the things that are most alive, that speak to me or attempt to speak to me through their beauty, tenderness and love. A bowl of oranges on my kitchen table. The sharp scent of a can filled with *campaxiuchil,* marigold flowers for Day of the Dead. The opening notes of an Agustin Lara bolero named *"Farolito."* The night sky filled with moist stars. *Mi'ja,* they call out to me, and my heart floods with joy.

Joining in the Conversation

1. Explain how Spanish is connected with Cisneros's father. How has speaking Spanish in an English-speaking world been detrimental to some people?
2. Cisneros mixes her writing strategies, using an informative style combined with personal experiences. She also writes in both English and Spanish when she feels it is appropriate. Discuss your thoughts with your class about whether the mixing of writing styles and language enhances or detracts from the article. Explain your feelings.
3. What is your understanding of the Day of the Dead? Complete some research about this cultural festival and be prepared to discuss different elements surrounding its celebration, such as sugar skulls, skeletons, altars, *pan de muerto*, marigolds, and so forth. If you have access to some of the artifacts, bring them to class to use in your explanations. How is Day of the Dead similar to and different from Halloween?

Speaking Spanish

Sarah Cortez

Sarah Cortez, a graduate of the University of Houston with a Masters of Science in Accountancy and of the University of Texas at Austin with a Master of Arts in Classical Studies, teaches creative writing courses in the Center for Mexican American Studies at the University of Houston. Among her recent publications, Cortez has a forthcoming poem in TimeSlice: Houston Poetry 2005, *two poems in* Riding Low on the Streets of Gold: Latino Literature for Young Adults *(2003), and a poem "How to Undress a Cop" in* Collected Poems *(2000). She was also the editor for* Urban-Speak: Poetry of the City *(2001). Cortez wrote the following article for this book.*

✦

In 1948 after my father had received his honorable discharge, my young parents moved away from both of their extensive families in South Texas to the thriving city of Houston. My birth a few years later brought me into a growing city where our green-shingled, ranch-style house, our Catholic church, my grade school, and all our friends were in an Anglo neighborhood.

The only times I heard Spanish were during the frequent trips to the homes of my grandparents, where the adults would stay up late sitting around the kitchen table or in metal lawn chairs under the oak trees talking and laughing long past the children's bedtimes. How I hated Spanish. Its soft, lilting and mysterious syllables seemed to be used solely when the adults wanted to exclude us children. As a treasured only child in our orderly Houston household, I wasn't accustomed to being left out.

Sometime around my fourteenth birthday, I decided to try learning Spanish in school. My hidden hope was that in knowing the language I would become privy to all the inscrutable secrets it contained. Secrets as yet uncommunicated to me, and, apparently, so potent that in my Houston family they were no longer spoken. On a trip to Laredo, my father proudly informed Grandpa that I was learning Spanish. Like most important news, it had been saved until almost the time of good-byes.

As we were leaving, Grandpa drew up his huge bulk out of the worn, brown Naugahyde armchair. This rare maneuver preceded his speaking directly and only to me. Was this the first time he had spoken solely to me? All my other memories show him surrounded by hordes of my dad's handsome half-brothers and raucous half-sisters, and their infinite number of babies scooting across area rugs in huge, ruffled diapers, while I stood silent and shy in the background. Yes, my stately and dignified grandfather was looking me straight in the eye and speaking. I sensed that what he was telling me was important, but I couldn't understand a word of the solemn Spanish. My parents were standing at the side already dressed in comfortable clothes for the nine-hour drive home from dusty Laredo. They stood smiling and awaited my reaction. I smiled a stopgap smile, hoping for a word of translation from either of my parents. None came. Slowly, Grandpa pointed his index finger directly in my face. "*Aprende*," he said emphatically. The syllables' secret hung in the air louder than the swoosh of the boxy, metal air coolers angled in the doorways. I panicked; I didn't know what to say. I smiled at my parents; they smiled back. I guessed at its meaning and shook my head from left to right "No," I said.

My parents almost visibly sagged. I, their studious and respectful daughter, had said, "No," when the Cortez family patriarch had simply and lovingly said, "Learn"—as I found out later. Someone else, a younger child from one of the stepfamilies who all spoke a fast, trilling Spanish, laughed at me, and darted into the freedom of the yard or kitchen.

* * *

My reconciliation with the Spanish language has happened slowly. It's unbroken code of beautiful sounds has remained aloof toward me, although it was my parents' first language. Even the acute embarrassment of not being able to reply when other Mexican Americans speak Spanish to me hasn't been enough to propel me into mastering difficult tense changes and the idiosyncrasies of Mexican slang. For me, Spanish has remained an elusive beauty.

Yet recently my relationship to speaking Spanish changed radically. While teaching (in English) in central Mexico, I became friends with a retired Texas couple—both Anglos. One day as I accompanied them to complete some business in this town they had settled in two years previously, I heard a conversation between one of my new friends and a Mexican store owner.

Oh, my goodness—all the sounds in my friend's Spanish were wrong. The r's weren't rolled, the "ll" was not pronounced like a "y," the internal "d's" weren't soft but thudded with all the grace of a falling cow patty. To my ear, it was ludicrous and terrible. But there amid the smell of ripe mangoes and tiny, fragrant limes, I saw that this friend made himself understood, got his business done, was polite, and was listened to politely by the store owner. I was flabbergasted. I now saw that my concern over having the exact accent, correct pronunciation, right verb choice, and the perfect one of those pesky personal pronouns had only kept me from using the language. And, by not using it, I would never be able to get comfortable with it. I had never been brave enough to try to touch its graceful beauty embodied in the soft consonants and even softer vowels. I had given up too soon.

And, yes, I did thank my retired CPA (Certified Public Accountant) Texas friend for helping me realize that I don't have to speak perfect Spanish, I just have to speak Spanish.

Joining in the Conversation

1. How did you feel about Cortez's response to her grandfather's comment? Have you ever been in a situation similar to hers? Explain. How do you feel about her attitude to speaking Spanish before she went to teach in Mexico? Have you ever been in a similar situation? Explain.
2. Cortez wrote an essay that incorporates personal experiences and ends with a moral. Analyze this essay for other strategies that she uses to support her thesis and develop her essay.
3. Using Cortez's essay as a model, write about an experience you had from which you learned a lesson at the end. Use various strategies to help develop your essay.

Testing "English Only" Rules

Miriam Jordan

Miriam Jordan wrote this article for the November 8, 2005 issue of The Wall Street Journal. *Jordan has been writing about Latino affairs and immigrants for* The Wall Street Journal *since returning to the United States two years ago after spending 17 years abroad as a reporter. Previously, she worked as a correspondent for* The Wall Street Journal *in Sao Paulo, Brazil; New Delhi, India; and Hong Kong. She started her career with Reuters News Agency, having worked in Mexico, Brazil, and Israel for the agency. While overseas for* The Wall Street Journal, *she wrote about business, health, gender, and poverty-related issues. A native of New York, Miriam was*

Source: Miriam Jordan, "Testing 'English Only' Rules: Employers Who Require Workers to Speak English Can Face Discrimination Suits," *Wall Street Journal,* November 8, 2005, p. B1.

raised partly in Brazil and has dual U.S.–Brazilian citizenship. She is currently based in Los Angeles, where she lives with her husband, Jonathan, and two children, Maya and Daniel. Their favorite pastime is traveling.

EMPLOYERS WHO REQUIRE WORKERS TO SPEAK ENGLISH CAN FACE DISCRIMINATION SUITS

Hispanic employees at a Sephora store in New York say their ability to speak Spanish was crucial when they were selling lipstick and eye shadow to well-heeled Chilean and Argentine tourists. But they say that if they uttered any Spanish to each other, even in the lunch room, they were reprimanded by managers.

As immigrants flock to the U.S. in record numbers, the nation's work force is becoming more multilingual. But some companies have responded by creating ad hoc language policies that can land them in court.

That's what happened to Sephora USA. Five employees filed a complaint against the division of luxury-goods maker LVMH Moet Hennessy Louis Vuitton with the U.S. Equal Employment Opportunity Commission in 2003. The commission, in turn, filed a lawsuit on behalf of the five and a class of Hispanic employees in a Federal District Court in Manhattan.

"This is the type of double standard we want to prevent," says EEOC attorney Raechel Adams. "Hispanic employees are expected to speak Spanish with customers but at the same time are reprimanded for speaking Spanish in their free time."

Sephora says it "considers the EEOC's allegations to be groundless." It denies that it ever had "an 'English-only' rule," but it says it does expect workers to speak English to customers unless the customer wishes otherwise. In September, a judge ruled that the company's written policy on English usage is "permissible," but the case is still pending on the issue of whether the employees were discriminated against when they were told not to speak Spanish.

Cases involving English-only policies are mounting at the EEOC, the federal agency that enforces antidiscrimination laws in the workplace, as well as at private law firms across the country. Complaints filed with the agency jumped to 155 in 2004 from 32 in 1996. More grievances—they usually involve Spanish—are likely being handled by private attorneys. Still, most instances of language discrimination go unreported because employees fear retaliation, such as job loss, or, if they are illegal immigrants, even deportation.

In the 2000 census, 47 million people—18% of all U.S. residents—reported speaking a language other than English at home, up from 14% in 1990. To accommodate immigrants, many states offer driver's license tests, hospital questionnaires and election ballots in foreign languages. Because of the increase in Spanish speakers, the U.S. Census Bureau is testing a bilingual questionnaire in preparation for the 2010 census.

But amid a heated national debate over what to do with 11 million illegal immigrants, employers may be feeling emboldened to crack down on those who speak Spanish, in particular, lawyers and civil-rights advocates say. They also say that language discrimination cases are emerging in states that have long absorbed immigrants relatively successfully, such as New York and Texas, they say.

Federal law doesn't prevent employers from requiring workers to speak only English if it is justified by business necessity or safety concerns, such as work in a hospital surgery room or an air-traffic control tower. But an English-only rule can get an employer in trouble if it's applied as a blanket policy, prohibiting workers from speaking another language during their breaks, for example, or when the language being spoken doesn't make a difference in the performance of the job. Workers who feel they are being treated unfairly can file a complaint with the EEOC, which then chooses whether to investigate, mediate or litigate the case. If merited, the EEOC takes legal action based on Title VII of the 1964 Civil Rights Act, which bans discrimination on the basis of national origin.

"Employers must understand that discriminatory English-only rules can hurt productivity, morale and ultimately their bottom line," says Kimberlie Ryan, a Denver attorney who is litigating several cases.

But some businesses fear that English-speaking clients will feel alienated if too many employees speak a foreign language. Other companies worry that use of a foreign language by one group of workers can undermine overall morale by making other employees feel they are being slighted.

Highland Hospital in Rochester, N.Y., asked its housekeeping staff to stick to English after it received complaints from several non-Spanish speaking workers who "were feeling ostracized by a group of Hispanic workers and [a] supervisor," says Cindy Becker, the hospital's chief executive officer.

In July, the EEOC filed suit against the hospital and its owners on behalf of a group of Hispanic employees who say they were subjected to an English-only rule and disciplined for violating it. The suit seeks financial compensation for past humiliation and emotional distress. "No one can argue that these janitors needed English to sweep the floors," says Sunu Chandy, an EEOC attorney.

The hospital denies that it ever enforced an English-only policy. According to Ms. Becker, the Hispanic plaintiffs all speak English and were asked to communicate in a "common language." But the EEOC maintains that most of the claimants have limited English proficiency. The workers, who are still employed by the hospital, won't comment on the case while it's in litigation.

Groups concerned about preserving English object to multilingualism whether it's practiced in offices or on assembly lines. They believe it threatens the dominance of English by tacitly encouraging newcomers to retain their own languages and to avoid assimilating into American society.

"As this country becomes more diverse ethnically, it is even more important to have a common language than it was 50 years ago," says K.C. McAlpin, executive director of ProEnglish, a group that lobbies to make English the official language of the U.S. The group is helping to finance the defense of at least two employers sued for insisting that English be spoken on the job.

But Ms. Ryan, the Denver attorney, says: "This is not about whether people should learn English. It's about not using language as a weapon of harassment." She says a large number of her clients require psychological counseling because of the emotional distress they suffer.

In March, Ms. Ryan reached a settlement with the Children's Medical Center in Dallas and the food-services company Sodexho Inc. on behalf of eight cooks and cafeteria workers at the facility. According to the complaint filed in Federal District Court in Dallas, the employees were subjected to a no-Spanish rule and harassed by the managers who had imposed it.

Juan Garrido, the lead plaintiff in the case, had been working at the facility for 18 months, preparing special meals for children with cancer, when a supervisor told him to speak only in English. When he declined, he says, he was warned that he was being "insubordinate." He eventually received a written notice that deemed him "unprofessional" and "unethical" for speaking Spanish. But Mr. Garrido, who speaks broken English, says that communicating with workers who spoke only Spanish was essential. "We were making food for children with special diets," he says in an interview.

Ultimately, the Guatemalan immigrant says, only eight of the 32 Hispanic kitchen staffers decided to seek legal recourse. The rest feared reprisal. To comply with a confidentiality provision, the parties declined to disclose the size of the settlement. The hospital declined to comment on the case.

Mr. Garrido, who is 29 years old, says he eventually quit his job at Children's Medical Center because the stress he felt at work was undermining his health. He has since taken a job as a cook at another Dallas hospital. There, he says, there are no restrictions on Spanish usage by the Latino kitchen staff.

Joining in the Conversation

1. According to Jordan, what are some of the reasons given for requiring Spanish-speaking employees to speak English only? What are the counter-arguments?
2. Jordan offers an essay that presents arguments in favor of and against an English-only policy on the job. Analyze the article for the sides she uses and determine whether the article favors or opposes English-only policies. Explain how you arrived at your decision.
3. Determine your own views on the subject of English-only policy at work and the reasons why. When would the policy be of benefit and when would it be harmful? Then contact several of your local or state leaders to discover those leaders who hold different views of English-only policies in the workplace compared to yours. Prepare a strong argument stating and defending your own views about English-only legislation and contact those public officials with your own proposal.

Where Do I Go With Spanish?

Lucy Hood

Lucy Hood wrote the following article for the September 2005 issue of Career World. *Hood is based in Washington, D.C. and is a freelance writer who writes about education and international issues. Her articles also appear in* DistrictAdministration: A Magazine for K-12 Education Leaders.

✦

Si puede leer esta frase, podría tener una maravillosa carrera profesional. If you can read that sentence, you may have a very bright career ahead of you. (In fact, that's what the sentence means.) Just about every field—including business, community service, travel, real estate, education, and health care—has a growing need for Spanish-speaking professionals. U.S. Census Bureau figures show that the Hispanic immigrant population grew more than 64.2 percent between 1990 and 2002. Hispanics, who now comprise more than 12 percent of the U.S. population, are expected to make up 24 percent of the population by 2050.

"Individuals with a solid knowledge of the Spanish language and Latino culture have career opportunities in 24 countries," says Luis Pablo Martinez, a spokesperson for the Hispanic Alliance for Career Enhancement. "Some of the professional opportunities include teaching, translating for government and corporate entities, law, [and] unique management opportunities with international corporations. Spanish is rapidly becoming the linguistic currency of the new century."

"The demand for bilingual skills in our business is phenomenal," adds Tom Young, a Houston-based manager for the recruiting and staffing firm Robert Half International. "I know that we have a demand [for Spanish-speaking employees] that we can't meet."

Where can you go with Spanish? Almost anywhere. *Career World* explores six possible routes.

MARKETING AND ADVERTISING

As a group, Latino Americans have a purchasing power of nearly $700 billion. So when advertisers want to create advertisements that appeal directly to Latinos, they turn to someone like Laura Sonderup, director of a marketing company in Denver that specializes in reaching Latino audiences. Sonderup studies what consumers want and creates targeted messages for advertisements, billboards, and mass mailings. When a local college wanted to recruit more Latino students, for example, Sonderup's group crafted a slogan: "Have you decided what to do with your life? *Permítenos ayudarte* [Let us help you]."

Laura Sonderup says she and her marketing staff are "absolutely bilingual, binational, and bicultural."

In marketing and advertising, as in many other fields, a professional level of Spanish fluency is a must. "I have high expectations," says Sonderup. Whether for a television ad, a billboard, or a mailing, the use of Spanish must be impeccable. Mistakes can reflect poorly on both client and agency.

Sonderup, who grew up speaking Spanish and has lived in Mexico, encourages young Latinos not only to be proud of their heritage but also to see it as a real asset in the job market. "As they become adults," she said, "that will give them a very distinct advantage in the marketplace."

For people interested in Latino marketing and advertising, opportunities abound, especially in the top Hispanic markets (Los Angeles, New York, Miami, Chicago, Houston, San Francisco, and Dallas).

Hot Job!

The Hispanic advertising industry has been growing at an average rate of 17% per year over the past five years. . . .

"Alto!" "Su licensia y registre, por favor," These are among the things that police officers in Des Moines, Iowa, are learning to say—the Spanish equivalents of "Stop!" and "Your license and registration, please."

Community police officers work with residents to ensure safety within a neighborhood. In Des Moines, as in many cities across the United States, community police officers must be able to communicate with the city's rapidly growing Latino population. Recruits at the police academy must meet a new Spanish language requirement. "We've incorporated Spanish into the curriculum," says Sgt. Vince Valdez, "not so much to make [officers] fluent but just to give them some phrases, words, and listening skills they could use on a daily basis."

Knowing Spanish helps officers get basic information from people in the community, fill out reports, and handle emergencies. Part of the community policing effort is outreach. Each month, officers hold meetings at community centers to update and inform residents about traffic, zoning, and criminal laws. In turn, residents share their concerns with the police. In order for the police and the community members to fully understand one another, Spanish language ability is crucial. The goals are to alleviate concerns residents might have about dealing with police and to help bridge the cultures. Valdez says the combination of coming to a new country, not speaking English, and dealing with police can be intimidating. "If you're coming from Latin America," Valdez notes, "the [Latin American] police can be very brutal and corrupt."

Sgt. Vince Valdez . . . and police officers in Des Moines, Iowa, help Latino residents feel secure in their community.

TRAVEL

Flight attendants are responsible for passenger safety and comfort on airline flights. They may occasionally be called on to attend to first aid and medical problems.

In all those instances, communication skills are key—and a knowledge of Spanish may prove valuable.

Delta Air Lines flight attendant Beatrice Pickert already spoke three languages when she signed up for Spanish classes. As a child growing up in Switzerland, she mastered English, German, and French. "Why Spanish?" she muses. "There's not much left. There's Chinese." And, she says, she can use Spanish on the job.

Learning Spanish is a smart move for Pickert. Her work schedule takes her from Atlanta to Montreal and back, and both cities have large Latino populations. "We get a lot of Spanish speakers on the airplane," she notes.

Eventually, Pickert can take a test to become an "onboard speaker" with Delta. If she passes the test, Pickert will be qualified to work on flights bound for Latin America.

Bilingual employees are valuable to any travel organization. "As the face of the United States changes, we in the travel industry have to be aware and respond to these demographic changes," says Daryl Krause, a spokesperson for Southwest Airlines. "Being bilingual allows you to have a broader reach with customers, employees, shareholders, and the media. . . . At Southwest Airlines, speaking Spanish is a plus for any flight attendants we hire, as they can provide outstanding customer service to both our English- and Spanish-speaking customers."

HEALTHCARE

A patient came to the primary health-care clinic in San Luis, Ariz., a small town on the Mexican border. He spoke only Spanish and couldn't tell an English-speaking health-care provider about his health background. Enter nurse-practitioner Rudy Valenzuela, a native Spanish speaker who grew up in Mexico. Once the patient could speak to someone in Spanish, he revealed the drug use that was the root of his illness.

Valenzuela says his ability to speak Spanish can lead to a more precise diagnosis and better care. "In trying to get really personal, intimate information from the patient," he notes, "you wouldn't be able to get that in English."

Most of Valenzuela's patients are native Spanish speakers. "A lot of them are bilingual," he said, "but their preferred mode of communication is Spanish." As a nurse-practitioner, Valenzuela can make a diagnosis and prescribe medicine, which registered nurses cannot. Nurse-practitioners are required to have a master's degree.

Clear communication between patient and healthcare provider is vital for an accurate diagnosis.

When prospective employees apply for jobs at the clinic where Valenzuela works, the first question they're asked is whether they speak Spanish. "If they don't," he says, "that's a big barrier in providing care to this population."

Hot Job!

More new job openings are expected to be created for nurses—especially for those with advanced education and training—than for any other occupation.

INTERNATIONAL BUSINESS AND TRADE

If you've come across a beautiful hand-knit Peruvian sweater in a shop, you might wonder how that sweater happened to get from Peru to your local store. Coordinating the journey from artisan to U.S. marketplace is Michelle Cote's job.

Cote is a program officer for Aid to Artisans, a nonprofit organization that helps craftspeople in developing nations create and sell their products in U.S. and European markets. As the liaison between the marketing staff in the Hartford, Conn., office and the staff based in Peru, she keeps each group updated on the other's work and needs. "All of that communication is done in Spanish, both over the phone and via e-mail," says Cote.

Cote enjoys occasional trips to Peru, where she meets with the artisans and sees how they produce their crafts. "I talk to them about the different challenges that they're facing and build that into the strategies for our overall project," she explains. On one visit, Cote traveled to a remote village to meet and speak with ceramicists whose pottery methods have been passed down from their ancestors over the past 1,000 years.

Cote began studying Spanish in college, when she developed an interest in Latin American culture. A study trip to Ecuador confirmed her interest. Cote notes that spending time abroad and interacting daily with Spanish speakers have sharpened her language skills.

TEACHING

Helping children is what Caryl Komornik's work is all about. Komornik is an English as a second language (ESL) teacher who helps English language learners adapt to—and succeed in—an English-speaking school environment. Komornik works at a Stamford, Conn., elementary school where one-third of the students are learning English as a second language.

The job outlook for ESL teachers is very good. Teachers need, at minimum, a bachelor's degree and state teaching certification. Many teachers pursue master's degrees.

Komornik helps students develop the language tools they will need for future success, both in school and in the world. That means being able to speak, read, write, and think fluently in both English and Spanish. "I always encourage my students, as young as they are, to never forget how important it is to be bilingual," she says. "Having a second language that you know well is an asset."

Every day, Komornik works with English language learners on reading, writing, spelling, vocabulary, and communication skills. She says her greatest challenge is working with students who have trouble reading and writing in their first language. "That makes the transition [to English] difficult, cumbersome, and frustrating for them," she says. "If it's frustrating for them, it's frustrating for me."

Komornik's Spanish language skills, honed during time spent in Colombia, help her connect to students who are often more comfortable chatting with her in their native language. "The children have lots to share—cultural information about their backgrounds, everyday information about what's going on at home," she says. "It's a sharing that I think only someone who has two languages is privileged to share."

ESL teacher Caryl Komornik teaches her students that being bilingual is an asset.

HOW WILL SPANISH HELP *YOU* IN THE FUTURE?

Career World asked advanced-placement Spanish students in McLean, Va., to share where they're going with Spanish. Rebecca White, 18: "We're [north of] an entire continent that speaks almost entirely Spanish. Speaking Spanish helps to widen your perspective to what's out there." White would like to go into counseling or civil service work. "I want to be involved in helping immigrant families." Annie Matsko, 18: Matsko wants "to do something in public service," and, she says, her Spanish language skills will serve her well. "When you speak someone's language," she says, "you can communicate so much better with them." Ray Kang, 18: "I've always considered Spanish the most versatile language. . . . I want to be a journalist. It would be a great help to have [Spanish] under my belt and use it when I can." Madeline Williams, 18: "I want to be a teacher. I want to teach ancient history. But speaking Spanish or any other language will definitely help with teaching and working with [Spanish-speaking] students." Shama Essa, 17: Originally from Los Angeles, Essa says, "I realize it's very important to be bilingual, at least." Essa is considering a career in psychology or sociology. "I'm not sure if I want to go back to L.A., but knowing another language will be helpful anywhere."

PUTTING SPANISH TO WORK FOR YOU

Want to go somewhere with Spanish? These three tips will take you far.

1. SPEND TIME ABROAD. When honing your language skills, there's no substitute for spending time abroad. "It's very difficult to market yourself as bilingual without having spent time in a Spanish-speaking country," says Tom Young of Robert Half International. Young studied Spanish for eight years but says he did not feel truly bilingual until he'd spent time living in Mexico.
2. KNOW THE CULTURE. Whether you are trying to connect with a Latino student or patient or to reach a broad audience with an ad, you need to understand the audience's culture. "I can't stress that enough," says nurse-practitioner Rudy Valenzuela. The connotations of a word and the subtle differences between one culture and another, he notes, make understanding Spanish and the people who speak it so important.
3. PERFECT YOUR PROFESSIONAL SPANISH. There is a "social" Spanish that can be used for informal or basic communication. But to move ahead in the professional world, a more formal level of Spanish fluency is required.

FAST FACT

According to a study by researchers at the University of Florida and the University of Miami, bilingual workers in Florida earn $7,000 more per year than their monolingual colleagues.

Joining in the Conversation

1. The title of this article is written as a question. List several different answers that Hood offers in the article to answer the question. What tips does she also provide? Do you think they are feasible for Spanish-only speakers? For English-only speakers?
2. After reading the article, who do you think Hood's audience is? What makes you think so? Has she done an effective job, in your opinion, of addressing her audience? List aspects of the article that make this article effective for the intended audience.
3. Using Hood's article as the foundation of your work, prepare an oral presentation that you might give to a group of high school students at a Career Night talk. Also create visual aids, such as charts, brochures, statistics, handouts, and so forth, that provide information that they can take away from the presentation and that will give them accurate information about a career involving speaking Spanish.

Additional Topics of Conversation

1. Immigrants to the United States often look to the school districts to provide not just mainstream classes geared to the traditional English-speaking student but also classes tailored more to special needs, whether those needs involve English as a Second Language (ESL) courses, bilingual classrooms, Head Start programs, or other supportive measures. But what would happen if the roles were reversed, that is, if an English-speaking student went to a foreign country for an elementary or high school education? What types of special needs classes or programs are available to that student in Mexico or in Central or South America? To find out, choose the country that best represents your own family's heritage outside of the United States and investigate the programs available to English-speaking students there. Then discuss your findings in an essay and conclude with a statement as to whether there is a reciprocal or even exchange of opportunities for all students.
2. One of the hidden reasons why classes and programs are often curtailed or limited in a school district is because of budget concerns that include

the costs of hiring specially trained instructors, classroom space, teacher training sessions, and so forth. Select a school district in your region and review the programs offered and the budgetary concerns involved in those programs outside of the mainstream classroom. Compare also the school taxes and any increases made during the last five years to accommodate the rising costs of business today. Then, based on your findings, deliver a persuasive speech in which you argue as to the quality of education offered to those students requiring additional educational help in relation to the demands of budget restraints. Various sides should be presented.

3. One way to investigate the many factors involved in representing cultural diversity within the schools is to look at the list of authors, the cultural events, and holidays that are represented in the classes. For example, choose one school district or campus in your area and look at the Table of Contents for freshman through senior English textbooks to discover the cultural diversity offered through the authors represented. You may also want to look at a different field of study, such as history, to see what types of diversity are offered and what proportion of the entire text such diversity represents. If such a task is too difficult, you may want to investigate the web sites for the major publishers whose books are adopted for use in classrooms and use the Internet as your resource. Based on your findings, determine the level of cultural diversity represented through the readings in the district's area and whether such level is representative of your community as a whole.
4. Two of the articles in this chapter, Maria González's and Richard Rodriguez's, offer opposing views as to affirmative action in terms of not only educational opportunities but hiring practices as well. After reading the two articles, look at the make-up of your own school's administration, custodial staff, and faculty, not just in English, but in at least three different fields, for example, English, History, and Biology, to determine whether cultural diversity exists. Also investigate the statement of philosophy for your campus and, if available, its mission statement; both statements reflect the guiding principles of your campus. Then, based on your review of the administrators, staff, and faculty membership and the guiding statements, determine whether the two are compatible.

Borders

The image that most people visualize or think about when they hear the term *border* is geographical: an official dividing line that separates two countries. In fact, the *Longman Advanced American Dictionary* (2000) cites that as the first definition. Today, with an emphasis on Homeland Security, the discussion of borders, both in the abstract and in the concrete, has become an important political topic as well involving securing our borders, border patrols, and air–space borders. If we turn on CNN or news on any television station, pick up a newspaper, or read magazines such as *Newsweek* or *Time,* the subject of geographical and political borders are spoken and written about prominently.

Today, many authors and journalists are writing about the U.S.–Mexican border and the problems arising from immigration. However, the borderlands also provide a sense of beauty and safety for many who live there or for those who have grown up in its environment. Furthermore, the cultural activities and beliefs practiced by residents on either side of the border introduce many to different ways of viewing life and its many joys: birth, coming of age, prosperity, and so forth. The articles in this chapter not only celebrate the positive elements that border life can bring but they also display the cruel realities that coexist with the beauty, both of which combine to paint a broad picture of what the *border* means to those who live there and to those who are distant from it. Furthermore, because of the opportunities that sometimes arise from disaster, borders appear to be expanding as migrant workers cross not only national borders but also state borders into areas that once did not have the "need" for their talents and their labor.

The Homeland, Aztlán

El otro México

GLORIA ANZALDÚA

Gloria Anzaldúa defined the border between Texas and Mexico in her famous work Borderlands/La Frontera: The New Mestiza *(1987). Anzaldúa was one of the first Chicana writers to enter the conversations challenging the mainstream culture as well as her own Mexican-American background in areas of feminism, heritage, sexuality, and literary style. Her words were controversial and politicized in 1987 when mainstream feminists were excluding the problems of women of color from their agendas. Anzaldúa provides an answer that today reverberates in the works of many theorists—mainstream and Chican@ alike. Even though she died in 2004, her works, her words, her ideology, and her memory will be studied and revered for years to come. The following is an excerpt from Chapter 1 of* Borderlands/La Frontera: The New Mestiza. *Other works by Anzaldúa include* Making Face, Making Soul/Haciendo Caras: Creative and Critical Perspectives by Women of Color *(1990) and* This Bridge We Call Home: Radical Visions for Transformation *(2002). She also wrote several children's books such as* Prietita Has a Friend—Prietita tiene un Amigo *(1991) and* Friends from the Other Side—Amigos del otra lado *(1993).*

The U.S.-Mexican border *es una herida abierta* where the Third World grates against the first and bleeds. And before a scab forms it hemorrhages again, the lifeblood of two worlds merging to form a third country—a border culture. Borders are set up to define the places that are safe and unsafe, to distinguish *us* from *them.* A border is a dividing line, a narrow strip along a steep edge. A borderland is a vague and undetermined place created by the emotional residue of an unnatural boundary. It is in a constant state of transition. The prohibited and forbidden are its inhabitants. *Los atravesados* live here: the squint-eyed, the perverse, the queer, the troublesome, the mongrel, the mulato, the half-breed, the half dead; in short, those who cross over, pass over, or go through the confines of the "normal." Gringos in the U.S. Southwest consider the inhabitants of the borderlands transgressors, aliens—whether they possess documents or not, whether they're Chicanos, Indians or Blacks. Do not enter, trespassers will be raped, maimed, strangled, gassed, shot. The only "legitimate" inhabitants are those in power, the whites and those who align themselves with whites. Tension grips the inhabitants of the borderlands like a virus. Ambivalence and unrest reside there and death is no stranger.

> In the fields, *la migra.* My aunt say, *"No corran,* don't run. They'll think you're *del otro lado."* In the confusion, Pedro ran, terrified of being caught. He couldn't speak English, couldn't tell them he was fifth generation American. *Sin papeles*—he did not carry his birth certificate to work in the fields. *La migra* took him away while we watched. *Se lo llevaron.* He tried to smile when he looked back at us, to raise his fist. But I saw the shame pushing his head down, I saw the terrible weight of shame hunch his shoulders. They deported him to Guadalajara by plane. The furthest he'd ever been to Mexico was Reynosa, a small border town opposite Hidalgo, Texas, not far from McAllen. Pedro walked all the way to the Valley. *Se lo llevaron sin un centavo al pobre. Se vino andando desde Guadalajara.*

During the original peopling of the Americas, the first inhabitants migrated across the Bering Straits and walked south across the continent. The oldest evidence of humankind in the U.S.—the Chicanos' ancient Indian ancestors—was found in Texas and has been dated to 35000 B.C.[1] In the Southwest United States archeologists have found 20,000-year-old campsites of the Indians who migrated through, or permanently occupied, the Southwest, Aztlán—land of the herons, land of whiteness, the Edenic place of origin of the Azteca.

In 1000 B.C., descendants of the original Cochise people migrated into what is now Mexico and Central America and became the direct ancestors of many of the Mexican people. (The Cochise culture of the Southwest is a parent culture of the Aztecs. The Uto-Aztecan languages stemmed from the language of the Cochise people.)[2] The Aztecs (the Nahuatl word for people of Aztlán) left the Southwest in 1168 A.D.

> Now let us go.
> *Tihueque, tihueque,*
> *Vámonos, vámonos.*
> *Un pájaro cantó.*
> *Con sus ocho tribus salieron*

De la "cueva del origen."
Los aztecas siguieron al dios
Huitzilopochtli

Huitzilopochtli, the God of War, guided them to the place (that later became Mexico City) where an eagle with a writhing serpent in its beak perched on a cactus. The eagle symbolizes the spirit (as the sun, the father); the serpent symbolizes the soul (as the earth, the mother). Together, they symbolize the struggle between the spiritual/celestial/male and the underworld/earth/feminine. The symbolic sacrifice of the serpent to the "higher" masculine powers indicates that the patriarchal order had already vanquished the feminine and matriarchal order in pre-Columbian America.

* * *

At the beginning of the 16th century, the Spaniards and Hernán Cortés invaded Mexico and, with the help of tribes that the Aztecs had subjugated, conquered it. Before the Conquest, there were twenty-five million Indian people in Mexico and the Yucatán. Immediately after the Conquest, the Indian population had been reduced to under seven million. By 1650, only one-and-a-half-million pure-blooded Indians remained. The *mestizos* who were genetically equipped to survive small pox, measles, and typhus (Old World diseases to which the natives had no immunity), founded a new hybrid race and inherited Central and South America.[3] *En 1521 nació una nueva raza, el mestizo, el mexicano* (people of mixed Indian and Spanish blood), a race that had never existed before. Chicanos, Mexican-Americans, are the offspring of those first matings.

Our Spanish, Indian, and *mestizo* ancestors explored and settled parts of the U.S. Southwest as early as the sixteenth century. For every gold-hungry *conquistador* and soul-hungry missionary who came north from Mexico, ten to twenty Indians and *mestizos* went along as porters or in other capacities.[4] For the Indians, this constituted a return to the place of origin, Aztlán, thus making Chicanos originally and secondarily indigenous to the Southwest. Indians and *mestizos* from central Mexico intermarried with North American Indians. The continual intermarriage between Mexican and American Indians and Spaniards formed an even greater *mestizaje.*

El destierro/The Lost Land

Entonces corre la sangre
no sabe el indio que hacer;
le van a quitar su tierra,

la tiene que defender,
el indio se cae muerto,
y el afuerino de pie.
Levántate, Manquilef.

Arauco tiene una pena
más negra que su chamal,
ya no son los españoles
los que le hacen llorar,
hoy son los propios chilenos
los que le quitan su pan.
Levántate, Pailahuan.

—Violeta Parra,
"Arauco tiene una pena"[5]

In the 1800s, Anglos migrated illegally into Texas, which was then part of Mexico, in greater and greater numbers and gradually drove the *tejanos* (native Texans of Mexican descent) from their lands, committing all manner of atrocities against them. Their illegal invasion forced Mexico to fight a war to keep its Texas territory. The Battle of the Alamo, in which the Mexican forces vanquished the whites, became, for the whites, the symbol for the cowardly and villainous character of the Mexicans. It became (and still is) a symbol that legitimized the white imperialist takeover. With the capture of Santa Anna later in 1836, Texas became a republic. *Tejanos* lost their land and, overnight, became the foreigners.

Ya la mitad del terreno
les vendió el traidor Santa Anna,
con lo que se ha hecho muy rica
la natión americana.
¿Qué acaso no se conforman
con el oro de las minas?
Ustedes muy elegantes
y aquí nosotros en ruinas.

—from the Mexican *corrido,*
"Del peligro de la Intervencíon"[6]

In 1846, the U.S. incited Mexico to war. U.S. troops invaded and occupied Mexico, forcing her to give up almost half of her nation, what is now Texas, New Mexico, Arizona, Colorado and California.

With the victory of the U.S. forces over the Mexican in the U.S.-Mexican War, *los norteamericanos* pushed the Texas border down

100 miles, from *el río Nueces* to *el río Grande*. South Texas ceased to be part of the Mexican state of Tamaulipas. Separated from Mexico, the Native Mexican-Texan no longer looked toward Mexico as home; the Southwest became our homeland once more. The border fence that divides the Mexican people was born on February 2,1848 with the signing of the Treaty of Guadalupe-Hidalgo. It left 100,000 Mexican citizens on this side, annexed by conquest along with the land. The land established by the treaty as belonging to Mexicans was soon swindled away from its owners. The treaty was never honored and restitution, to this day, has never been made.

> The justice and benevolence of God
> will forbid that . . . Texas should again
> become a howling wilderness
> trod only by savages, or . . . benighted
> by the ignorance and superstition,
> the anarchy and rapine of Mexican misrule.
> The Anglo-American race are destined
> to be forever the proprietors of
> this land of promise and fulfillment.
> Their laws will govern it,
> their learning will enlighten it,
> their enterprise will improve it.
> Their flocks range its boundless pastures,
> for them its fertile lands will yield . . .
> luxuriant harvests . . .
> The wilderness of Texas has been redeemed
> by Anglo-American blood & enterprise.
>
> —William H.Wharton[7]

The Gringo, locked into the fiction of white superiority seized complete political power, stripping Indians and Mexicans of their land while their feet were still rooted in it. *Con el destierro y el exilio fuimos desuñados, destroncados, destripados*—we were jerked out by the roots, truncated, disemboweled, dispossessed, and separated from our identity and our history. Many, under the threat of Anglo terrorism, abandoned homes and ranches and went to Mexico. Some stayed and protested. But as the courts, law enforcement officials, and government officials not only ignored their pleas but penalized them for their efforts, *tejanos* had no other recourse but armed retaliation.

After Mexican-American resisters robbed a train in Brownsville, Texas, on October 18, 1915, Anglo vigilante groups began lynching

Chicanos. Texas Rangers would take them into the brush and shoot them. One hundred Chicanos were killed in a matter of months, whole families lynched. Seven thousand fled to Mexico, leaving their small ranches and farms. The Anglos, afraid that the *mexicanos*[8] would seek independence from the U.S., brought in 20,000 army troops to put an end to the social protest movement in South Texas. Race hatred had finally fomented into an all out war.[9]

My grandmother lost all her cattle,
they stole her land.

"Drought hit South Texas," my mother tells me. *"La tierra se puso bien seca y los animales comenzaron a morirse de se'. Mi papá se murió de un* heart attack *dejando a mamá* pregnant *y con ocho huercos,* with eight kids and one on the way. *Yo fui la mayor, tenía diez años.* The next year the drought continued *y el ganado* got hoof and mouth. *Se cayeron* in droves *en las pastas y el* brushland, *panzas blancas* ballooning to the skies. *El siguiente año* still no rain. *Mi pobre madre vieuda perdió* two-thirds of her *ganado*. A smart *gabacho* lawyer took the land away *mamá* hadn't paid taxes. *No hablaba inglés,* she didn't know how to ask for time to raise the money." My father's mother, Mama Locha, also lost her *terreno*. For a while we got $12.50 a year for the "mineral rights" of six acres of cemetery, all that was left of the ancestral lands. Mama Locha had asked that we bury her there beside her husband. *El cementerio estaba cercado.* But there was a fence around the cemetery, chained and padlocked by the ranch owners of the surrounding land. We couldn't even get in to visit the graves, much less bury her there. Today, it is still padlocked. The sign reads: "Keep out. Trespassers will be shot."

In the 1930s, after Anglo agribusiness corporations cheated the small Chicano landowners of their land, the corporations hired gangs of *mexicanos* to pull out the brush, chaparral, and cactus and to irrigate the desert. The land they toiled over had once belonged to many of them, or had been used communally by them. Later the Anglos brought in huge machines and root plows and had the Mexicans scrape the land clean of natural vegetation. In my childhood I saw the end of dryland farming. I witnessed the land cleared; saw the huge pipes connected to underwater sources sticking up in the air. As children, we'd go fishing in some of those canals when they were full and hunt for snakes in them when they were dry. In the 1950s I saw the land, cut up into thousands of neat rectangles and squares, constantly being irrigated. In the

340-day growth season, the seeds of any kind of fruit or vegetable had only to be stuck in the ground in order to grow. More big land corporations came in and bought up the remaining land.

To make a living my father became a sharecropper. Rio Farms Incorporated loaned him seed money and living expenses. At harvest time, my father repaid the loan and forked over 40% of the earnings. Sometimes we earned less than we owed, but always the corporations fared well. Some had major holdings in vegetable trucking, livestock auctions and cotton gins. Altogether we lived on three successive Rio farms; the second was adjacent to the King Ranch and included a dairy farm; the third was a chicken farm. I remember the white feathers of three thousand Leghorn chickens blanketing the land for acres around. My sister, mother and I cleaned, weighed and packaged eggs. (For years afterwards I couldn't stomach the sight of an egg.) I remember my mother attending some of the meetings sponsored by well-meaning whites from Rio Farms. They talked about good nutrition, health, and held huge barbecues. The only thing salvaged for my family from those years are modern techniques of food canning and a food-stained book they printed made up of recipes from Rio Farms' Mexican women. How proud my mother was to have her recipe for *enchiladas coloradas* in a book.

El cruzar del mojado/Illegal Crossing

> *"Ahora si ya tengo una tumba para llorar,"*
> *dice Conchita,* upon being reunited with
> her unknown mother just before the mother dies.
>
> —from Ismael Rodriguez' film,
> *Nosotros los pobres*[10]

LA CRISIS *Los gringos* had not stopped at the border. By the end of the nineteenth century, powerful landowners in Mexico, in partnership with U.S. colonizing companies, had dispossessed millions of Indians of their lands. Currently, Mexico and her eighty million citizens are almost completely dependent on the U.S. market. The Mexican government and wealthy growers are in partnership with such American conglomerates as American Motors, IT&T and Du Pont which owns factories called *maquiladoras*. One-fourth of all Mexicans work at *maquiladoras;* most are young women. Next to oil, *maquiladoras* are Mexico's second greatest source of U.S. dollars. Working eight to twelve hours a day to wire in backup lights of U.S. autos or solder minuscule wires in TV sets is not the Mexican way. While the women are in the *maquiladoras*, the children are left on their own. Many roam the street, become part of *cholo* gangs. The infusion of the values of the white culture, coupled with the exploitation by that culture, is changing the Mexican way of life.

The devaluation of the *peso* and Mexico's dependency on the U.S. have brought on what the Mexicans call *la crisis. No hay trabajo.* Half of the Mexican people are unemployed. In the U.S., a man or woman can make eight times what they can in Mexico. By March, 1987, 1,088 *pesos* were worth one U.S. dollar. I remember when I was growing up in Texas how we'd cross the border at Reynosa or Progreso to buy sugar or medicines when the dollar was worth eight *pesos* and fifty *centavos*.

LA TRAVESÍA For many *mexicanos del otro lado,* the choice is to stay in Mexico and starve or move north and live. *Dicen que cada mexicano siempre sueña de la conquista en los brazos de cuatro gringas rubias, la conquista del país poderoso del norte, los Estados Unidos. En cada Chicano y mexicano vive el mito del tesoro territorial perdido.* North Americans call this return to the homeland the silent invasion.

> *"A la cueva volverán"*
>
> —E1 Puma *en la canción "Amalia"*

South of the border, called North America's rubbish dump by Chicanos, *mexicanos* congregate in the plazas to talk about the best way to cross. Smugglers, *coyotes, pasadores, enganchadores* approach these people or are sought out by them. "*¿Qué dicen muchachos a echársela de mojado?*"

> "Now among the alien gods with
> weapons of magic am I."
>
> —Navajo protection song,
> sung when going into battle.[11]

We have a tradition of migration, a tradition of long walks. Today we are witnessing *la migración de los pueblos mexicanos,* the return odyssey to the historical/mythological Aztlán. This time, the traffic is from south to north.

El retorno to the promised land first began with the Indians from the interior of Mexico and the *mestizos* that came with the *conquistadores* in the 1500s. Immigration continued in the next three centuries, and, in this century, it continued with the *braceros* who helped to build our railroads and who picked our fruit. Today thousands of Mexicans are crossing the border legally and illegally; ten million people without documents have returned to the Southwest.

Faceless, nameless, invisible, taunted with "Hey *cucaracho*" (cockroach). Trembling with fear, yet filled with courage, a courage born of desperation. Barefoot and uneducated, Mexicans with hands like boot soles gather at night by the river where two worlds merge creating what Reagan calls a frontline, a war zone. The convergence has created a shock culture, a border culture, a third country, a closed country.

Without benefit of bridges, the "*mojados*" (wetbacks) float on inflatable rafts across *el río Grande,* or wade or swim across naked, clutching their clothes over their heads. Holding onto the grass, they pull themselves along the banks with a prayer to *Virgen de Guadalupe* on their lips.: *Ay virgencita morena, mi madrecita, dame tu bendición.*

The Border Patrol hides behind the local McDonalds on the outskirts of Brownsville, Texas or some other border town. They set traps around the river beds beneath the bridge.[12] Hunters in army-green uniforms stalk and track these economic refugees by the powerful nightvision of electronic sensing devices planted in the ground or mounted on Border Patrol vans. Cornered by flashlights, frisked while their arms stretch over their heads, *los mojados* are handcuffed, locked in jeeps, and then kicked back across the border.

One out of every three is caught. Some return to enact their rite of passage as many as three times a day. Some of those who make it across undetected fall prey to Mexican robbers such as those in Smugglers' Canyon on the American side of the border near Tijuana. As refugees in a homeland that does not want them, many find a welcome hand holding out only suffering, pain, and ignoble death.

Those who make it past the checking points of the Border Patrol find themselves in the midst of 150 years of racism in Chicano *barrios* in the Southwest and in big northern cities. Living in a no-man's-borderland, caught between being treated as criminals and being able to eat, between resistance and deportation, the illegal refugees are some of the poorest and the most exploited of any people in the U.S. It is illegal for Mexicans to work without green cards. But big farming combines, farm bosses and smugglers who bring them in make money off the "wetbacks'" labor—they don't have to pay federal minimum wages, or ensure adequate housing or sanitary conditions.

The Mexican woman is especially at risk. Often the *coyote* (smuggler) doesn't feed her for days or let her go to the bathroom. Often he rapes her or sells her into prostitution. She cannot call on county or state health or economic resources because she doesn't know English and she fears deportation. American employers are quick to take advantage of her helplessness. She can't go home. She's sold her house, her furniture, borrowed from her friends in order to pay the *coyote* who charges her four or five thousand dollars to smuggle her to Chicago. She may work as a live-in maid for white, Chicano or Latino households for as little as $15 a week. Or work in the garment industry, do hotel work. Isolated and worried about her family back home, afraid of getting caught and deported, living with as many as fifteen people in one room, the *mexicana* suffers serious health problems. *Se enferma de los nervios, de alta presíon.*[13]

La mojada, la mujer indocumentada, is doubly threatened in this country. Not only does she have to contend with sexual violence, but like all women, she is prey to a sense of physical helplessness. As a refugee, she leaves the familiar and safe homeground to venture into unknown and possibly dangerous terrain.

This is her home
this thin edge of
barbwire.

Endnotes

1. John R. Chávez, *The Lost Land: The Chicano Images of the Southwest* (Albuquerque, NM: University of New Mexico Press, 1984), 9.
2. Chávez, 9. Besides the Aztecs, the Ute, Gabrillino of California, Pima of Arizona, some Pueblo of New Mexico, Comanche of Texas, Opata of Sonora, Tarahumara of Sinaloa and Durango, and the Huichol of Jalisco speak Uto-Aztecan languages and are descended from the Cochise people.
3. Reay Tannahill, *Sex in History* (Briarcliff Manor, NY: Stein and Day/ Publishers/Scarborough House, 1980), 308.
4. Chávez, 21.
5. Isabel Parra, *El Libro Major de Violeta Parra* (Madrid, España: Ediciones Michay, S.A., 1985), 156–57.

6. From the Mexican *corrido, "Del peligro de la Intervencíon"* Vincente T. Mendoza, *El Corrido Mexicano* (México, D.F.: *Fondo de Cultura Económica,* 1954), 42.
7. Arnoldo De León, *They Called Them Greasers: Anglo Attitudes Toward Mexicans in Texas, 1821–1900* (Austin, TX: University of Texas Press, 1983), 2–3.
8. The Plan of San Diego, Texas, drawn up on January 6, 1915, called for the independence and segregation of the states bordering Mexico: Texas, New Mexico, Arizona, Colorado, and California. Indians would get their land back, Blacks would get six states from the south and form their own independent republic. Chávez, 79.
9. Jesús Mena, "Violence in the Rio Grande Valley," *Nuestro* (Jan./Feb. 1983), 41–42.
10. *Nosotros los pobres* was the first Mexican film that was truly Mexican and not an imitation European film. It stressed the devotion and love that children should have for their mother and how its lack would lead to the dissipation of their character. This film spawned a generation of mother-devotion/ungrateful-son films.
11. From the Navajo "Protection Song" (to be sung upon going into battle). George W. Groyn, ed. *American Indian Poetry: The Standard Anthology of Songs and Chants* (New York, NY: Liveright, 1934), 97.
12. Grace Halsell, *Los ilegales,* trans. Mayo Antonio Sánchez (*Editorial Diana Mexica,* 1979).
13. Margarita B. Melville, "Mexican Women Adapt to Migration," *International Migration Review,* 1978.

Joining in the Conversation

1. What scenario does Anzaldúa create for those who cross the border illegally from Mexico before and after they arrive in the United States? The ending seems to be somewhat abrupt. How do you account for it? Do you like the ending or would you change it? Explain.
2. Anzaldúa uses various strategies to develop her ideas. Identify two or three strategies within the article. Do you find them effective? Explain your position.
3. In this chapter, Anzaldúa uses the border between Mexico and the United States; however, there are other metaphorical borders that have been constructed that are just as damaging to those whom they separate. In groups, select several borders other than the geopolitical one between Mexico and the U.S. that have been constructed between people and discuss them. Share your selections with the class and determine how far the border metaphor develops Anzaldúa's essay.

Cross Purposes

JONATHAN KANDELL

Jonathan Kandell is a former foreign correspondent for The New York Times *and the author of several books,* LA Capital: The Biography of Mexico City (1990) *and* Passage Through El Dorado: Traveling the World's Last Great Wilderness (1984) *as well as articles for the* Smithsonian *(June 2005) where the following article appeared.*

On a windy Sunday morning, I get off a subway train in Queens, New York, to join throngs of Mexican families headed into the mowed, shady groves of Flushing Meadows Park. Many are wrapped in Mexico's red, white and green national flag; others wear shawls imprinted with the image of the Virgin Mary. They have come, by the hundreds of thousands, to celebrate *Cinco de Mayo* (the fifth of May), the Mexican national holiday marking the day an invading French Army was defeated in 1862.

Inside the park, a steel globe of the earth and water-stained concrete pavilions, left over from the 1964 world's fair, suggest the ruins of a bygone civilization. On a stage just beyond these structures, costumed dancers and drummers evoke another lost civilization—the Aztec Empire. Following their performance, more contemporary acts predominate: mariachi musicians, cowboy balladeers, tropical torch singers, rock bands and comedians.

Between acts, radio talk-show hosts pay homage to the various states constituting the Republic of Mexico. The cheers of the crowd reach earsplitting decibels at the mention of Puebla, the small, 13,187-square-mile state (roughly the size of Maryland) due east of Mexico City. Little wonder, considering that *Poblanos*, as natives of Puebla are called, account for at least 80 percent of the estimated 600,000 Mexicans living in the New York City metropolitan region. And this is, in a sense, their day; the 1862 defeat of the French invaders took place in Puebla.

Nowadays, of course, it's the Mexicans who are often portrayed as invaders, illegal immigrants pouring across the 1,951-mile-long border with the United States. In fact, the presence of undocumented Mexicans, who account for perhaps 60 percent of the 12 million or so foreigners living illegally in this country and for

15 percent of the 2.1 million Latinos in New York City, remains the most contentious issue between the United States and its southern neighbor. For decades, undocumented Mexicans have taken the jobs that nobody else seemed to want, while fending off charges they were not only depriving Americans of gainful employment but were also lowering the wage for some blue-collar jobs.

The surprising reality, however, is that Mexico's immigrants—a population exemplified by the half-million or so *Poblanos* living in the New York area, with another 500,000 concentrated mainly in Los Angeles, Houston and Chicago—fuel a complex economic dynamic, both here and at home. In taking on menial work in this country, Mexicans have not only raised their standard of living and that of their families, they've also created a flow of capital back to villages across Mexico, especially towns throughout Puebla. That transfer of wealth—around $17 billion last year, double what it was only four years ago—has transformed life across the border, where new housing, medical clinics and schools are under construction. "Many government officials both in the United States and Mexico would argue that these remittances have accomplished what foreign aid and local public investment failed to do," says Oscar Chacón, director of *Enlaces América,* a Chicago-based advocacy group for Latin American immigrants. As this transformation has taken place, many of the assumptions—or even stereotypes—held in this country regarding Mexican immigrants are being challenged.

"Getting into the U.S. was so much simpler and safer when I first came here," says Jaime Lucero, 48, one of the organizers of the *Cinco de Mayo* festivities. Lucero, from the small Puebla community of Piaxtla, was 17 when, in 1975, he waded across the Rio Grande into Texas and hopped a bus to New York City to join an older brother washing dishes in a Queens restaurant. He became legal under President Reagan's 1986 amnesty program, which granted residency to illegals who had resided in the U.S. before 1982 and imposed sanctions on employers who hired undocumented workers. He became a citizen in 1988. Today, he is the millionaire owner of both a women's apparel company in New Jersey and a factory in Puebla. "I came in through the backdoor," he says. "But I never intended to be a burden to this country." . . .

In January 2004, President Bush proposed granting three-year visas to illegal foreigners who can show they hold U.S. jobs that Americans have turned down. The plan, now stalled in Congress, falls short of the permanent residence permits for immigrants that Mexican president Vicente Fox has been urging since 2001.

President Bush's proposal bears a resemblance to the *Bracero* (migrant farmworker) Program of 1942 to 1964, which allowed Mexicans to be given temporary contracts for agricultural work. Intended to address a World War II-era shortage of farm labor, the *Bracero* Program led to an unintended consequence: an upsurge in illegal border crossings. Millions of Mexicans—precise figures have never been calculated—entered the country illegally. "People who were unable to get *bracero* jobs just headed elsewhere in the United States," says Robert Courtney Smith, a sociology professor at the City University of New York (CUNY) and author of a forthcoming book on Puebla immigrants in New York. The first *Poblanos* to arrive in New York during the 1940s, he says, ended up in the city for this reason.

Once settled, the new arrivals often arranged menial jobs, and a place to sleep, for friends and relatives, most of them also illegal, who joined them from their hometowns in Puebla. Over the past six decades, the number of illegal *Poblanos* in New York has soared. But according to Francisco Rivera-Batíz, a Columbia University professor of economics and education, until the early 1990s, some 85 percent of all undocumented Mexicans in New York City returned home within five years. That figure, he says, has declined sharply in recent years to about 50 percent because of Mexico's sluggish economy—and, ironically because stricter border surveillance makes going back and forth between the two countries more difficult. As a result, the border controls that were designed to keep people out of the United States are also keeping illegals in.

Yet many *Poblanos* in the United States illegally are willing to risk apprehension; for those here legally, of course, visiting Mexico and reentering the United States poses [sic] few problems. "People from my hometown are constantly going back and forth," says Jesús Pérez Méndez, who was born in Tulcingo de Valle, Puebla, and is now an academic adviser at CUNY. *Poblanos* finance their round trips by acting as couriers, or *paqueteros*, for clothes, electronic goods and other gifts sent by immigrants to relatives in Puebla. Between visits to their villages, *Poblanos* keep in touch through discount phone cards, e-mail or Web sites. It was after listening to a live Internet radio broadcast on tulcingo.com that I decided to fly to Mexico to assess the effects of this symbiotic relationship for myself.

The Sierra Mixteca, a mountain chain, stretches across the southern portion of the state of Puebla. For much of the year, the region is hot and arid, with yellow grass blanketing farm plots and giant organ cactus spiking the hillsides. But I arrive in June, during the rainy season. . . .

But the Sierra Mixteca has also undergone dramatic transformations that have nothing to do with rain. In Piaxtla, most of the 1,600 inhabitants are either children or older adults. "Maybe three out of four of my constituents live in New York," says Manuel Aquino Carrera, the town's mayor. The cash they send home each month can be seen in new brick houses with satellite television dishes on their roofs. "As a child, I could count on my fingers the houses that were made of brick and concrete," says Aquino, 40. "Everything else was palm-thatched adobe." Many of the new houses sit empty, occupied only during summer months or at Christmas.

Efforts to create jobs that might keep younger adults in the Sierra Mixteca have largely foundered. In 2001, Jaime Lucero, the New Jersey-based clothing magnate and Piaxtla's most illustrious son, opened a factory in the Puebla town of El Seco; the facility employs more than 2,500 workers. He planned to open five more plants, but says he hasn't been able to do so. "So many young people have emigrated," he says, "that there isn't enough labor to set up another plant."

Emigration has also hit Puebla's long tradition of artisanry—ceramics, woodwork and weaving. Folk art pieces are increasingly mass-produced, and master craftsmen despair of passing on their skills. "Most young people aren't willing to work the long, lonely hours, and for something that with few exceptions is badly paid," says César Torres Ramírez, 52, one of Puebla's leading ceramists. Although his exquisitely glazed plates and vases—embellished with feathery, blue patterns and animal motifs—win national awards, to make a living Torres must work from dawn to sunset six days a week in a small home studio.

"These master artisans are an endangered species," says Marta Turok Wallace, a Mexico City anthropologist who runs Amacup, a cooperative that connects Mexican artisans with collectors, interior designers and retailers. Turok and her colleagues try to locate and encourage younger artists, such as Rafael Lopez Jiménez, 20, a mask-maker in Acatlán de Osorio, a 45-minute drive east of Piaxtla. . . .

As elsewhere in Mexico, the craft of mask-making survived thanks to Spanish missionaries who adapted it to Roman Catholic iconography. Jaguar masks "are associated with ancient Indian rituals asking the gods for rain around the time of the planting of corn," says anthropologist Turok. And Puebla is one of the earliest sites of corn cultivation. In 1960, the late American archaeologist Richard S. MacNeish, excavating in Puebla's arid Tehuacán Valley, uncovered ancient corncobs 4,000 years old. . . .

But if the ancient *Poblanos* were able to master corn cultivation and make it the foundation of their lives, their modern-day descendants must struggle against price controls that the government began to impose in the early 1980s to keep tortillas cheap. In addition, since the advent of the North American Free Trade Agreement (NAFTA) in 1994, *Poblano* farmers have been unable to compete with imports of new corn hybrids, produced by high-tech, low-cost U.S. farms. All along the highway connecting Piaxtla with Tulcingo 30 miles to the south, cornfields lie fallow, even at the height of the growing season. The gradual demise of small-scale farming here has also fueled emigration to the United States. . . .

The town of Tulcingo de Valle is a 40-minute drive south of Piaxtla. Its 8,000 residents have thus far resisted New York City's temptations only slightly more successfully than those in Piaxtla, though the money returned to Tulcingo's coffers by its emigrants has helped restore the town church, damaged in an earthquake in 1999, and caused the Hong Kong and Shanghai Banking Corporation, a global financial giant, to open a branch here. Remittances have been invested in restaurants and cybercafés that have replaced *pulquerías*, old-time saloons with swinging doors.

Signs of newfound affluence are everywhere. There are dozens of taxis—though the town can be traversed on foot in less than 20 minutes—and repair shops of all types, for cars, bicycles, television sets and stereos, have sprouted like cactuses. Video games are so popular that parents complain their kids have given up sports and grown too sedentary. Main streets have been asphalted. . . .

On my last day in the Sierra Mixteca, I drive back to Piaxtla to meet with a man who reputedly arranges to smuggle people across the border. Often called "*coyotes*," most smugglers prefer the term *pollero*—someone who guards chickens. My instructions are to wait for him at the edge of the weekly street market next to a folk healer's stand.

The healer, Cobita Macedo, hawks herbal cures, some of them handed over the centuries. For kidney disease, she offers a gnarled clump of dried flower that, she explains, must be boiled in water. "You drink a cup of the broth twice a day, and you will pass any kidney stone within weeks," she promises. Other herbal concoctions, she says, treat gastrointestinal, pulmonary and heart ailments. But in recent years, she adds, the most sought-after remedies have been for hypertension and diabetes—illnesses associated with the more stressful lifestyles (and eating habits) of expatriate *Poblanos*.

When the reputed *pollero*, a slim man in his 40s, at last shows up, he suggests we have breakfast in the market, where local farmers have set up scores of stands selling all manner of fruits, vegetables and freshly prepared foods. We share a plate of barbacoa—kid goat that has been barbecued in an underground pit and served with chile sauce, cilantro and roasted scallions, wrapped in freshly made tortillas.

In the Mexican and U.S. media, *coyotes* are routinely and adamantly denounced for trafficking in human lives. But my breakfast companion claims that "most people think my profession is a necessary and honorable one. They entrust me with their sons and daughters and friends." (He also says that while his vocation is widely known, he has never been bothered by the police.) His job, as he describes it, is to escort the departees to the border and there turn them over to someone who will smuggle them into the United States and arrange for transportation to their ultimate destination—usually New York City. His fees range from a rock-bottom 1,800 pesos ($160) for *Poblanos* who want only to get across the border, to 10,000 pesos ($900) for door-to-door shepherding, including airfare, from Piaxtla to New York City.

As I sit with him, I recall my dinner at MacD, at which Jaime Peñafort, 26, talked of having paid the cheapest rate to be smuggled across the border, led on foot across the Arizona desert, and then driven in stages to Houston, where he worked as a dishwasher for more than a year. "Each leg of the trip requires paying somebody hundreds more pesos," said Peñafort, who now runs a tortilla business in Tulcingo. "You feel like you're getting sold over and over again."

Piaxtla's mayor, Manuel Aquino, says he has not once contemplated making that hazardous crossing. He decided a long time ago, he tells me, never to try to enter the United States illegally. His father, a farmer, insisted that all seven of his children take up professions and remain in Mexico, which every one of them did, unlike most of the mayor's friends and neighbors. But once elected mayor, Aquino says, he felt a duty to go to New York City to meet with constituents. Two years ago he applied for a tourist visa, giving his reasons to American consulate officials. "And," says Aquino with a slow smile, "they turned me down."

Joining in the Conversation

1. Explain what *Cinco de Mayo* celebrates. What was the *Bracero* Program? What were some of the problems with the Program? How does emigration affect the towns in the state of Puebla? Explain the artisan situation in Puebla.
2. Kandell writes an essay in which he incorporates primary source information gathered from the people in the villages he spoke with. Examine carefully the way he presents his information: presenting historical information about the people, gathering information about the town, interviewing individuals about their situation, and allowing the reader to draw conclusions. Discuss Kandell's procedure and evaluate its effectiveness.
3. In 2004 and 2005 several states along the Gulf and East Coasts suffered from enormous hurricane damage. In addition to that, other towns were victims of massive floods that were not caused by the hurricanes. In Southern California, residents had to be evacuated in several areas because of wild fires and mud slides. If you live in any of these areas, investigate the same kinds of issues that Kandell explores in his essay. If your city/town has not been in danger of any natural disasters, explore a topic of concern that your City Council is working on and how it will affect residents. Use the same strategies that Kandell uses in his article.

A Sense of Place

Rolando Hinojosa

Rolando Hinojosa, a professor of English at the University of Texas in Austin, began his academic career as a professor of Spanish in Minnesota. Hinojosa was the first Chicano author to win a major international literary award, Premio Casa de las Americas, *for his novel* Klail City y sus alrededores (Klail City) *(1976) that is part of his novel series "The Klail City Death Trip," which focuses on the lower Rio Grande Valley of Texas. Hinojosa has frequently been compared to William Faulkner because both authors focused on and immortalized in their works parts of the country where they grew up, the Rio Grande Valley, Texas, and Lafayette County, Mississippi, respectively. Hinojosa also wrote a war novel,* The Useless Servants *(1993), and several mystery novels. In the following article, Hinojosa celebrates his corner of the world and tells how he, as well as some other writers, creates a "sense of place." This article was published in* Texas Journal *(1994).*

✦

> I have sworn to be a good Texan; and that I will not forswear. I will die for what I firmly believe, for I know it is just and right. One life is a small price for a cause so great. As I fought, so shall I be willing to die. I will never forsake Texas and her cause. I am her son.

This quotation is from a man imprisoned for his participation in the Texas-Santa Fe Expedition of 1841; while in his cell in Mexico City, he spurned Santa Anna's offer of freedom in exchange for renouncing the Republic of Texas. These words of 1842 were said by a man who had signed the Texas Declaration of Independence and who had served in the Congress of the Republic. Later on, he was to cast a delegate vote for annexation and contribute to the writing of the first state constitution. He would win election to the state legislature and still later would support secession.

The man was José Antonio Navarro, the same Navarro for whom the Texas county is named. Historian James Wilson once wrote that Navarro's name is virtually unknown to Texas school children and, for the most part, unknown to their teachers as well.

The year 1983 marked the one hundredth anniversary of the birth of my father, Manuel Guzmán Hinojosa, on the Campacuas Ranch, some three miles north of Mercedes, down in the Valley; his father was born on that ranch, as was his father's father. My mother arrived in the Valley at the age of six weeks in the year 1887 as part of the first Anglo American settlers enticed to the mid-Valley by Jim Wells, one of the early developers on the northern bank. As you may already know, it's no accident that Jim Wells County in South Texas is named for him.

One of the earliest stories I heard about Grandfather Smith was a supposed conversation he held with lawyer Wells—you are being asked to imagine the month of July in the Valley with no air conditioning in 1887. Wells was extolling the Valley and said that all it needed was a little water and a few good people. My grandfather replied, "Well, that's all Hell needs, too."

The story is apocryphal—it has to be—but living in the Valley, and hearing that type of story, laid the foundation for what I later learned was to give me a sense of place. By that I do not mean that I had no feel for the place; no, not at all. I was not learning about the culture of the Valley but living it, forming part of it, and, thus, contributing to it.

But a place is merely that until it is populated, and once populated, the histories of the place and its people begin. For me and mine, history began in 1749 when the first colonists began moving into the southern and northern banks of the Rio Grande. That river was not yet a jurisdictional barrier and was not to be until almost 100 years later; but, by then, the border had its own history, its own culture, and its own sense of place: it was Nuevo Santander, named for old Santander in the Spanish Peninsula.

The last names were similar up and down on both banks of the river, and as second and third cousins were allowed to marry, this further promulgated and propagated blood relationships and that sense of belonging that led the borderers to label their fellow Mexicans who came from the interior as *fuerenos*, or outsiders; later, when people from the North started coming to the border, these were labeled *gringos,* a word for foreigner and nothing else until the *gringo* himself, from all evidence, took the term as a pejorative label. For me, then, part of a sense of the border came from sharing: the sharing of names, of places, of a common history, and of belonging. One attended funerals, was taken to cemeteries; and one saw names that corresponded to one's own or to one's friends and neighbors and relatives.

When I first started to write, and being *empapado*—drenched, imbibed, soaked, drunk—with the place, I had to eschew the romanticism and the sentimentalism that tend to blind the unwary, that get in the way of truth. The border wasn't paradise, and it didn't have to be. But it was more than paradise, it was home; and (as Frost once wrote) home, when you have to go there, is the place where they have to take you in. It was also home to the petty officeholder elected by an uninformed citizenry, a home for bossism, and for smuggling as a way of life for some. But it also maintained the remains of a social democracy that cried out for independence and for the continuance of a sense of community.

The history one learned there was an oral one. Many of my generation were raised with the music written and composed by Valley people, and we learned the ballads of the border, little knowing that it was a true native art form. And one was also steeped in the stories and exploits of Juan Nepomuceno Cortina and of the Texas Rangers, and then, as always, names, familiar patronymics: Jacinto Treviño, Aniceto Pizana, the Seditionists of 1915. My father would mark for me the spot where the Seditionists had camped half a generation before. These were men of flesh and bone who lived and died there in Mercedes, in the Valley.

And then there were the stories of the Revolution of 1910, and of the participation in it for the next ten years off and on by Valley *Mexicanos* who fought alongside their south bank relatives, and the stories told by exiles, men and women from Mexico who earned a living by teaching us school on the northern bank while they bided their time to return to Mexico.

But we didn't return to Mexico; we didn't have to. We were borderers with a living and unifying culture born of conflict with another culture, and this, too, helped to cement further still the knowing of exactly where one came from and from whom one was descended. The north bank border Mexican couldn't "go back to where you came from." The borderer was there and had been before the interlopers. But what of the indigenous population prior to the 1749 settlement? Since Nuevo Santander was never under the *presidio* system and since its citizens did not build missions that trapped and stultified the indigenous people, they remained there and, in time, settled down or were absorbed by the colonial population. And this, too, fostered that sense of place.

For the writer—this writer—a sense of place became essential. And so much so, that my stories are not held together by the *plotas* as much as by what the people who populate the stories say and how they say it; how they look at the world out and the world in. The works, then, become studies of perceptions and values and decisions reached by them because of those perceptions and values which in turn were fashioned and forged by the place and its history.

It is not impossible for a writer to write about a place, its history, and its people if the writer is not from that particular place; it can be done, and it has been done. What I am saying is that I needed a sense of place, and that this helped me in the way that Américo Paredes, Larry McMurtry, Fred Gipson, William A. Owens, and Tomás Rivera were all helped by a sense of place. To me, these writers and others impart a sense of place and a truth about the place and about the values of that place. It isn't a studied attitude but rather one of a certain love, to use that phrase, and an understanding for the place that they capture in print for themselves.

I am not making a medieval pitch for the shoemaker to stick to his past here, but if the writer places a lifetime of living in a work, the writer sometimes finds it difficult to remove the place of provenance from the writings. What spine one has is formed early in life, and it is formed at a specific place. Later on when one grows up, one may mythologize, adopt a persona, become an actor, restructure family history, but the original facts of one's formation remain, as facts always do.

It's a personal thing, because I found that after many years of hesitancy, and fits and spurts, and false starts, that despite what education I had acquired, I was still limited in many ways; that whatever I attempted to write came out false and frail. Now, I know I wanted to write, had to write, was burning to write—and all of those things that some writers say to some garden clubs—but the truth and heart of the matter were that I did not know where to begin. And there it was again, that adverb of place—the where.

And then I got lucky: I decided to write whatever it was I had, in Spanish, and I decided to set it on the border, in the Valley. As reduced as that space was, it too was Texas with all of its contradictions and its often repeated one-sided telling of Texas history. When the characters stayed in the Spanish-speaking milieu or society, the Spanish language worked well, and then it was in the natural order of things that English made its entrance when the characters strayed or found themselves in Anglo institutions. In cases where both cultures would come into contact, both languages were used, and I would employ both, and where one and only one would do, I would follow that as well. What dominated, then, was the place, at first.

Later on I discovered that generational and class differences also dictated *which* language as well. From this came the *how* they said *what* they said. As the census rolls filled up in the works, so did some distinguishing features, characteristics, viewpoints, values, decisions, and thus I used the Valley and the border, the history and the people. The freedom to do this also led me to use folklore and anthropology and whatever literary form I desired and saw fit to tell my stories: dialogues, duologues, monologues, imaginary newspaper clippings, and whatever else I felt would be of use. It was the Valley, but it remained forever Texas.

It was a matter of luck in some ways, but mostly it was the proper historical moment; it came along, and I took what had been there for some time, but which I had not been able to see, since I had not fully developed a sense of place. I had left the Valley for the service, for formal university training, and for a series of very odd jobs, only to return to it in my writing. My decision to write what I write and where I choose to situate the writing is not based on anything else other than to write about what I know, the place I know, and the language used, the values held. When someone mentions universality, I say that what happens to my characters happens to other people of the world at given times, and I've no doubt on that score.

What has also helped me to write has been a certain amount of questionable self-education, a long and fairly misspent youth in the eyes of some, an acceptance of certain facts and some misrepresentations of the past which I could not change but which led to a rejection, not of those unalterable facts but of hypocrisy and the smugness of the self-satisfied. For this and other reasons, humor creeps into my writing once in awhile, because it was the use of irony, as many of us know, that allowed the borderer to survive and to maintain a certain measure of dignity.

Serious writing is deliberate as well as a consequence of an arrived-at decision. What one does with it may be of value or not, but I believe that one's fidelity to history is the first step to fixing a sense of place, whether that place is a world-wide arena or a corner of it, as is mine.

Joining in the Conversation

1. Hinojosa tells a story that gave him a "sense of place." Explain that story and describe how a "sense of place" is created. Where does Hinojosa's "sense of the border" come from? How does he define "borderer"? How does this article give the reader an insight into Hinojosa's novels?
2. Hinojosa writes an article that gives readers directions about how to write a piece that gives a "sense of place." Rather than listing point after point, he develops the article through definition and personal narrative. Analyze the article finding points that can be extracted from the article and listed for someone who wants to write a piece that gives readers a "sense of place." Make the list and compare your points with points found by others in your class. Compile a master list that gives as many points as possible without being repetitive.
3. Using Hinojosa's method of writing, select one place that you know very well whether it is your home, a special place you go to be alone, a vacation spot that your family visits, or some other place that gives you a "sense of place" and write as much about it as you can. Include many of the qualities of that location that Hinojosa discusses as giving one's writing a "sense of place." If using a language other than English helps you express yourself better as you are writing, do so.

At 15, a Step Ahead

Jesse Sendejas

Jesse Sendejas, a correspondent for the Houston Chronicle, *wrote this article for the August 2, 2001 issue.*

✦

QUINCEAÑERAS CELEBRATE PASSAGE TO WOMENHOOD.

Wendy Fuentes nearly passed on an experience she now says she'll never forget.

Xochitl Rendon said the experience so moved her that she started attending church more regularly.

And Jessica Bazan said it was a passage to womanhood.

The three 15-year-old friends were together one afternoon discussing the events surrounding their recent *quinceañeras*. A traditional coming-of-age celebration in Hispanic communities—with its roots in Mayan and Aztec cultures—the *quinceañera* commemorates the 15th birthday of Hispanic girls in various fashions.

Quinceañeras may be simple affairs or opulent extravaganzas. They might follow the traditions handed down from generations before or be tailored to the modern tastes of today's young Latina. Teens celebrating the event may call them *quinceañeras* or may refer to them as "fifteens."

Bazan, Fuentes and Rendon are parishioners at Prince of Peace Catholic Community. Located at 19222 Tomball Parkway, the 30-year-old church serves more than 4,000 families in northwest Harris County.

A major focus of the church is Hispanic and youth ministries, according to Gina Pasket, associate director of youth ministries for Prince of Peace. She said roughly one-third of the parish is Hispanic, and the church performed as many as 30 *quinceañera* masses last year. Bazan, Fuentes and Rendon celebrated theirs last month.

The celebration comes after each celebrant completes five two-hour classes, a community service project and a two-day retreat.

"Basically, it is a growth and renewal of one's own identity. It offers the family the opportunity to share their faith and culture in a liturgical context," Pasket said. "It ministers to Hispanic families within the church, is a renewal of baptism promises and gives thanks to God for the gifts of life, family and community."

A *quinceañera* closely resembles a wedding ceremony. There usually is—but doesn't have to be—a religious observation the morning or afternoon of the celebration. The birthday celebrant always wears an elegant dress.

Following the church ceremonies, there may be a photo session of the celebrant, her escort—also known as the *chambelan*—and the couples she selects to participate. Generally, there are 14 couples of escorts (young men) and *damas* (young women), each signifying a year in the celebrant's life.

Following a photo session, there may be a dinner reception and dance. At either, some traditional elements of the *quinceañera* are observed. Each girl and family is free to decide which elements will be included and which won't, but most include mariachi bands performing songs, including the traditional *Las Mañanitas*.

The celebrant may have a tiara placed on her head, and some have their parents change their footwear, from flat shoes to heels, representing the parents' acceptance that their daughter is now a young woman.

A newer trend is a choreographed dance the celebrant, her escort and the court perform for those in attendance.

Bazan, Fuentes and Rendon each had a mass, dinner and dance. All served barbecue at their dinner receptions and all had deejays rather than bands at their dances.

Bazan said an ice sculpture was a unique touch at her event. She also was presented her last doll at the celebration, a traditional and symbolic gift given at many *quinceañeras*. Rendon said hers featured a photo session at Williams Tower's water wall—a favored local spot for such photo shoots—a low rider car procession, *mariachis* and a *charro*, performing a lariat routine in her honor. No matter the particulars, one constant is that the *quinceañera* seems to leave a lasting impression on those involved.

"For me, it's a day that I'll remember for the rest of my life. One thing I got out of it was not to ever forget where I came from. I think the most important thing that I learned was to give thanks for everything that you have and, most important, to not be ashamed of your culture," Fuentes said.

"It's an incredibly emotional thing," said Dr. Marie Theresa Hernandez, an assistant professor in the School of Social Work at the University of Houston. Hernandez has taught Mexican-American culture courses at the university.

"I've seen 20- and 21-year-old women bring in their crowns and their *quinceañera* pictures and just cry over them. They're just incredibly attached to the experience.

"It is their day. They're the most important person that day. Everything revolves around them. Relatives and people have come from all over that day just to honor them," Hernandez said. "It's so very, very special because it's a gift from the family and it's a special gift because it is a day for themselves."

In spite of that, Hernandez said many of today's Latinas balk at the idea of a *quinceañera*.

"Some of my more cynical students feel it's a way for mainstream society to make Latinos spend money uselessly," she said.

"There are instances where parents are willing to spend $15,000 on a *quinceañera,* but there's nothing in the college fund."

The costs of the *quinceañeras* for Bazan, Fuentes and Rendon ranged from $1,500 to $6,000. They took between two weeks and 18 months to plan.

"I didn't want to have a party, all I wanted was the mass. But, my mom always told me she always wanted me to have whatever she didn't have, so she said she was throwing the party for me," Fuentes said. "I think if I wouldn't have had the party I would have regretted it afterwards, so I'm really happy I did have it."

"When I was a little girl I always had imagined having one of these parties," Rendon said. "When I started getting older, I was thinking more toward going for a car. When I turned 13, I finally decided I wanted to have the party. It was like a traditional ceremony, and I didn't want to regret missing it."

"I got into the spirit of being a person with more faith. I really wasn't a person who liked going to church, but after going to the sessions it hit me I should have more faith and I should give thanks to God for everything I have now that my parents didn't have when they were younger," Rendon said. "It also helped my family come together and helped me come out of my shell, not to be a person who is shy, to be a person with more confidence."

"I remember, when I was little I used to go to my older cousins' *quinceañeras* and I thought it was really cool," Bazan said. "First, I wanted to do it because of this big dress and because everybody's giving you gifts. When I got older and I went to the classes, I thought, 'This is really neat.'"

"It wasn't just for the dress, it was to show you're becoming more responsible, more of a young lady."

Joining in the Conversation

1. How does the church play a role in *quinceañeras*? Explain the communal importance of the *quinceañera*.
2. Sendejas writes his article for the newspaper and answers all the journalistic questions necessary for a good piece. However, he gives his reader a view of the event with only a contemporary perspective. Conduct research to find out more about *quinceañeras* and the culture. You might look for articles by Norma Cantú and KarenMary Davalos that combine both historical background with personal experiences. Then develop a presentation that explores as many aspects of the *quinceañeras* as possible.
3. Choose a cultural ritual that you are familiar with and write about it from both your own perspective and from a researched perspective showing its

origin, how it has changed, how it is celebrated today, and how you have participated in it. Be sure to integrate the personal and the researched material rather than simply writing one part from personal experience and one from researched information. If you know anyone else who has celebrated this same ritual, interview the person and use material from that celebration as well.

They Die in Brooks County

MARY JO MCCONAHAY

Mary Jo McConahay is a contributing editor to New America Media *and an independent journalist whose works have appeared in the* Pacific News Service *and* The Texas Observer *in which the following article appeared on June 1, 2007. In this article, McConahay explores the dangers faced by both the illegal immigrants crossing into the United States and the American residents whose own security and way of life are now in jeopardy.*

✦

There is a human toll to illegal immigration. The corpses of men, women, and children who perished trying to enter the country are routinely found in Brooks County. They are photographed by law enforcement officials and private citizens. Police use the photos to investigate the deaths. Private citizens bring the photos to their elected officials and urge action.

At the Side Door Café in Falfurrias, Texas, body counts enter conversations as naturally as the price of feed, or the cost of repairing torn fences. "I removed 11 bodies last year from my ranch, 12 the year before," said prominent local landowner Presnall Cage. "I found four so far this year." Sometimes, Cage said, he has taken survivors to a hospital; mostly, however, time and the sun have done their jobs, and it is too late.

As increased U.S. border security closes certain routes, undocumented migrants continue to come but squeeze onto fewer, more dangerous and isolated pathways to America's interior. One of these is the network of trails that bypasses the last Border Patrol checkpoint traveling north on Hwy. 281, in Brooks County. That change is having a dramatic ripple effect on the county (total pop: 7,685), and on people who have lived here for generations.

For one thing, the dead are breaking the budget. County officials earmarked $16,000 in fiscal 2007 for handling deceased indigents. That category includes the remains of undocumented Mexicans and other would-be migrants found within county lines. But by May, Brooks County had already spent $34,195 on autopsies and burials, "and we're just heading into the hot months now," said County Judge Raul Ramirez. It's also rattlesnake mating season, noted the judge, who grew up on the King Ranch. It's the time when the serpents move around most, biting the unwary and those who walk in grass and sand without high boots.

"Don't get me wrong. I'm glad to do this. I'd spend $120,000 if I had to because it's the right thing to do," Ramirez said in his modest office on Allen Street in Falfurrias (population 5,020), the county seat. "But we could be helping more of our own." About a third of Brooks residents live below the poverty line; average household income is $21,000; jobs are just plain scarce.

Pictures of the dead are kept discreetly in certain places in this town, a collective album that tells an important part of what Brooks County—which used to be better known for oil, watermelon, and a Halliburton facility—has become in the last couple of years: a grave for the weak or unlucky.

Luis M. Lopez Moreno, Mexico's consul in McAllen, said there are other changes that may add to the death toll. Since the border has become so difficult to cross, working men who moved back and forth annually are now stuck in the north, and family members unaccustomed to the trek are "trying to reunite" by traveling to the States. Women, arguably less able to withstand the journey, sometimes caring for children, are represented more in the migrant stream. Young migrants, the majority of those who come, are likely to be better educated and more urban now, less aware of how to manage themselves under extreme conditions.

"Hank," a guide for high-end hunters who doesn't want his real name used, thinks he saves lives. Unobtrusively, he turns hunters' blinds away from nearby trails so the "illegals" don't get shot by accident. This is also an attempt "to protect the psychological state of the hunters." They may be men fearless in high finance and politics—Washington figures including both Bush presidents have hunted here, with Air Force One parked incongruously on the county airstrip. And the gentlemen may have the confidence big wallets can bring, paying well over $1,000 a day to stalk deer, spring turkey, quail, wild pig, and imported exotic animals, and to stay at lodges with gourmet meals, bars, and wireless. Surprised in the wild by local human traffic, however, they can quake.

"Hunters, they get scared and panic, especially if it's something like a group of 30 coming through," Hank explained. "The illegals got so bad last year we had to buy two-way radios." Hunters can use the radios to call their guides for help. Hank's job has changed in other ways, too. "Before there was downtime to be in the truck, kick back, park in a pasture, and wait for the hunters." No more. "We stay within 100 yards."

At home, Hank reaches into the bed of his pick-up and pulls out a black backpack like the ones he finds "most every day." Inside are dirty clothes, a comb, deodorant, a razor, mirror, a pair of tweezers. It's typical of a pack left behind as a migrant emerges at a highway pick-up point, ready to blend in to America. Inside the house with his wife and two small children, Hank displays a silver-handled .380, which he started carrying only recently for protection, after 14 years on a job he used to love. *Coyotes,* those who guide the migrants for high fees, are vicious, he says. That's a good reason for not wanting to use his real name. They're not just from Mexico but are home-grown too, some from right here in town. But that's nothing compared to gang members he began to see two years ago. MS-13, he said, tattooed from head to toe and skinheads. Unlike other illegals, "they never talk to you." Hank never expected to see the kinds of things he sees now, and reluctantly plans to move on to another job someday, although he would like to spend a few more years at this one. "If I can last," he said.

Brooks County is some 70 miles from the U.S.-Mexico border. The checkpoint here tallies more interceptions and drug confiscations than any other in the nation. Migrants are either dumped just south of the checkpoint by *coyotes,* or they reach Brooks after walking all the way from *la linea,* which takes about 60 hours. They enter the ranches and desert stretches, avoiding the checkpoint until hours later—ideally for them—they reach highway pick-up spots around the town of Falfurrias or nearby ranches. The local Minuteman-type group calls one path west of 281 the Ho Chi Minh Trail because it's so heavily traveled. Other trails traverse hot sands, or in winter are mercilessly cold and wet. The unfit, those held back by children, the old, and anyone else who can't keep up the brisk pace, are at risk. *Coyotes* don't wait. A kind of frontier law forbids those lost and left behind from attaching themselves to another coyote's group. This stark and stunning landscape, this once-welcoming town far from where immigration laws are made, is where the reality of U.S. immigration policy, or lack of policy, plays out darkly, in a way almost invisible to the outside world.

"Washington, D.C., and even Austin don't have any idea what goes on," said Brooks County Sheriff Balde Lozano. "Worst is the deaths. We get there and sometimes they've been dead minutes, sometimes months. Some I'm sure are never found."

Small habits, the kind that make up the comforting weave of a life one knows, are changing. Corina Molina, the county auditor, used to come out to the driveway in the mornings and start her engine while she returned inside to gather up a child, or exchanged pleasantries with neighbors doing the same thing. Since an undocumented migrant under pursuit grabbed one of the running cars and took off, the women of the neighborhood dropped the custom. Another county employee, Katy Garza, said she had witnessed a police action that very morning at one of the safe houses used by smugglers to keep migrants overnight. "I guess I'll be having to lock doors now," said Garza. "I have a granddaughter who plays out front—maybe that will have to change too."

Two women professionals in their fifties did not want their names used because—like "Hank"—they feared retribution from local *coyotes* if they spoke to a reporter. Locals who collaborate with the trafficking network are few, but "it's a small town," neighbors say, and some do not want to cross others they grew up with, or recognize on the street. "I thought with the National Guard on the border it would be okay, but the number [of migrants] is growing, and now I won't stay home alone," said one, an accountant whose home is in a rural area. She had her refrigerator raided, and shampoo swiped, but no jewelry or money. A few weeks back young women emerged from the brush and approached her husband, a backhoe operator, begging rides to Houston. Returning late from a party with office companions, all women, the accountant said she "realized something else new."

"Nobody wanted to go out and open the gate alone," she said.

Presnall Cage grew up on the family ranch, 46,000 acres of it. "We had them come through for years, agricultural workers, only men," he said. "They hailed you and asked, 'Do you have work or food?' They walked, all the way from Mexico, singly, or maybe in twos, and they knew where the cowboy camps were, where they could pick up some coffee or a meal. Six months later we'd see them walking back, going home to join their families." Today big groups pass through the ranch, he said, and the guide has a cell phone and GPS. Cage spends more than $50,000 a year to repair property damage caused by the migrants, who bend or cut fences, break pipelines to get water, and leave gates open, which means cattle stray or get mixed up. His cowboys—and this isn't the job they signed up for—go out Fridays on litter patrol, collecting hundreds of pounds of plastic bags, jugs, backpacks, and other detritus. Cage thinks back to the old days, before the recent immigrant surge, and looks thoughtful. "We never had a body, all those years."

The Texas Border Volunteers, most of them armed, track and surround migrants and *coyotes.* They're a civilian group like the Minutemen, better equipped than local lawmen, and partly funded by ranchers, they say. Their stated aim is to communicate the location of illegals for authorities, "to report intel to the Border Patrol." They reckon 1,000 people come through daily, a number used by other sources, and only some are captured by the undermanned agents. "What gets me is their total disregard for our property, for state and federal laws," local veterinarian, rancher, and the group's founder, Dr. Mike Vickers said of the "aliens." "I don't blame them for wanting to come, but do it legally. I'm mad. They're stealing our country."

Sheriff Lozano said that for civilians to surround migrants might be detaining them against their will, which could be against the law, "but no one has complained about it." Vickers admits the Volunteers dressed in camouflage appear like enforcement authorities, and the presence of the dogs they take with them is intimidating. But the aliens are technically free to keep walking, and if they don't know that, well, too bad. The Border Patrol says it doesn't encourage private citizens to do its job, which is dangerous.

But the Volunteers claim they disrupt *coyotes'* deliveries of human beings, save lives by finding the lost and straggling, and are on the spot to receive anyone who wants to "surrender" because they can't go any farther. Most of all, the Volunteers want the feeling they are *doing* something about uninvited newcomers.

In McAllen, Consul Lopez Moreno says the Mexican government supports a temporary worker program of some kind because it revives a system that worked well until the big U.S. immigration reforms of 1986 and 1996. "This was a revolving door. The United States opened or closed it as it needed," said Lopez. "Breaking the cycle is what has caused the problem." That "circularity"—when workers went back and forth more easily between labor in the States and family in Mexico—worked for both countries, he said. The United States needs workers. Mexicans need work. "But this way they're candidates for death," he said.

One-third of the consul's staff works in the Protection Department, which handles searches for those reported missing by families in Mexico, and repatriation of the deceased. It's a job that takes a daily toll, and McAllen is classified for diplomatic staff as a hardship post. José Luís Diaz Mirón Hinojosa, who goes to the field when remains are found, now attends 40 to 50 cases a year. "I can give certainty to people," Diaz says, returning the bodies of the missing. At least the dead from Brooks County are easier to identify than some—about 80 percent can be sent home; around the Rio Grande the percentage is fewer, because remains deteriorate faster in the river.

THE ACCIDENTAL *COYOTE*

The seduction of easy money, $1,500 for a quick trip to Houston with an undocumented passenger, and no checkpoints to cross—has been too tempting for some residents of Falfurrias. "Bill," 43, a heavy equipment operator with a wife and daughter, became a criminal two years ago, an accidental *coyote*. Someone offered him big money to take an illegal immigrant who had just made it through the desert for a no-risk ride—he'd start from north of the last Border Patrol checkpoint—and the extra cash became a habit. Recently he's started working with a more serious, deliberate *coyote*, now running him down to Mission twice a week for $700 each time—again no risk, since Border Patrol isn't likely to stop a car traveling south. There are probably fewer than a dozen such local *coyotes*, authorities and Bill say, and probably half of them would be doing something illegal anyway, running small amounts of dope, for instance. But Bill had never been in jail in his life, except for a few hours in high school for speeding. He's not one of the despicable *coyotes* who lie and would just as soon leave someone to die when he's squeezed off schedule. "I was trying to start a septic tank business. If I do it seven more months I think I can start."

But the extra cash has helped Bill revive an old cocaine habit. And when a cop stopped him for an out-of-date tag and found an undocumented person in the car, Bill was warned and released but it went on his record, so he lost his good regular job and has settled for one that pays less. Starting the septic tank business may take more time than he thought.

He should quit or be extra careful; if he's caught again he goes to jail. But now he's a little afraid, just like some townspeople are cautious about local *coyotes*, lest they be connected to mean ones. "They should be afraid," suggests Bill. Not of him, he insists, of others. "We each work with a chain and if you steal someone off another one's chain or do something else they don't like they say, 'The mafia will take care of you.' That's the Mexican mafia."

Bill doesn't think he'd make it in prison. "I'm not the prison type," he said.

Joining in the Conversation

1. What are the main effects that illegal immigration has on the residents of Brooks County and the surrounding area? What are some of the dangers that are faced by the illegal immigrants themselves? Do you think McConahay is fair in her representation of both sides? Explain.
2. McConahay discusses several very emotional aspects of the illegal immigration process by using various writing techniques. Find several examples in the article where she uses personal narrative or stories as a way to get her point across, making sure to point out specific words used to make the story more emotional. Then find examples where she uses logic as a technique by supplying numbers and dates to support her ideas. After you have collected your examples, compose an informative essay in which you discuss your findings and conclude your essay with your opinion about which writing technique (emotional personal narrative or logical facts) was most convincing for you.
3. Investigate the various processes available through the federal government for entering the United States legally. Which visas or other documents are used for work? For residence? For education? For medical and other "hardship" cases? Then investigate the same process in another country, such as Mexico, Japan, or Sweden. Based on your findings, compose a comparison/contrast paper in which you explain each country's immigration process and determine which country is most generous in opening its doors to foreigners.

Mexican-Americans Struggle for Jobs

CHARLIE LEDUFF

Charlie LeDuff has been a reporter for The New York Times *since 1995. In 2001, LeDuff, along with several other reporters, won a Pulitzer Prize for* The New York Times *series, "How Race Is Lived*

Source: Charlie LeDuff, "Mexican-Americans Struggle for Jobs," New York Times, October 13, 2004.

in America." In the following article that appeared on October 13, 2004, LeDuff explores the problems NAFTA has created for employees working for companies that have moved to other countries to continue producing their goods.

✦

WORKERS WHO CAME NORTH, ONLY TO SEE THE WORLD HEAD SOUTH

Ernestina Miranda left Mexico for the United States in 1979 in the trunk of a car.

She found a job sewing blue jeans in one of the dozens of clothing factories here. Work was steady, six days a week, 12 hours a day. She married and bought a trailer—without running water or electricity—on a plot of land. She was awarded citizenship in the late 1980's.

Now, those blue jeans jobs that brought Mrs. Miranda and thousands of others like her north have gone south, to Mexico.

"My American dream has turned into a nightmare," she said, over a glass of strawberry Kool-Aid in her listing trailer. Until recently, she had made a life on $7.50 an hour. She has become a temporary worker in a plastics plant that used to be based in Michigan, earning minimum wage, no benefits, no security. Her husband, Miguel, is unemployed. The mortgage on the slapdash home is in peril.

"I worry about the future," she said, echoing the sentiment of blue-collar and increasingly of white-collar workers from Los Angeles to Detroit, people who find their jobs being shipped to countries where wages are a small fraction of theirs.

When VF Jeanswear, the maker of Wrangler and Lee jeans, announced in September that it was moving the last of its jeans production and more than 1,000 jobs to Mexico, it was the death of that industry in a town once known as Blue Jean Capital, U.S.A. Levi Strauss, Sun Apparel, Wrangler, Lee and Farah do not make jeans here anymore.

Proponents of increased international trade say that it ultimately creates more jobs in the United States and lowers prices for consumers here.

But in the 11 years since the North American Free Trade Agreement, known as NAFTA, was ratified, more than 17,000 garment manufacturing jobs have gone away, according to the Texas Workforce Commission, some to Mexico, some to China, and some to China by way of Mexico. Gone, too, is the good American life described by women like Mrs. Miranda, who has two teenage children. The $7- to $10-an-hour job, the health insurance, McDonald's double cheeseburgers, the $200 apartments in the back of a day care center with a communal toilet, all gone.

In a strange post-industrial twist, most people who have lost their jobs in the garment industry here are first-generation Mexican women. They typically are illiterate and speak little English. They came to El Paso in the 60's, 70's and 80's, when the American factories moved down from the Northern states in search of cut-rate border labor.

With those factories having moved out of El Paso, these American citizens find they are members of the obsolescent class.

"I cannot move back to Mexico," said Soledad Renteria, 51, who waded across the Rio Grande with her son on her back nearly two decades ago. "My life is here, and my family there is poor," Ms. Renteria said. "My son wants to work, but I tell him he has to stay in school or he'll end up like me, working as a janitor."

In this election year, the presidential candidates debate the benefits of free trade mostly in the rust-belt swing states like Pennsylvania, Michigan and Ohio that have been battered by the loss of manufacturing jobs.

Yet NAFTA has affected the low-skilled, low-wage Latino workers near the border more than any other place. According to an analysis by the Economic Policy Institute, which focuses on labor issues, California lost 116,000 jobs from 1993 through 2002 because of NAFTA, many of them textile jobs. The federal government has certified that 7,800 workers in El Paso County were displaced by NAFTA over the past three years, more than double the number displaced in Cook County, Ill., which was second.

Immigrants elsewhere find their jobs being shipped back to their motherland. In September, the San Francisco Sewing Association closed its doors after 22 years. Once a provider of clothing for Gap, Esprit and Koret, the company lost the last of its contracts to China. Its 200 unionized employees, almost all Chinese and Mexican, were sent to the breadline.

"We lost the business because Mexico and China are a lot cheaper," said Steven Lau, co-owner of the factory. "One day's salary here is one month's salary in China."

Economists frequently describe how the departure of low-wage jobs to other places leads to the creation of yet better jobs in the United States, but not everyone displaced is a candidate for these proverbial new jobs. And with Texas safely in Republican hands and polls showing that California is poised once again to vote Democratic, presidential candidates are not rushing to assure these workers that help is on the way.

Raquel G. Ortiz, the daughter of immigrants who stole across the Rio Grande, speaks English and can write in both English and Spanish. But at 56, she is unattractive to new employers and scared, she said, after 21 years at VF Jeanswear.

"Who wants to hire a broken-down old lady?" she asked. "I'd like to be an embalmer. That seems nice and peaceful. But they don't offer training classes for that."

She recently wrote a letter addressed to 1600 Pennsylvania Ave.:

President Bush:

"I respectfully need your attention in the matter of my termination from VF Wrangler Jeans. The factory is leaving to Mexico for cheap labor. I have three complaints.

1. The company wants to give me $110 for each year service.
2. No extension of health benefits.
3. No implementation of promises in the NAFTA treaty to help American workers. I need training for a real job that exists here."

Ms. Ortiz said: "There's nothing left here, and I'm too old to go anywhere else. What am I supposed to do?

The decision to move its manufacturing jobs to Mexico was a simple economic one, according to an executive with VF Jeanswear. "We are the last major apparel supplier to move manufacturing out of the United States," said Sam Tucker, vice president for human resources. "If we could, we would stay. But in order to make products competitive, we don't have much choice."

As part of NAFTA, the federal government promised retraining programs for workers who lost their jobs to foreign competition, so that they could obtain a new job that pays at least 80 percent of what they earned previously.

The El Paso seamstresses are suing the federal Department of Labor, saying they got only remedial English classes and a course, in Spanish, to earn their graduate equivalency diploma. The Association of Border Workers, which filed the complaint, says that the workers should be in bilingual vocational schools or in on-the-job training.

"What do we need with a G.E.D.?" Ms. Oritz asked. "They trained a bunch of people to be nurse's aides, and then all of the sudden there were so many nurse's aides and no jobs for nurse's aides. It's ridiculous."

El Paso is a border town, and along with Juarez, Mexico, makes up one of the biggest international urban centers. But El Paso is one of the poorest urban centers in the country, where three of four households speak Spanish and almost a third of the population cannot speak English at all and where one-quarter of the work force has not completed the ninth grade. Unemployment hovers around 7.5 percent, and median household income is $37,000, $20,000 less than the national average, according to Census figures.

El Paso has cheap, willing labor. But Juarez has cheaper, more willing labor. And so the older American workers, particularly from the immigrant classes, are the throwaways in the new economic order, said Eliot Shapleigh, the state senator from El Paso County, who is trying to bring new industry to El Paso.

"The promise of America is that with drive, with heart, with quality education, anyone can succeed," Mr. Shapleigh said. "We did not make good on our promise to Americans to keep that dream alive."

There are still some jobs related to the garment industry in El Paso, at laundries and distribution centers. One garment plant is still hiring because it makes military uniforms, which are required by law to be made in the United States. Beyond that, the garment workers scratch out a living sewing hospital scrubs for minimum wage or doing temporary work with no benefits.

And Mrs. Miranda, the marginally educated woman now earning $5.15 an hour—who is unable to speak English and who failed her G.E.D. exam by five points—summed up the economic situation for blue-collar workers as well as anyone.

"The problem in the United States is bad," she said. "It is worse in Mexico."

Joining in the Conversation

1. Explain how NAFTA has been beneficial for American industry but a nightmare for the employees of those companies. Give specific examples.

2. This is clearly an informative essay written with a slant. Take the essay and rewrite it so that it is a persuasive essay, one that attempts to make the reader take action based on an existing situation. You will have to determine what the current article is trying to convince you to believe, whether you believe the author, and whether you want to try to persuade your audience to do something based on the opinion being expressed. If you want to take a different side, you will also have to find evidence to support your position.
3. Write an investigative, informative essay that describes the economic changes in terms of financial gains and/or losses that have occurred in one manufacturing company of your choice since its move out of the United States to produce the same products. Investigate what changes the company has had to make, such as the costs incurred in the move, the changes or no changes in the prices of their primary products since the move, the differences in pay scale to their laborers in their new country, the cost of public relations (advertising), and any other elements that affect the company financially. After you have presented your information, draw conclusions.

Hospitals Feeling Strain From Illegal Immigrants

DANA CANEDY

Dana Canedy has been an assistant editor for the The New York Times–*National Desk since 2003. She began her career as a reporter for consumer products for* The Times *and went on to become* The Times's *Miami bureau chief. Her career also includes writing for the* Cleveland Plain Dealer *and* The Wall Street Journal. *In 2000, Canedy's article "Between the Lines, a Measure of Hurt" was part of* The Times's *Pulitzer award-winning series, "How Race Is Lived in America."*

✦

Source: Dana Canedy, "Hospitals Feel Strain from Illegal Immigrants," *New York Times,* August 25, 2002.

"FREE" CARE STAGGERS PROVIDERS AT BORDERS

In the two and a half years since Luis Jiménez arrived at the Martin Memorial Medical Center emergency room with severe brain damage from a head-on car collision, the hospital here has become his home.

In that time, Mr. Jiménez, 30, a former gardener, has emerged from a coma, had two birthdays and accumulated medical bills of almost $1 million. By all accounts, he is well enough to be discharged, but the hospital and advocates for the patient are in a conflict over his mounting medical bills and future care that makes his release unlikely without a court order.

A penniless illegal immigrant from Guatemala, Mr. Jiménez has no health insurance, and his injuries have left him with limited mobility and the mental capacity of a 3-year-old. Martin Memorial wants to send him back to his homeland for any remaining medical care. But Mr. Jiménez's advocates insist that he must remain at the hospital until it can find a suitable place in the United States or Guatemala that is willing to care for him.

The impasse is at the center of a national debate over who is ultimately responsible for illegal immigrants who require extensive medical care but have no means to pay for it. The issue has become an increasing concern for health care providers, particularly in Florida and border states with growing numbers of illegal immigrants.

Federal law requires hospitals to provide emergency care to critically ill or injured patients regardless of their immigration status. But because many illegal immigrants work in low-wage jobs that offer no benefits, and cannot qualify for Medicaid, they use emergency rooms as their primary source of routine and critical health care. As the number of such patients increases sharply in states like Florida, California, Texas and Arizona, so too does the financial burden on health care centers that treat them, hospital administrators say.

"We have people coming to our country in good faith to work, but we have no system in place as a nation as to what to do when these people get sick," said Pat Austin, a spokeswoman for Martin Memorial. "Each hospital is left to kind of figure out what to do for itself."

The hospitals insist that they are not turning away critically ill or injured people, but they are becoming more aggressive in seeking ways to release them. Some hospitals are going to court seeking permission to discharge patients like Mr. Jiménez. Federal lawmakers are seeking financial aid to reimburse hospitals for treating indigent illegal immigrants, and some hospitals have taken unusual steps, including putting nurses on planes to fly the patients back to their own countries.

Such measures, though, have done little to stem the rising costs, the health care providers say. "We have tried to work on this for years, but the problem has gotten more acute," said Sheri Jorden, senior policy director for the Arizona Hospital and Healthcare Association. "Hospitals have been writing these bills off with great difficulty."

According to a study released last month by the National Association of Counties, 86 percent of 150 counties nationwide reported an increase in uncompensated health care expenses in the last five years. Of those reporting an increase, 67 percent cited a growing number of immigrants as a factor in the rising costs for county hospitals and rescue services.

"Most of the counties receive money from the state and federal government," said Jacqueline Byers, director of research for the association, "but it is not nearly enough to meet the growing need."

According to the Immigration and Naturalization Service, the number of illegal immigrants in the United States increased to as many as eight million in 2000, the last year for which figures are available, from five million in 1996. By some estimates, hospitals are collectively writing off as much as $2 billion a year in unpaid medical bills to treat the illegal immigrants, who, unlike American citizens and permanent residents, are ineligible for Medicaid.

In one case at Martin Memorial that was resolved in February, an illegal immigrant from Jamaica arrived at the emergency room with a sore on his leg and stayed in the hospital for 17 months.

"He said he had a green card but couldn't find it," Ms. Austin said. "The doctors found a serious vascular disease and he had to have both legs amputated."

"After his surgeries, when he was well enough, we had a great deal of difficulty figuring out what to do next," Ms. Austin added. "We eventually found some relatives and a physician in Jamaica who was willing to accept him, and one of our nurses flew with him to Jamaica. By the time all that happened, it had cost us probably over half a million dollars."

In the case of Mr. Jiménez, Martin Memorial says it has already incurred nearly $900,000 in expenses for which it has no hope of being paid.

"We feel there needs to be a national program of some sort that would cover these individuals with insurance," Ms. Austin said, "or in the case of catastrophic events, allow the hospital a chance of repayment."

Martin Memorial has been unable to release Mr. Jiménez because the patient's guardian and the hospital cannot agree on a discharge plan. The hospital has petitioned a judge for permission to send Mr. Jiménez back to Guatemala. No state medical center will accept him, since his immigration status makes him ineligible for Medicaid.

Mr. Jiménez's lawyer contends that the hospital has not provided enough information about where the man will be placed and who will treat him. Mr. Jiménez's family in Guatemala does not have the money to pay for his care.

"The hospital is saying he's occupying a bed and we need to get him out," said Michael Banks, a lawyer who has donated his services to Montejo Gaspar, Mr. Jiménez's cousin by marriage and his court-appointed guardian. "We have made it unequivocally clear that we have no problems sending Mr. Jiménez to Guatemala, but we feel a plan is not in place."

In Arizona, where hospitals have grappled with similar problems, the University Medical Center in Tucson wrote off more than $3 million in costs between July 2000 and June 2001 that it incurred from treating uninsured immigrants, said John Duval, chief operating officer for the center. "I don't know that there's a societal solution to the problem," Mr. Duval said, "but we are doing an enormous amount of heavy lifting with no compensation."

Another Arizona hospital, Southeast Arizona Medical Center in Douglas, filed for bankruptcy and nearly closed in 1998 because of the rising costs of treating illegal immigrants. The problem has become so bad in Arizona that a state program that provided free dialysis and chemotherapy for legal and illegal immigrants will run out of money in a couple of months.

The issue has prompted hospitals in several states to seek assistance from sympathetic lawmakers. Senator Jon Kyl, Republican of Arizona, introduced a bill in January 2001, co-sponsored with Senator John McCain, Republican of Arizona, and Senator Dianne Feinstein, Democrat of California, that would provide $200 million a year for four years to reimburse health care providers in border regions.

Representative Jim Kolbe, Republican of Arizona, introduced a similar measure in June 2001 that would establish a $50 million reimbursement program for hospitals and ambulance services in his state. The Border Hospital Survival and Illegal Immigrant Care Act would guarantee that medical providers are compensated for treating illegal immigrants. Both bills are stalled in committees.

"It is not a top priority for many," Mr. Kolbe said. "It does happen everywhere, but where you see it every day is here along the border."

Joining in the Conversation

1. Canedy's article tries to give both perspectives on the issue of medical care costs for immigrants in America. What points does she use to support each side of the argument? Do you think she succeeds in giving a "balanced," that is, a fair discussion of both sides? Defend you answer with examples from the article.
2. According to Canedy's article, the U.S. government has passed a law that "requires hospitals to provide emergency care to critically ill or injured patients regardless of their immigration status." However, the article also points out the other side of the problem: "many illegal immigrants work in low-wage jobs that offer no benefits, and cannot qualify for Medicaid." Looking at these two statements, do you think that one of the policies should be changed or should some other system be put into place to care for individuals such as the ones Canedy describes? That is, should the federal government quit requiring emergency care if someone is illegal, should illegal immigrants be allowed to apply for Medicaid, or should some other system of care be allowed?
3. Using the Internet, research the federal government's requirements for applying for Medicaid, including how someone becomes eligible for Medicaid, what forms are needed, and what benefits are extended to individuals. Then prepare a report explaining the process involved in applying and the benefits and limitations of the program. Conclude your report with one recommendation to improve the Medicaid system.

La Nueva Orleans

Gregory Rodriguez

Gregory Rodriguez is a longtime contributing editor to the Los Angeles Times *and an Irvine Senior Fellow at the New America Foundation. He wrote the following article for the September 25, 2005 edition of the* Los Angeles Times.

LATINO IMMIGRANTS, MANY OF THEM HERE ILLEGALLY, WILL REBUILD THE GULF COAST—AND STAY THERE

No matter what all the politicians and activists want, African Americans and impoverished white Cajuns will not be first in line to rebuild the Katrina-ravaged Gulf Coast and New Orleans. Latino immigrants, many of them undocumented, will. And when they're done, they're going to stay, making New Orleans look like Los Angeles. It's the federal government that will have made the transformation possible, further exposing the hollowness of the immigration debate.

President Bush has promised that Washington will pick up the greater part of the cost for "one of the largest reconstruction efforts the world has ever seen." To that end, he suspended provisions of the Davis-Bacon Act that would have required government contractors to pay prevailing wages in Louisiana and devastated parts of Mississippi, Alabama and Florida. And the Department of Homeland Security has temporarily suspended sanctioning employers who hire workers who cannot document their citizenship. The idea is to benefit Americans who may have lost everything in the hurricane, but the main effect will be to let contractors hire illegal immigrants.

Mexican and Central American laborers are already arriving in southeastern Louisiana. One construction firm based in Metairie, La., sent a foreman to Houston to round up 150 workers willing to do cleanup work for $15 an hour, more than twice their wages in Texas. The men—most of whom are undocumented, according to news accounts—live outside New Orleans in mobile homes without running water and electricity. The foreman expects them to stay "until there's no more work" but "there's going to be a lot of construction jobs for a really long time."

Because they are young and lack roots in the United States, many recent migrants are ideal for the explosion of construction jobs to come. Those living in the U.S. will relocate to the Gulf Coast, while others will come from south of the border. Most will not intend to stay where their new jobs are, but the longer the jobs last, the more likely they will settle permanently. One recent poll of New Orleans evacuees living in Houston emergency shelters found that fewer than half intend to return home. In part, their places will be taken by the migrant workers. Former President Clinton recently hinted as much on NBC's *Meet the Press* when he said New Orleans will be resettled with a different population.

It is not the first time that hurricanes and other natural disasters have triggered population movements. In 1998, Hurricane Mitch slammed into Central America, sending waves of migrants northward. The 2001 earthquakes in El Salvador produced similar shifts. The effects of Hurricane Andrew may better foretell New Orleans' future. The 1992 storm displaced 250,000 residents in southeastern Florida. The construction boom that followed attracted large numbers of Latin American immigrants, who rebuilt towns such as Homestead, whose Latino population has increased by 50% since then.

At the same time, U.S. construction firms have become increasingly reliant on Latino immigrant labor. In 1990, only 3.3% of construction workers were Mexican immigrants. Ten years later, the number was 8.5%. In 2004, 17% of Latino immigrants worked in the business, a higher percentage than in any other industry. Nor is this an exclusively Southwest phenomenon. Even before Katrina, more and more Latin American immigrant workers were locating in the South, with North Carolina and Arkansas incurring the greatest percentage gains between 1990 and 2000. This helps explain why 40% of the workers who rebuilt the Pentagon after the 9/11 attack were Latino.

Reliance on immigrant labor to complete huge projects is part of U.S. history. In the early 19th century, mostly Irish immigrant laborers, who worked for as little as 37½ cents an hour, built the Erie Canal, one of the greatest engineering feats of its day. Later that century, Italian immigrants, sometimes making just $1.50 a day, were the backbone of the workforce that constructed the New York subway system. In 1890, 90% of New York City's public works employees, and 99% of Chicago's street workers, were Italian.

After Congress authorized construction of the transcontinental railroad in 1862, one of the most ambitious projects in U.S. history, Charles Crocker, head of construction for Central Pacific railroad, recognized that the Civil War was creating a labor shortage. So he turned to Chinese immigrants to do the job. By 1867, 12,000 of Central Pacific's 13,500 workers were Chinese immigrants, who were paid between $26 and $35 for a six-day workweek of 12 hours a day. At the turn of the 20th century, Mexican immigrant laborers did most of the railroad construction in Southern California, Arizona, New Mexico and Nevada.

Mexican workers were also essential in turning the Southwest into a fertile region, which by 1929 produced 40% of the United States' fruits and vegetables. They cleared the mesquite brush of south Texas to make room for the expansion of agriculture, then played a primary role in the success of cotton farming in the state. A generation earlier, German immigrants from Russia and Norwegians had busted the prairie sod to turn the grasslands of North Dakota into arable fields.

The major difference between then and now is that neither the American public nor the government will admit their dependence on a labor force that is heavily undocumented. When Mexican President Vicente Fox offered to provide Mexican labor to help rebuild New Orleans—"If there is anything Mexicans are good at, it is construction," he said—the federal government ignored him. At the same time, some of the undocumented Mexicans who have cleaned up and begun to rebuild Biloxi, Miss., are wondering whether they deserve at least a temporary visa so they can live in the U.S. legally.

Last week, the White House said it will push its plan to allow illegal immigrants already in the U.S. to become legal guest workers. Good. Hurricane Katrina exposed the nation's black-white divide. Post-Katrina reconstruction will soon spotlight the hypocrisy of refusing to grant legal status to those who will rebuild the Gulf Coast and New Orleans.

Joining in the Conversation

1. In addition to Latinos, list the other immigrant groups who have helped build and/or rebuild parts of the United States over the years. What hypocrisy has been revealed according to Rodriguez about using Latinos to help rebuild New Orleans?
2. Rodriguez uses a historical strategy to support his claim. Identify his claim and list specific points that he uses to support and develop his article. Does the article convince you to agree with Rodriguez's main points or does it persuade you not only to agree with him but to act as well? Do you agree or disagree with Rodriguez's main points and why?
3. Go to the databases in your library and find as many articles as you can on the tension between Latinos and New Orleans residents regarding the rebuilding of the city. Also investigate what Mayor Ray Nagin has said about repopulating New Orleans. What is the difference between what is happening and what is being said? Using the various opinions, arrive at a position that describes a possible projection for the future of the New Orleans population. Support your projections from your sources. If you know any New Orleans evacuees, you might ask if you can interview them for their perspectives.

Additional Topics of Conversation

1. Two of the authors in this section Rolando Hinojosa and Jonathan Kandell, explores some aspect of the environment and how it has been affected by the cultural changes brought about by immigration between Mexico and the United States. Explore these articles to see how the environment has been impacted and the effects of such impact on the people involved. Then, investigate further on the Internet the issue you have chosen. When finished, organize your thoughts for presentation to the class.
2. One aspect of border space is that of change. Review LeDuff's and Canedy's, articles, to understand further how the intersection of cultures can alter even such powerful forces as employment and health care. Then, interview individuals from two separate generations of the same cultural background, for example, grandparents and teenagers. See what types of changes, if any, have occurred not only in these two fields, but in other cultural aspects as well, such as gender codes, education, and even fashion. Present your findings in a class discussion that shows the differences and similarities between the expectations and standards of the two generations.
3. Often small communities are not aware of more pressing regional or national issues affecting them. Interview members of an organization in your area that deals with U.S.-Mexican interests, whether nonprofit or corporate, to discover some of the issues between the countries that exist now. Such areas could involve finance, relief work, scientific research, educational exchanges, and so forth. Present your findings in a variety of ways, including charts and other visual forms, that describe the situation, and as a class or in groups, determine a workable solution to the problems.
4. The Internet is often seen as a "borderless" area because it has no physical boundaries to it. However, it also participates in the cultural and psychological border discussions between Mexico and the United States. For background information, research two web sites that promote Mexican interests and two that promote those of the United States. The areas can vary widely, for example, sports or theater. Then prepare a travel brochure for each country promoting tourism based on your findings.
5. The topic of women as a cultural issue has been mentioned in a few articles in this chapter. In groups, brainstorm the U.S. cultural expectations that women must meet and then determine what you can about the cultural expectations of Chicanas based on your readings. If these articles do not provide enough information, search the Internet or go to the library for further cultural information about women's lives and the expectations the culture has for them. Take one area of the culture (being a wife, being a mother, being a career woman, etc.) and make a presentation to the class about the differences between U.S. expectations of American women and Mexican expectations of Latinas. You might also interview several Latinas and Latinos to find their cultural beliefs about Latinas.

Everyday Issues

On the evening of February 23, 2007, many Houstonians turned their television on to one of the favorite local stations, KTRK-TV, an affiliate of ABC13 Eyewitness News, and were greeted with an array of news items ranging from freeway closures, immigration issues in the city, and sports to the difficulties of meeting medical expenses and how a group of school workers found the image of the Virgin Mary on a pizza pan used at their public school. The news item regarding the pizza pan, although highly interesting, was not as unusual as one would think. Less than two years earlier, an image of Jesus Christ was reported by a family to be in one of the trees in their front yard and merited several days of news exposure and community interest.

These news items highlight on a miniature scale the complexity and diversity of everyday life in the United States today and just how interactive many of those cultural ties are. Images that one culture sees may be interpreted differently by another or given no significance at all. In the case of the image of Our Lady of Guadalupe, unless you were culturally exposed to the image, you may see only an impressionistic view of a woman's face and attach no religious significance to it at all. A transnational perspective, that is, a viewpoint about one's life that spans two national cultures, operates continuously in the United States. Newly arrived immigrants have to learn not only the basics, such as where to buy groceries and exchange currency, but also a host of cultural issues, such as the food value of french fries or which TV channels they prefer to watch.

Although critics have examined many of the major problems, such as education and immigration, the more everyday issues have not received as much attention. What the news broadcasts point out is another perspective to consider. How does one go about his or her everyday life in a new country where technology reaches into every aspect of its citizens' lives, where the opportunity exists to expand one's diet to include cheap and readily available fast food, and where more social and economic opportunities for both adults and youth also carry a personal and cultural price? This chapter addresses the issues of life on a day-to-day level and how the choices one makes can have significant ramifications for one's self and family. While there are many issues that come up in the everyday life of Chican@s in America, this chapter focuses on several that have long-range consequences. How do Chican@s adapt to the Internet revolution that now reaches into all parts of American life? How does one balance medical needs between the U.S. medical system and traditional *curanderismo*, and, if the Chican@s' diet in other countries is healthy, why is there an increase in childhood obesity in U.S. Chican@ families? How do limitations in language affect one's work environment, especially in the dangerous field of construction where Chican@s excel? And finally, how does a shift in location to the United States and its economic and social benefits affect Chican@ families for generations? As the old saying goes, "It's the little things that count most." Technology, health, work, and family certainly are not "little things," but choosing fries over a salad at a fast-food restaurant is a small matter that can have enormous repercussions down the road. As you read, consider the small daily choices and options you make and how they will affect you later in life.

A Latino Internet Revolution

LEE ROMNEY

Lee Romney, a long-standing staff writer for the Los Angeles Times *and a freelance writer, wrote the following article for the June 22, 1999 issue of the* Los Angeles Times.

✦

Source: Lee Romney, "A Latino Internet Revolution," *Los Angeles Times*, June 22, 1999, p. 1A.

ONCE SEPARATED FROM THE AMERICAN MAINSTREAM BY A VAST DIGITAL DIVIDE, SPANISH-SURNAMED HOUSEHOLDS ARE CONNECTING TO THE WEB AT RECORD RATES. AND THE RUSH IS ON TO CATER TO THIS NEW MARKET

Patricia and Jose Cucufate bought their first computer 18 months ago, eager to keep their three children competitive in the classroom and gain them entry into the Information Age. But Patricia soon left her kids in the dust. With computer prices plunging, she purchased a second machine last year and kicked her business into high gear.

Today she receives about 30 online requests a week for shipments of her restaurant's *pupusas*—Salvadoran corncakes stuffed with cheeses, pork and *loroco,* a Central American palm blossom. The restaurant's Spanish-language Web site offers a menu and maps directing customers to *Los Chorros'* two locations in Inglewood and Hawthorne. An online order form will soon let Internet customers buy frozen *pupusas* with the click of a mouse. Queries have come from Panama and Mexico, as well as from homesick Salvadoran emigres in Washington state.

Cucufate boasts that *Los Chorros* may be the first Salvadoran eatery in cyberspace. But she is an unknowing trendsetter in other ways—part of a virtual Latino stampede into the online world.

Once separated from the American mainstream by a vast digital divide, Latino households are now purchasing computers at twice the rate of the overall population. They also are connecting to the Internet at record rates. Though only 2 percent of U.S. Latinos were online in 1994, 15 percent of Latino households—or an estimated 4.5 million users—were connected in 1998, according to one recent study. The surge moves Latinos closer to the roughly one in four American households online. Other studies reveal an even higher percentage of wired Latinos accessing the Internet through work, school and libraries.

The statistics have dealt a swift blow to the long-held notion of Latinos as low-tech, triggering a rush to cater to the new consumers both in Spanish and in English.

"The explosion has been just mind-blowing," said Arturo Villar, publisher of *Hispanic Market Weekly,* a New York-based trade publication. "There was a misconception . . . about Internet usage and computer purchasing by Hispanics in the U.S. and by Latin Americans."

A key pioneer of the Latin Internet is StarMedia Network Inc., a New York–based Spanish- and Portuguese-language portal that went public last month and saw its shares nearly double in the first day of trading. Monday the company's market value topped $2.6 billion. The company first gained its footing with customers in Latin America. Competitor *Quepasa*.com, a Phoenix-based start-up targeting U.S. Latinos, is expected to launch its public offering in the coming weeks after a month's-long promotional blitz on Spanish-language radio and television.

Other portals—one-stop Web sites that serve as gateways to the Internet and feature targeted content and services—are pulling in private capital, tailoring services to everyone from Spanish-speaking immigrants who crave news of their home countries to acculturated Latinos who prefer their content in English. Mainstream corporate players such as Yahoo Inc., America Online Inc. and Prodigy Communications Corp. have joined the mix, along with several Spanish-language media conglomerates.

The prospect of a Latino online revolution is also enticing the advertising world, which views the Internet as a promising way to target a diverse and fragmented community with an estimated $340 billion in annual U.S. spending power.

"Once the content becomes relevant, it is the perfect medium, because you can deliver such segmented interests," said Tony Dieste, president and chief executive of Dieste & Partners, a Dallas-based Latino ad agency. "You have Los Angeles Mexicanos, Tejanos in Texas, Central Americans in Chicago, Cubans in Miami, Puerto Ricans in New York."

The same week as StarMedia's public offering, Dieste launched Samba Interactive, which will build brands for Latinos on the Internet through Web advertising and kiosks in Latino neighborhood malls. Most ad agencies in the mainstream market have already formed or acquired interactive divisions, but Samba is the first in the Latino market.

DRAMATIC TRANSFORMATION

Already, the cyberworld is transforming the Latino community. Chat rooms and discussion groups are allowing English-speaking Latinos in Ohio suburbs to engage in political debate with big-city peers on San Francisco–based LatinoLink's site. Spanish speakers in Miami, Spain and Argentina banter about vampire novels through Miami Beach–based Yupi.com. And Latino cultural events posted on the Web are drawing Netizens from surrounding states.

"You have gay Hispanics online, you have women, . . . poets, political people and social organizations," said Isaac Cubillos, founder and editor of San Diego–based Latino Beat, an English-language news and information service. "You're seeing the whole community coming together."

Entrepreneurs like Cucufate are tapping into long-distance commerce through *MundoLatino*.com, a mall created by Duarte-based Web Enterprises that aims to link entrepreneurs here with Latin America and Spain.

"I think [the Internet] will take us to the next level," said Cucufate, who for Mother's Day bought her mother an online Pizza Hut pizza, delivered shortly thereafter to her San Salvador home.

The spread of Internet technology to the nation's 30-million-strong Latinos—many with global ties—heralds a new era for communications, said Ana Maria Fernandez Haar, immediate past president of the Assn. of Hispanic Advertising Agencies.

"The Internet is the ultimate border-less Hispanic market, and in that case it's the biggest market in the hemisphere," she said. "Current numbers indicate that the growth is taking place now—geometrically."

Key to the boom is the growing number of computer owners and Internet users in the Latino community, which in 1994 lagged nearly a decade behind white non-Latinos, according to the Claremont-based Tomas Rivera Policy Institute. The institute began tracking the issue in 1996 to ensure Latinos access to the information superhighway.

A report released last year showed a dramatically shifting landscape, with Latino households accessing computers at nearly double the rate of non-Latino homes. While only one Latino household in eight possessed a computer in 1994—compared with one in four for the nation as a whole—an estimated 30 percent of Latino households possessed a computer in 1998. About half of U.S. households overall are believed to have computers now, studies show.

The studies also showed that while only 2 percent of Latinos were online in 1994, 15 percent were connected in 1998. Other studies show even greater growth: A March study released by Forrester Research Inc. in Cambridge, Mass., showed 36 percent—or 3.3 million—Latino households online at the end of 1998, compared with 33 percent of all U.S. households. Skeptics call those figures overly optimistic but say a steady growth among Latino users is undeniable.

"Latino households are probably the fastest-growing" among Internet users, said Jeffrey Cole, director of UCLA's Center for Communication Policy, which recently announced plans for a long-term study to track Internet use in 18 countries. The U.S. study will also be conducted in Spanish.

Statistics on Latin American users have been equally explosive. Figures compiled by IDC, a Framingham, Mass.–based market research company, projected 7 million Internet users by the end of 1999, a figure expected to grow to 10 million next year. Other studies place the current number of Latin American Internet users at 13 million.

Key to the growth here are falling computer prices and an emerging Latino middle class accessing technology through home, college and work. A full 77 percent of Latino Internet users in the Tomas Rivera study had gone to college, and 40 percent earned more than $50,000 a year. Of college-educated Latinos, 66 percent owned computers in 1998, up from 39 percent in 1994.

"The booming economy we've had . . . is a rising tide that has lifted all boats, and more Hispanics have come into the middle class," said Tomas Rivera President Harry P. Pachon. "Forty percent of computers last year were below $999, and those two trend lines came together."

The sudden celebrity of well-capitalized players such as StarMedia, *Quepasa* and Yupi.com has given the industry a burst of momentum. But some smaller players have been chipping away at the market for years.

"I'm feeling vindicated lately," said LatinoLink President Lavonne Luquis, who launched her company in 1995. "People are finally realizing that Hispanics are indeed online."

It wasn't always so.

Five years ago, Allan Ortegaray called a group of friends to his Walnut living room to talk about the future. The Nicaraguan-born Ortegaray, who ran a computer repair and sales company, saw the Internet hatching and wanted to bring it to fellow Latinos.

Of all who gathered at his home that evening, only one signed on to the task—fellow Nicaraguan Tito Lagos. Together they launched Web Enterprises, designing business sites and later creating *MundoLatino* to promote them. They also held seminars for Central American entrepreneurs.

"The people did not know the Internet," Lagos said. "They didn't know if it was a food or an antibiotic or what. . . . We had to do little drawings and explain what is 'www.'"

FAST FORWARD AND THE PICTURE CHANGES DISTINCTLY

Eduardo Vertiz couldn't get through lunch recently without his cell phone ringing. "We just got another site," said Vertiz, director of business development for Woodland Hills-based Net*Fuerza,* the only U.S. Internet advertising representative dedicated to the Latino market in the United States, Latin America, Spain and Portugal. The company helps Latino-oriented Web sites secure advertising.

A division of AdSmart, Net*Fuerza* was formed last fall just as StarMedia raked in $80 million in financing from the likes of Chase Capital Partners and David Rockefeller. Net*Fuerza* has since seen its number of clients grow to 50, from just four in December, although StarMedia is not among them. The lunchtime addition: *Hispanico*.com, a Pittsburgh-based site that sells Latino books music and videos.

Many of the big portals began their odyssey in the burgeoning Latin American market and are just now turning to Spanish speakers here.

StarMedia co-founder Fernando Espuelas was first on the scene in 1996, building brand dominance in Spanish and Portuguese-speaking Latin America for his portal, which offers e-mail, chat and discussion rooms, as well as searches and guides to the Internet. StarMedia's move to New York gave it access to capital markets and the ability to lure U.S. Latinos into its pan-regional mix.

"What I saw was a moment in history—the opportunity to reunify the Latin community across the world," Espuelas said.

A number of competitors have since emerged in Latin America or are expanding there from Spain. Others have headquartered here, with strategies to sweep the Spanish- and Portuguese-speaking worlds, including U.S. Latinos in the mix.

SMALLER PLAYERS AT DISADVANTAGE

The global approach has paid off in volume. Yupi.com, which last month acquired entertainment and online community site *Ciudad*

Futura, boasts of 80 million page views a month, StarMedia 60 million.

But others warn that U.S. Latinos—even those who want Spanish services—will ultimately favor content that addresses their multiculturalism. Bilingual *Quepasa*.com, the Phoenix start-up, is banking on that. In recent months, the company has teamed up with potentially powerful partners, including Spanish-language television network *Telemundo,* which owns a stake in the portal and will provide some content and advertising.

Smaller players are also vying to serve more-acculturated Latinos. And others yet are weighing in with niche sites that cater to distinct interests or geographic zones.

"Even my sister is going to launch a competitive service," joked StarMedia's Espuelas.

The myriad small players, however, may find themselves in a crowded market once media giants with greater resources and technology savvy move in.

Yahoo is already serving Spanish and Portuguese speakers. America Online recently partnered with a Venezuelan media conglomerate to target Latin America. In April, Prodigy launched a Spanish-language version of its Internet access service for U.S. Latinos. And leading Spanish-language television network Univision is expected to launch Univision Online this fall, tapping the network's entertainment expertise.

Other online services catering to Spanish-speaking Latinos are cropping up almost daily. Last month, for example, Bloomberg launched *Negocios* Bloomberg, a bilingual personal finance portal for U.S. Latinos. But Pachon and others say the digital divide—while closing—is still broad.

Middle- and upper-class Latinos may be catching up fast, but lower-income Latinos still lag noticeably, Pachon said. To change that, technology—and instruction—must be more available through schools, libraries and community centers, he said.

Furthermore, hardware and software manufacturers have overlooked the Latino market in the U.S., pushing products more forcefully to Spanish speakers in Latin America, industry watchers say.

"There's a misconception that the Hispanic in the U.S. is a poor immigrant with lack of resources, and monolingual," said Gene Bryan, president of HispanicAd.Com, a news site for industry professionals launched in February. "That has thwarted the interests of major corporations that have focused [instead] on Latin America."

Others point out that the Latino Internet landscape remains wide open, despite the recent frenzy. Specialty niches must be filled if the online world is to become as indispensable to Latinos as it has to the mainstream population.

"The more sites we can create, the more we can generate a buzz about this," said Markos Alberto Moulitsas, a Boston law student who founded the online Latino/Hispanic News Service last year.

This fall he will join San Francisco-based *VivaMedia*, which last month launched *Picosito*.com, a bilingual portal targeting acculturated Latinos in the U.S.

"People are starting to realize we're the largest minority group in this country if you include the undocumented, and there's nothing out there. If you try to find a Latino sports site, there's nothing, which is bizarre because there's a site for everything. There's not even a [Latino] Sammy Sosa fan page."

THE BOOMING LATINO INTERNET

A sampling of Internet portals, directories and Web sites catering to Latinos here and abroad:

U.S. corporate players

America Online, in a joint venture with Venezuelan media conglomerate to enter Latin American market.

Yahoo's Yahoo *en Espanol* at http://*espanol*.yahoo.com and Portuguese-language Yahoo Brasil at http://br.yahoo.com.

Prodigy Communications' Spanish-language version of the Internet access service at http://*espanol*.prodigy.com/. Part-owned by Mexican investor Carlos Slim.

Helu, who also owns controlling stake in phone giant Telmex and part of online U.S. music retailer CDNow.

Targeting national audience

QuePasa.com, Phoenix-based Spanish- and English-language portal at http://www.quepasa.com.

Oyeme.com, New Jersey-based Spanish- and English-language portal at http://www.oyeme.com.

Picosito.com, San-Francisco-based Spanish- and English-language portal at http://www.*picosito*.com.

LatinoLink, San Francisco-based English-language portal at http://www.latinolink.com.

LatinoWeb, Montebello-based English-language directory at http://www.latinoweb.com.

Latin American portals

Infosel en linea, Mexico City–based portal and Internal service provider at http://www.infosel.com.

Universo Online, Brazil-based portal at http://www.uol.com.br.

El Sitio, Argentina-based portal at http://www.elsitio.com.

Niche sites

Latino Beat, San Diego-based English-language news and information service at http://www.latinobeat.net.

LatinoLA.com, Los-Angeles based English-language arts, culture and community site at http://www.latinola.com.

LaMusica.com, New York-based English-language Latin music site recently acquired by Miami-based radio conglomerate Spanish Broadcasting Systems, at http://www.lamusica.com.

Musica Virtual Online, Los Angeles-based Spanish-language Latin music site at http://www.musicavirtual.com.

Negocios Bloomberg, bilingual personal finance portal for U.S. Latinos launched by Bloomberg at http://www.*negocios*.bloomberg.com.

Joining in the Conversation

1. Explain what the "digital divide" is. What does it have to do with Latinos? Explain what a "Latino online revolution" means in terms of this article.
2. Romney listed numerous URLs that readers can access. Visit two or three different sites and write a review of them, explaining their contents, what language they use, if they have English access, if they were interesting to you and why, and what accounts for their popularity. If you know of any other Latino URLs, visit them and share their qualities with your class along with the ones you visited from the article.
3. Although the statistics in this article are dated, the basic idea is that Latin@s have begun connecting to the Internet and more Latin@s have bought computers for their households. Complete some research through the Internet and through personal interviews with Latin@s to discover how widespread computer ownership and connections to the Internet have become among families in your community. Present the statistics you find, making sure that they are as up-to-date as possible and remembering that most statistics you find published in hardcopy will be at least one to two years old. How do the statistics you find compare with the "projected 7 million Internet users by the end of 1999"?

Town's-Eye View of Immigration Debate

PETER SLEVIN

Peter Slevin is a staff writer for The Washington Post *and is based in Chicago. He writes about politics and about creation and evolution theories. The following article came from* The Washington Post, *April 3, 2006 issue.*

Harold Hogsed wonders how his grandchildren learn anything in school, with all the time their teachers spend instructing Hispanic immigrants on basic English. A drawling Georgia native, he cannot understand what the Spanish-accented adults are saying. He sees them as a drain on his tax dollars and he wishes they would all go home.

"How many people can this country hold?" Hogsed asked. "I don't have the solution to it, but something's got to be done."

Hogsed is not alone in struggling to wrap his mind around the tide of Latin American workers who have remade this north-Georgia town. City schools are now 55 percent Hispanic. More children arrive each day with their undocumented parents, often directly from Mexico. The Yellow Pages include 41 pages in Spanish. St. Michael Catholic Church, which once drew 25 people to a monthly Spanish mass, now has 6,000 Hispanic families on its parish registry.

Their numbers show just how rooted the predominantly Mexican immigrants have become in Gainesville and throughout the South. They have put pressure on public services while becoming essential players in the local economy. Amid anxiety on all sides, neighbors, advocates and the new residents are assessing their presence and their future in a debate that resonates nationally.

Source: Peter Slevin, "Town's-Eye View of Immigration Debate: In GA, Influx Fills a Gap in Workforce," *Washington Post,* April 3, 2006, p. A1.

Proponents of more generous accommodations for illegal immigrants staged a one-day economic boycott on March 24 [2006] that shuttered businesses and boosted morale. Business and farming leaders declared that immigrants are keeping them solvent. At a Mass on Thursday night dedicated to the immigrants, Rev. Fabio Sotelo urged 300 parishoners to persevere, pray and write the governor.

Gov. Sonny Perdue (R) is considering a strong anti-immigration bill delivered last week by the Georgia legislature. Congress is considering significant federal legislation, with Gainesville's congressman, Nathan Deal (R), among the firmest supporters of tightened borders and toughened measures. Lawyers for U.S.-born carpet workers will argue to the Supreme Court this month that a Georgia manufacturer conspired to drive down wages by importing illegal laborers.

Gainesville advertises itself as "the poultry capital of the world" and it is the chicken-processing plants that are driving much of the city's startling growth. Since 1990, the official population has nearly doubled to 32,000 and the number of Hispanics has quadrupled to compose nearly half the registered population—and far more when illegal immigrants are considered.

When the shift changes at the factories on Industrial Boulevard, hundreds of workers in hairnets stream through the doors of Koch Foods and Pilgrim's Pride. Their origins are reflected in the Spanish banter, the salsa tunes blasting from car radios, and the young ice-cream vendor who calls his cart *La Paleteria Lulu.*

"Reality speaks and it says that, absent Hispanic workers, we could not process chicken," said Tom Hensley, chief financial officer for Gainesville's largest chicken plant, Fieldale Farms. "There aren't enough native American people who want to work in a chicken plant at any wage. We'd be put out of business."

A dozen years ago, Fieldale employed fewer than 100 Hispanics. Today, Hispanics total 3,000 in a 4,700-person workforce that transforms live birds by the thousand into boneless chicken flesh. To win jobs that start at about $10 an hour, applicants must present at least two identity documents from a government list of 18.

"If the documents appear to be legitimate, we accept them," Hensley said.

Two workers said they got jobs at Fieldale with fake documents, a practice considered an open secret. One longtime laborer, who spoke on the condition of anonymity, said he is counting on Congress—"in a free country, a democracy"—to design a compromise that legalizes needed and reliable undocumented residents.

Praised for excellence by President Bush in his 2004 Republican National Convention speech, Gainesville Elementary greets one new student a day in a school already 70 percent Hispanic. Nine in 10 students qualify for subsidized meals. Educators draft letters in two languages and visit homes to urge parents to support the students.

"We're not going to ask, 'Are you legal?' That's not our concern," said Principal Priscilla Collins. "We let them know that no one is going to come into our schools and do raids. That's not how America works."

Raids are much on people's minds. The telephones at St. Michael have been ringing in the past two weeks as anxious residents tracked rumors prompted by legislative activity in Atlanta and Washington. Is it true, they asked, that immigration agents grabbed 300 people at Wal-Mart? Was there a roundup of 500 along Jesse Jewel Parkway? Will agents raid the schools on Friday?

No, no, and no, Lucia Martin answered.

Martin was sneaked into the country from Mexico at age 3. She remembers being tucked under the seat of a truck and told to keep quiet. Her family moved to Chicago. Twenty years ago, she arrived in Gainesville when her husband found work on the chicken line. She works at the church.

"There's a supply. There's a demand. There's an opportunity and you take it. It's human instinct," Martin said. When white residents complain that the new immigrants should wait their turn, she answers, "Did your ancestors get a visa?"

Martin's worry is that new rules will make it easier for government authorities to target immigrants unfairly—by arresting people on a pretext to investigate their legal status. Angel Rojas, a Catholic Social Services worker, raised the same issue in advising an overflow crowd of educators and community workers to study the potential impact of proposed legislation.

"The main thing we need to understand is this affects everybody," Rojas said. He noted that one proposal would make it a crime to help an undocumented resident remain in the United States. A number of Mexicans, he said, have told him they would rather return home with their worldly goods than risk losing all during deportation.

That would be cheerful news to legislators who have said they hope to increase pressure and create a deterrent. It also jibes with the thinking of Joe Merck, a working-class Gainesville native and advocate for the homeless who describes the city as "overrun."

"I don't blame 'em coming up here, but half of 'em are illegal. We're taking care of 'em. They're having all these babies one right after another," Merck, 71, said. "You can go buy your credentials, it's a known fact, but nobody does anything about it. We need to send 'em back home."

Waiting for a ride, kitchen worker William Morton griped that he cannot obtain some restaurant jobs because he speaks no Spanish.

"This country's not right," said Morton, 38. "The economy's went down for us and gone up for them, and we're supporting Mexico."

Merck and Morton can be counted in the potential audience for the immigration proposals that have suddenly dominated the state and national debate. Deal, a seven-term congressman who received an A-plus career rating from Americans for Better Immigration, a group that favors stricter controls, said the Untied States is "a nation of law."

"To make sure we have the confidence of the American public behind us, we have to show we're going to enforce our law first and foremost," Deal said. The nation's estimated 11 million illegal immigrants "are going to have to go home."

Trinidad Avila, 44, is among those who consider that impossible.

Avila, who darted across the Mexican border as a teenager and later obtained residency, expects a compromise permitting workers and their families to remain, but wonders when. His two teenage children hold hands at the dinner table and pray for friends who are here illegally.

"People don't know what they're going to do," Avila said. "They're just wishing for the government to do something for them."

Julia Perilla, who studies grass-roots Latino issues at Georgia State University, describes a "love-hate relationship" between the new immigrants and many Georgians, especially business people.

"On the one hand, they want us very badly. They are very, very dependent on Latino labor. On the other hand, there's an incredible amount of xenophobia that's on the rise in Georgia," Perilla said. "It's extremes. Nobody is in the middle."

Joining in the Conversation

1. Discuss the population increase in Gainesville and what those numbers do to the economy, the schools, the need for utilities and housing, and the general living conditions in a town not necessarily ready for that kind of population explosion.

2. Slevin writes this as an expository article, one that gives information about a particular situation. In it, he interviews various individuals who are proponents of the immigration situation and those who are opponents. In fact, one interviewee explained that there is a "'love-hate relationship' between the new immigrants and many Georgians." Analyze the article and determine whether Slevin is focusing on the "love" or the "hate" aspect of the relationship and what spin he is putting on the topic. If there is a clear position he is taking, explain what it is and select quotations to support your assertions.
3. Create a role-playing situation in your classroom in which three other classes have lost their instructor and the students, 20–25 in each class, are transferred into your classroom in the middle of the semester. Brainstorm the issues that might arise if this were to happen. Also discuss the problems that might arise and suggest solutions that could be used to combat them. Write a paper that describes the situation and offers a proposal for dealing with the new students as well as with the attitudes of the original students.

Bush's Spanish Lessons

Richard Wolffe, Holly Bailey, and Evan Thomas, with Andrew Murr in Yuma and Eleanor Clift

Richard Wolffe is the Senior White House Correspondent for Newsweek. *Holley Bailey is a White House Correspondent for* Newsweek, *and Evan Thomas has been the Assistant Managing Editor for* Newsweek *since 1991. Wolffe has written numerous cover stories and contributed to a major news item that helped* Newsweek *win the National Magazine Award for General Excellence for 2002 and 2004. This article appeared in the May 29, 2006 issue of* Newsweek.

✦

Source: Richard Wolffe, Holly Bailey, and Evan Thomas, "Bush's Spanish Lessons: For President Bush, Immigration Isn't a Dry Policy Debate, It's Personal." From *Newsweek,* May 29, 2006.

FOR PRESIDENT BUSH, IMMIGRATION ISN'T A DRY POLICY DEBATE. IT'S PERSONAL. START WITH THE MEXICAN-BORN AMERICAN CITIZEN WHO TENDS HIS HOUSE AND HELPED RAISE HIS KIDS

President George W. Bush seemed unusually heartfelt when he addressed the nation last week on immigration reform. For the president immigration is not just a matter of politics or policy, it's personal. Bush has always been drawn to stories of Latino immigrants who came up by their bootstraps. In an interview with *Hispanic Magazine* in 2004, he described Paula Rendon, "who came up from Mexico to work in our house" when Bush was a boy growing up in Midland, Texas. "She loved me. She chewed me out. She tried to shape me up," said Bush. "And I have grown to love her like a second mom." Bush recalled Rendon's pride in seeing "her grandkids go to college for the first time."

Bush has another inspiring example close to home. For more than a decade, Maria Galvan, 53, has worked for Bush, looked after his daughters, befriended his wife and won the affection of the First Family for her loyalty, decency and hard work. As governor of Texas, Bush encouraged his housekeeper to become a U.S. citizen. Bush's own brother, Florida Gov. Jeb Bush, married a Latino, and Jeb's eldest son, George P. Bush, is seen as a candidate to go into the family business.

Bush has a history of promoting Latinos, most notably Attorney General Alberto Gonzales, who recently told CNN's Wolf Blitzer that "it's unclear" whether his grandparents emigrated legally from Mexico. Bush has always spoken emotionally about Gonzales, the son of hard-working but uneducated migrant workers. Bush recognized early on that inspiring Latino family stories could be a boon to the Republican Party. "He appreciates how close Latino families are with each other," says Israel Hernandez, an early campaign aide whom Bush hired after hearing his family story. "For a long time, he's talked about how these are the qualities he thinks the party represents. He has always talked about immigration in a very compassionate way." But the president's willingness to help illegal immigrants on the path to citizenship sets him apart from many vocal conservatives in the GOP. The divide could paralyze the effort to bring much-needed reform to the nation's immigration laws. The issue has become, in a way, too personal: a source of more heat than light in the body politic.

There is general agreement in Congress over the need to get control of the borders and enforce existing immigration laws. Last week Bush proposed a plan that could position up to 6,000 National Guard troops along the Mexican border for a year or so while beefing up the Border Patrol (from about 12,000 to 18,000 by 2008). The troops would not be sent to "militarize" the border with Mexico, Bush hastened to add, or even to arrest illegals coming over the border, but rather to provide logistical support, monitor surveillance cameras and do construction. Bush proposed building high-tech fences in urban corridors to help staunch the flow, as well as deploying a host of new gizmos like motion sensors and unmanned aerial drones.

Bush also put forth a "temporary-worker program" to "match willing foreign workers with willing American employers for jobs Americans are not doing." Such a program would probably be acceptable to House conservatives, according to a GOP leadership aide who declined to be identified discussing politically sensitive matters. But any plan that "smacks of amnesty"—that offers a way for the roughly 12 million illegal immigrants now in the United States to become citizens—is a nonstarter, according to this aide. The aide said that House Judiciary Committee chairman James Sensenbrenner would block a plan, proposed by Bush, that would let illegals apply for citizenship after spending five years in the United States, learning English and paying a fine and back taxes. (As a sop to conservatives, the Senate last week passed a bill making English the national language of the United States.)

"We must honor the great American tradition of the melting pot," Bush said last week. He has been dipping into it ever since he got into politics. His first campaign aide, when he was a managing partner of the Texas Rangers Major League Baseball team and thinking about a run for governor, was Hernandez. Born in a tiny border town, son of a Mexican immigrant, Hernandez was the first in his family to go to college. Driving around the state, "we would joke around and talk and sometimes switch into Spanish," recalls Hernandez, who is now assistant secretary of Commerce for trade promotion. As co-chairman of the 1996 Republican National Convention in San Diego, Bush was dismayed by the anti-immigration rhetoric of Pete Wilson, California's governor at the time, according to Hernandez. Bush saw that Hispanics shared the family values pushed by the Republican Party—and represented a growing voting bloc that Republicans ignored at their peril. During the 2000 election, Bush's catchphrase was "Family values do not stop at the Rio Grande."

Bush had his own housekeeper as an example. Emigrating from a small village in Mexico with her daughter sometime in the mid-'80s, Galvan worked as a domestic for several families in Austin, Texas, before getting a job at the Governor's Mansion just as Bush moved in with his family in 1995, when the twins were 12 years old. According to Anne DeBois, who was the mansion's chief administrator, Galvan taught herself English and how to read. Bush "encouraged her heavily to get her citizenship," says DeBois, who says that Galvan was a legal immigrant with a green card when she started work there. (The White House last week refused to comment on Galvan, except to say that she is a U.S. citizen; White House aides were silent on how she entered the country and what her legal status was at the time.) The Bushes liked Galvan so much that they brought her to Washington in 2001. She lives in the White House, travels with the First Family and looks after their beloved dogs. She has advised the White House chefs on the Bushes' favorite Mexican foods and is said by White House insiders, who refuse to be identified discussing First Family matters, to be "part of the family," which is unusual for staff in the formal, institutionalized Executive Mansion. Laura Bush has included Galvan as a guest at some of her social lunches.

Though the needs of Latinos have always been part of Bush's portfolio as a self-proclaimed "compassionate conservative," immigration reform took a back seat to education and national security during the first five years of the Bush presidency. Meanwhile, as illegal immigrants overwhelmed social services and drove up crime, not just in border states but across the country, a backlash was setting in. Last winter the House of Representatives passed a bill to make illegal immigration a felony, though how the House proposed to arrest and deport 12 million people was left unclear. At the time, the Bush administration apparently figured that the Senate would "fix" any immigration bill by adding provisions for guest workers and a plan to allow illegals to become citizens after paying their dues. But public anger at illegals is peaking. Radio-show host Rush Limbaugh is saying he has never seen his followers so riled up. And when Bush's political adviser Karl Rove met privately with House Republicans after the president's speech, the lawmakers were still in a rebellious mood. On two major occasions—the No Child Left Behind education law in 2002 and Medicare reform in 2003—Bush pressed the House to work with Democratic Sen. Edward Kennedy of Massachusetts. Never again, says GOP Rep. Ric Keller of Florida, who pungently told Rove: "If you get into bed with Ted Kennedy, you're going to get more than sleep." Bush is trying to take the high road. "We cannot build a unified country by inciting people to anger, or playing on anyone's fears or exploiting the issue of immigration for political gain," Bush said from the Oval Office. But at least half the House Republicans see a hard line on immigration as smart politics in an election year when the Democrats are threatening to win back control of Congress. With his approval ratings sagging into the mid-30s, Bush probably lacks the clout to force the House GOP to accept a Senate bill that includes steps for illegals to become citizens. The result would be no reforms at all, though it is possible that something could be salvaged in a lame-duck session after the November elections, when political passions have cooled a bit.

Meanwhile, angry citizens continue to take matters into their own hands. Five hours after Bush took off from Yuma, Ariz., where he had staged a photo op driving a dune buggy around the Mexican border, David (Flash) Sharrar stood in a dusty farmyard to brief a circle of so-called Yuma Patriots. They were preparing to go off on a nocturnal search for illegals coming across the border. Sharrar went over the rules and the checklist. No weapons, no altercations. The Patriots are armed only with bright flashlights, which they beam on the illegals as they radio the Border Patrol for help, and with Mace, in the unlikely event one of the intruders attacks them.

"I don't think the president is going to do a damn thing about Yuma," said Sharrar, 51, part owner of an auto-transmission shop. He launched the Yuma Patriots a year ago with his business partner after some illegals carjacked his 21-year-old son's Ford Explorer at gunpoint. The thieves also stole a cell phone and $700 in combat pay—Sharrar's son had just returned from serving as a soldier in Iraq.

Sharrar led the Patriots in prayer ("Lord, these great men and women are here to stop an epidemic that is destroying our country . . ."). Then the group, which claims to have caught and turned over 1,500 illegal migrants in the past year, went out and caught nine more. Until the borders are closed and the laws reformed, most of them will try to come back.

Joining in the Conversation

1. Discuss three of the suggestions President Bush has recommended to fight the immigration problems in the United States.
2. In the text, the authors show Bush as an individual who cares about "Latinos," and they give specific examples of those to whom Bush is close. However, the authors also suggest that "Bush recognized early on that inspiring Latino family stories could be a boon to the Republican Party." This assertion

gives a different spin to the president's attitude toward "Latinos." Analyze the remainder of the article and decide which spin, the personal or the political, comes closer to Bush's true feelings. Support your claim with quotations from the text.

3. President Bush suggested, among other things, a "temporary-worker program." This kind of system was attempted before. Research the *bracero* program and present an expository report that discusses the program, citing both its positive and negative sides. Then investigate Bush's "temporary-worker program," comparing and contrasting it with the earlier program. Take a stand on whether or not you think the new recommended program will work and why, based on its characteristics and the benefits and problems of the *bracero* program.

Curanderismo: Past and Present Viewpoints

ROBERT T. TROTTER, II
JUAN ANTONIO CHAVIRA

The following article comes from the book Curanderismo: Mexican American Folk Healing *(1997), which is the result of studies conducted by the authors Robert T. Trotter, II and Juan Antonio Chavira, and their assistants, working not only with individuals in the Lower Rio Grande Valley of Texas, but also with some individuals who live across the border in Mexico. The difference between this study and others that have been done in the past is that Trotter and Chavira interviewed the* curanderos *for their perspectives on the cultural issue of* curanderismo *rather than simply relying on the beliefs and thoughts of "outsiders." Currently, Robert T. Trotter, II is the Regent's Professor in the Anthropology Department of Northern Arizona University. His research focuses on such issues as health and prevention, as well as corporate anthropology. Juan Antonio*

Chavira is a Court Master in San Antonio, Texas, for the Fourth Administrative Judicial Region.

Curanderismo, the Mexican American folk-healing system, is an important source of health resources for Mexican Americans living in the Lower Rio Grande Valley of Texas and other places. The term *curanderismo* and the term *curandero* come from the Spanish verb *curar,* which means "to heal." Loosely, the word *curandero* could be applied to anyone who claims to have some skill in the healing arts, from a brain surgeon to a grandmother giving medicinal teas. However, for Mexican Americans the title *curandero* represents a healer who is part of a historically and culturally important system of health care. Therefore, in this book *curandero* is reserved for a person whose main profession and full-time work is as a healer, who sees more than five patients a day, and who uses all or some significant part of the theoretical system described here. . . .

Curanderos have long been a community health resource because the evolution and practice of *Curanderismo* parallel the historical and cultural evolution of Mexican Americans as a population. The *curandero* is often a person chosen from the community, who shares the same experiences, the same language, and the same socioeconomic status as his or her patients. The *curandero* is highly accessible, without the intervening variables of excessive social and spatial distance that sometimes affect the delivery of health care in the United States. Usually, the only major distinctions between the *curandero* and the patient are the *curandero's* healing powers and medical knowledge. The *curanderos'* office is in the community, normally in the healer's home. No appointments are necessary, referrals are not often required, no bureaucratic forms must be filled out, and no fees for services are charged (the patient gives a donation, using his conscience as his guide). The patient does not need to be covered by Medicare, Medicaid, Blue Cross, or the Kaiser plan to have access to the *curandero*.

Another characteristic that makes the *curandero* an important community health resource is the way that the healers use culturally appropriate methods of dealing with the patients, methods that activate the natural support system already existing in the community, rather than attempting to develop new or artificial support systems. The religious and spiritual aspects of the healing process capitalize on the patients' faith and belief systems. The use of herbs, fruits, eggs, and oils allow healing to occur through the use of everyday resources, products the patient can easily obtain. And by making themselves an integral part of the patients' existing social network, the *curanderos* can use the patient's family and peer group to support or implement the designated therapy.

The *curanderos'* practices and theories have evolved through centuries of services to patients in the community, often when the healer provided the only health care available. Within the past twenty years, at least in the Lower Rio Grande Valley, the socio-economic position of many Mexican Americans has improved so that modern medical resources are increasingly available; widely utilized, and appreciated by both *curanderos* and patients, since modern medicine offers excellent care for a number of medical problems. However, at least in the valley, this use of modern medical facilities by both *curanderos* and their patients has not had the effect expected by some social scientists. *Curanderismo* has not disappeared. It continues to exist, thrive, and even evolve creative new forms of dealing with health and misfortune, side by side with modern medicine and in (often silent) partnership with it. . . .

Certain data from previous studies were confirmed by the authors. These data include the existence and treatment of the so-called folk illnesses of Mexican Americans (*empacho, susto,* and so forth . . .); however, we found these illnesses to be of relatively minor importance in the healing system. The individuals we define as *curanderos* seldom treat these diseases because, as one informant put it, "anyone can take care of those things. We only see the ones that other people, the mother, the grandmothers, the neighbor, cannot cure." Instead, the *curanderos* are sought out to deal with problems of a much more serious nature.

The study also corroborated the information that the healers' perspective of health and illness contains a dual element of "natural" and "supernatural" illnesses. This duality forms the base upon which *curanderismo* is structured. "The members of La Raza [Mexican Americans] do not divide the natural and the supernatural into separate compartments as Anglos do. A harmonious relationship between the natural and the supernatural is considered essential to human health and welfare, while disharmony precipitates illness and misfortune" (Madsen 1964: 68).

The *curanderos'* concept of the natural source of illness overlaps extensively with the medical model. Such basic premises of modern medicine as the germ theory of disease are accepted. Natural illnesses are seen as being amenable to treatment by physicians, by herbal remedies, and occasionally through supernatural intervention, although the last is not the preferred mode since it takes time and energy that could be better spent on other cures.

The *curanderos* do not consider supernatural sources of illness amenable to treatment by the medical establishment. The *curanderos* indicated that any particular illness suffered by a patient could theoretically be caused by either natural or supernatural processes. This means that there is a natural form of diabetes and a form caused by a supernatural agent, such as a *brujo* (witch or sorcerer). The same is true for alcoholism, cancer, and so on. One of the key problems that the *curanderos* deal with is identifying the nature of the causal agent for a particular illness.

The *curanderos* recognize that their acceptance of magic and witchcraft makes them an object of ridicule from the scientific medical system. They feel this ridicule is not justified, and they fault the medical system for its lack of attention to the supernatural. One *curandero* went so far as to say that many of the people in mental institutions (he estimated 10 percent) were there because they were *embrujados* (hexed persons), but the doctors could not recognize this condition, so it went untreated. Supernaturally caused illnesses were most commonly said to be initiated by either evil spirits *(espiritús malos)* or by *brujos,* and these provoked illnesses form a significant part of the *curanderos'* work on the United States side of the border.

Some *curanderos* appear to identify more supernatural causes for illnesses than others do. A student once asked one of us to take him to a key informant. The student very strongly felt he was *embrujado* (hexed) by a former girl friend whom he had treated poorly. The student was in poor health; he was failing his courses; he was always tired. He presented these symptoms to the *curandero* and asked that the *trabajo* (magical work or hex) be removed. The *curandero* examined the student using his magical training and then asked him a series of questions about his habits: whether he went to many parties, how much he drank, how much he studied. The *curandero* very bluntly told the student that he could find absolutely no supernatural cause for his troubles. He said that the student's problems were directly the effect of too many parties, too much drinking, not enough studying, and lack of sleep. If he concentrated on work and study, the student's condition would improve enormously.

This also illustrates that the authors were able to confirm . . . reports that there is far less dichotomizing of physical and social problems within *curanderismo* than within the medical-care system.

The *curanderos* very clearly deal with social, psychological, and spiritual problems as well as with physical ailments. In many cases the problems overlap into two or more categories. Bad luck in business was a common problem presented to the *curanderos.* They also had to deal with marital disruptions, alcoholism, infidelity, bothersome supernatural manifestations, cancer, diabetes, and infertility. The list of problems presented to the *curanderos* is nearly inexhaustible. Obviously . . . *curanderismo* plays an important, culturally appropriate psychotherapeutic role in some Mexican American communities.

Another previously described element of *curanderismo* that was supported by the present study is the belief in the existence of "a gift of healing" (*el don*) that provides the *curandero* with his or her ability to heal. . . . The *don* is the basic difference between the healer and the non-healer; it allows the healer to practice his or her work, especially in the supernatural area. It is clear that the *don* for healing in the past was felt to be a gift from God. However, a secular interpretation of the presence of the *don* is now competing with the more traditional explanation. Many healers still refer to the *don* as a gift from God and support this premise by reference to biblical passages (for example, I Corinthians 12:7 and James 5:14). Other healers explain the *don* as an inborn trait that is common to and present in all human beings. They consider it to have the same basis as singing, running, or talking. Almost any human being can do these activities, but some obviously can do them better than others, and a few can do them extremely well. *Curanderos,* according to these healers, are simply the individuals with a better ability to heal than is normative for the population as a whole. The healers refer to this condition as having "developed abilities."

One element of Hispanic folk medicine that is present in most areas, the hot-cold syndrome . . . is missing in south Texas. . . . No healers who were raised in the area made use of the hot-cold dichotomy to explain illness, although it was used in organizing herbal cures by one informant who was born in central Mexico and migrated to the valley as an adult. The only elements of the hot-cold syndrome that the authors found were a few scattered beliefs about women not eating citrus when having their period, or not taking a cold shower after being in the hot sun. No systematic use of the hot-cold concepts were [sic] otherwise documented. . . .

Curanderos, like all health-care professionals, are perceived from at least three viewpoints. One viewpoint is that of the general nonparticipating public. In a multicultural or multiethnic environment, this viewpoint depends on whether the viewer has a cultural background similar to or different from the system of folk medicine being studied. In either case this viewpoint can be called the outsider's perspective. The second viewpoint is the perspective of those who are participant-patients of the *curanderos*. This can be called the client's perspective. The third viewpoint on *curanderismo* is the perspective of the *curanderos* themselves. This is the practitioner's perspective.

The most varied perspective on *curanderismo* is the view from the outside. For people with different cultural experiences, this view is often based on myth, superstition, and social stereotypes. In many cases there is a complete lack of information about *curanderismo* even among Anglo-Americans who have spent their entire lives in South Texas. In other cases the picture is distorted through a cultural filter and through incomplete experience or knowledge of the system. This is not unexpected, since this is the common condition for cross-cultural understanding in multiethnic environments, especially when one culture defines itself as superior to the other.

It would be nearly impossible to document all of the views which the general public holds regarding *curanderos*. For our purposes we have divided outsiders into three categories: the critics, the doubters, and the pragmatists. However, we will discuss only what may be considered the most salient features of each category, since most of these viewpoints tend to blend into each other.

The most outspoken and hostile critics of *curanderismo* are usually those who do not believe in the *curandero's* practices. The reasons for their skepticism vary: denial of the reality of what *curanderismo* is and what the *curanderos* do, disbelief in the moral validity of the system, rejection on the basis of sociocultural stereotypes of Mexican Americans, and concern over the effect of *curanderismo* on patients in need of medical care.

Those who reject *curanderos* on the basis of social stereotypes consider them purveyors of ignorance and superstition and major contributors to the existence of a culture that should have been discarded long ago. This rejection indicates a strong tendency toward assimilation. In essence, Mexican American culture is viewed by these people as being inferior; they tend to reject anything and anyone who continues to keep it alive. Therefore, they reject *curanderismo* because it reinforces and justifies the existence of what is thought to be ignorant superstition and mumbo-jumbo nonsense. Many of these people appear to accept modern medicine not because it is thought to be better or a more efficient system, but because it is a symbol of entrance into a superior culture.

Other people reject *curanderismo* because they believe *curanderos* to be frauds and quacks. Some believe all *curanderos* are frauds, preying on the gullibility of people and taking away their money by promising wondrous results. These people are often concerned that the *curandero's* clients may lose money to an unscrupulous healer whose only purpose is to make a quick buck. Others, viewing all *curanderos* as quacks, are concerned for their client's health. These people suggest that the sick lose time, money, and sometimes their lives by going to someone who really cannot help them. They are also concerned that people may be taking medication prescribed by the *curanderos,* which may be ineffective in relieving pain or may have harmful effects when used with drugs prescribed by a physician. Thus all *curanderos* are labeled as frauds, as quacks, because they are thought to harm rather than to help people.

Some people reject *curanderos* because of the mystery surrounding the source of their power; many consider them agents of the devil. Their healing powers, their magical powers, their source of knowledge, are all believed to be part of a cult or a false religion and in direct opposition to the tenets of various churches, especially the fundamentalist sects. The fundamentalists often view participating in *curanderismo* as analogous to worshipping idols and strange gods. In this case, the rector feels that the best thing to do is to keep away from *curanderos,* since they are inspired by the devil as a trap for unwary believers.

Some people are ambivalent toward *curanderismo:* those who are afraid someone may laugh at them for believing in a marginal superstition and those who are honestly not sure of *curanderismo's* value. Both of these groups tend to view the practices with some degree of skepticism but do not reject them outright. Examples of the acculturated doubter can be found in the ranks of Mexican American college students who come from very traditional *barrio* environments and how as children were at least partially initiated into this healing system. As adolescents they tend to leave their *barrio* culture seeking a new identity in a more acculturated school atmosphere. They generally admit the existence of *curanderismo* and probably have relatives and family members who are very much a part of the system. However, they are afraid to admit they have participated for fear of being ridiculed by others. Nonetheless, the family socialization process keeps their doubts from turning into utter disbelief despite their relatively high level of education. This type of doubting sometimes occurs among professionals and other working adults. . . .

There are many people in the community who are skeptical about *curanderismo* but want to know more about it. These skeptics can be divided into two groups: the scientifically oriented and spiritually oriented. The scientific skeptic is not sure if *curanderismo* works, but would like to empirically assess the *curandero's* theories and his therapeutic techniques. The spiritually oriented skeptic is interested in the *curandero's* premise that spiritual harmony is essential to good health, yet the source of the *curandero's* power to some degree either frightens him or makes him wary of pursuing his interest. . . .

The third group we call the pragmatists whose identifying characteristic is that they have the welfare of the sick as their primary goal. Their major concern is to include in the health-care system anything that will make the treatment of patients more effective. Some of these people believe that *curanderos* can help in the treatment of the sick and should therefore be incorporated into the medical system. Others want to find out first whether the *curanderos* really can provide therapeutic relief to the patients. If they can help either in actual treatment or in convincing people to seek treatment, then perhaps a system of cooperation should be established. If the *curanderos* do no harm they can be tolerated; if they harm rather than heal, then the necessary steps should be taken to prevent their being used as a health resource.

Several views of *curanderismo* are held by those who are either active or passive participants in the system. These views differ because not everyone goes to *curanderos* with the same expectations, nor are all treatments equally successful.

Some people participate in *curanderismo* because they are taken to the healers by friends and relatives who believe in the system. Others go merely to satisfy their own curiosity about *curanderos.* Those who seek *curanderos* out of a curiosity usually see neither harm nor benefit from their participation. Some even hover around the system, taking friends or relatives for help without actually seeking treatment for themselves. Other passive participants are those who have no control over their actions but are brought to the *curandero* by concerned relatives. These patients may be children, the elderly, the mentally retarded, or the mentally disturbed. These patients usually come from families who are strong believers or from families who go to the *curandero* as a last resort. Such people tend to have neutral attitudes toward *curanderismo* until their participation provides them with experiences that convince them about the good or the harm that *curanderismo* produces.

Many of the participants in the folk medical system are believers. Those who believe in *curanderismo* are often long-time users of the system. They seek *curanderos* because they believe in the *curandero's* theories and definitions of illness and because they have faith in the therapeutic techniques of the *curandero.* Moreover, the believers usually testify that they have been helped by the *curanderos.* They continue to seek *curanderos* because they are satisfied patients. By performing successful and sometimes apparently miraculous cures, *curanderos* reinforce the believers' already positive attitudes toward the folk-healing system.

Curanderismo, like all professions, has its share of quacks and con artists who are experts at exploiting the faith and inexperience of their clients. Patients who are cheated often come to the healer with a rather serious problem, expecting some kind of miracle. Dishonest *curanderos,* knowing the vulnerability of persons seeking quick solutions for serious problems, promise more than they can deliver in order to make a quick profit. Their patients not only lose money, but also fail to achieve their expectations. As a result they become doubly cheated—emotionally and financially—and they are usually vehement in their condemnation of *curanderismo*.

Many *curanderos* think of themselves as agents doing the work of God. These *curanderos* claim that their healing powers are a gift from God and that all their success can be attributed to the mercy and power of the Lord. As a gift from God, their powers can be neither exploited nor used to harm anyone. These *curanderos* feel that they have a moral obligation to help those in need, to relieve the misery of those who are suffering, and to counsel those in distress.

In reality *curanderos* can only try to live up to this ideal. Many difficulties intrude on their behavior. Survival is expensive now, so they must often charge for their services, whereas there is some indication that in the past no charges were made at all. Moreover, most *curanderos* have families and dependents who need the basic necessities of life, not only food and shelter but also attention and love. The pressures of having people calling at all hours of the day, every day of the week, can sometimes become a nuisance. As one of our informants told us, "Sometimes I wish I were like everyone else." He added that the responsibility of having so many people dependent on him for so many things is often too great. It deprives him of time with his family, especially his children, and of time to pursue his other interests. There are patients who become so dependent on him that they will not leave him alone. There are times when he wants to do something else so badly that he does not dedicate as much time as he feels he should to his patients.

Reference

Madsen, William. *The Mexican-Americans of South Texas.* New York: Holt, Rinehart and Winston, 1964.

Joining in the Conversation

1. Trotter and Chavira divide the nonbelievers into three groups. What does each of the groups believe about *curanderismo?*
2. This chapter is written as an informative text. Review the article for its research elements: thesis, supporting evidence, material that contradicts the beliefs, appeals to emotion and/or to logic, details, development of ideas, transitions, and so forth. Then determine how you would have researched the topic of *curanderismo* and how your methods might differ from Trotter and Chavira's and how they might agree.
3. Using the model above for a researched paper, choose a topic of interest and controversy in your community. Complete research by creating questions that you would ask interviewees and go to the library and to the Internet for further secondary source information. Check with your instructor about the details of the assignment and the method of documentation the instructor wishes you to use.

Work Place Health Disparities Increasing among Hispanics

Kim Krisberg

Kim Krisberg is a longtime writer for The Nation's Health. *The following article appeared in the March 2004 issue. In addition to Latino health concerns, Krisberg also writes about international gay issues, women's issues, and other public health care topics. Some of her articles have also appeared in* The Washington Blade Online.

✦

OUTREACH FOCUSES ON WORKERS' RIGHTS, SAFETY. AN IN-DEPTH LOOK AT CURRENT PUBLIC HEALTH ISSUES

Third in an in-depth series on health disparities in the United States, in conjunction with APHA's National Public Health Week 2004. The event, which will be held April 5–11, 2004, focuses on "Eliminating Health Disparities: Communities Moving from Statistics to Solutions."

While rates of occupational injuries, illnesses and fatalities have been falling in the United States for most populations, such incidents continue to rise for Hispanic workers, particularly immigrants. The issue is especially difficult to tackle, as such workers confront numerous barriers to standing up for their health and rights as workers.

Since 1992, occupational deaths among Hispanic workers in the United States have increased by more than 50 percent, according to the Centers for Disease Control and Prevention. Work-related fatalities among Hispanic workers rose by 12 percent in 2000 alone, especially among those in the construction industry. Laws and agencies, such as the U.S. Occupational Safety and Health Administration, are inadequate, according to several labor and workers' rights groups, and the United States lacks a reliable system of accurately tracking occupational disease and injury, especially data pertaining to certain ethnic and racial minorities. For many Hispanic workers, attempts to enforce available laws are often clouded by language barriers, immigration status, unfamiliarity with U.S. legal and health systems and high rates of uninsurance.

Hispanic immigrants working in the agricultural sector face additional problems. According to "Fields of Poison 2002: California Farmworkers and Pesticides," a study conducted by Californians for Pesticide Reform, agricultural workers face the greatest threats of pesticide-related illnesses, including long-term effects such as cancer and birth defects. Most agricultural work in the United States is performed by ethnic and racial minorities, and the large majority of migrant and seasonal farm workers are of Hispanic origin. According to CDC, Hispanics face high exposure rates to toxic substances, including chemicals in the work place.

"Farmworkers are pretty much at the bottom of the barrel in terms of the working poor—they are among the poorest," said

Virginia Ruiz, environmental health coordinator at the Farmworker Justice Fund, which has been working for more than 20 years to improve living and working conditions for migrant seasonal farmworkers and their families in the United States.

Ruiz's organization works with local organizations along the U.S./Mexico border to recruit people within farmworker communities, giving them information on environmental health and training them on how to conduct outreach work within their communities. The Clean Environment for Healthy Kids project operates in border communities on the U.S. side, training and supervising about 40 lay health promoters per year. The project also trains professional health promoters in the region on environmental health.

The lay health promoters try to educate about 20 people per month, Ruiz said, and keep in contact with the Farmworker Justice Fund, which attempts to track the number of people reached through the project. In terms of occupational health, lay health workers are taught how to prevent exposure to pesticides, how to prevent bringing home some of the toxins to their families and about their rights to a safe workplace. Ruiz said that some of the training also looks at toxic sources coming from Mexico, with the hope that the information finds its way across the border.

"The border is a such a fluid area that it makes sense to try to do outreach to both countries," she told *The Nation's Health*.

For example, according to Ruiz, in El Paso, Texas, the Farmworker Justice Fund is working with health authorities to warn people about using pesticides indoors. In Mexico, it's easier to buy dangerous pesticides, which are then brought across the border and used indoors to kill insects, she said.

When Ruiz talks to farmworkers along the border, she often hears complaints such as lack of pesticide safety training, not being provided with handwashing equipment, not being told when or where pesticides have been applied and, occasionally, stories of being directly exposed to pesticides. Ruiz noted that a good portion of the workforce are indigenous people from Mexico and parts of Central America, for whom Spanish is a second language, and they are often given the hardest and most difficult work.

Although farmworkers are entitled to certain rights under the law, many Hispanic workers don't come forward for fear of being fired or retaliated against by an employer, Ruiz said. Many are also undocumented and fear that their immigration status will be used against them.

"In general, the state laws are very weak and there's little enforcement," she said. "Even if there were a problem, the fines that employers have to pay are minimal. There's not a lot of incentive for employers to comply (with the law)."

Unfortunately, according to Erik Nicholson, Pacific Northwest regional director for United Farmworkers, a part of the AFLCIO, agricultural workers are not provided many of the same legal protections as other workers. While most workers are covered under OSHA, agricultural workers are the purview of the Environmental Protection Agency. Also, agricultural work is not covered by the National Labor Relations Act, said Nicholson, who is also a member of the Pesticide Program Dialogue Committee, an advisory committee to EPA's pesticide program. In fact, Nicholson's organization, along with a host of other groups, filed suit in January challenging EPA's approval of the use of two pesticides known to poison humans.

"Farmworkers work in a place where toxins are intentionally introduced, and what we see time and time again is that the standards that are set up to protect the workers are insufficient," he told *The Nation's Health*. "What adds insult to injury is that farm workers are seen and used as laboratory animals."

To fill the gaps overlooked by regulations, United Farmworkers, which has been working with agricultural workers for more than 30 years, conducts worker house visits, educating workers, the majority of whom are Hispanic, on the long-term chronic effects of pesticides, as well as trying to identify the kinds of pesticides that are being used in the workplace, Nicholson said. Providing misinformation to farm workers is far from new, he noted. For example, many workers actually use the Spanish word for "medicine" when talking about pesticides because they've heard their employers characterize pesticides as medicines for plants, Nicholson said.

"We know that parents can bring the pesticides back into the house—that kids and parents are eating products treated with pesticides," he said.

The United Farmworkers union also operates the Radio Campesina Network, a chain of Spanish-language radio stations along the West Coast originally designed to reach farmworkers even in the most isolated regions. The stations, which mostly broadcast music, also communicate occasional educational programming on pesticide use.

Nicholson called on health care professionals who serve agricultural workers to educate themselves on the occupational hazards of farm work. Many times, he said, providers will treat the symptoms of occupational disease and not ask when or how the patient got sick.

"Racism is alive and well in this country, and if a lot of things were happening to white people that are happening to Hispanics, this country would be in an uproar," Nicholson said.

URBAN WORK SETTINGS POSE DANGERS AS WELL

For Hispanic immigrants working outside the agricultural sector, work conditions are just as grim. According to Amy Vruno, JD, an Equal Justice Works fellow at the D.C. Employment Justice Center, about 12 percent of the center's overall clientele come in about a workplace injury, although among the overall Hispanic clientele, it's closer to 25 percent. The D.C. Employment Justice Center, which was founded in 2000, works to secure and enforce the rights of low-wage workers in Washington, D.C.

The main spine of the organization is the Workers' Rights Clinic, which sees about 1,500 workers every year via a free, walk-in legal clinic. About 25 percent of those who visit the clinic are Spanish-speaking, many of whom are day laborers with complaints about unpaid wages and questions about workers' compensation, Vruno said. About 80 percent of Hispanics who visit the clinic have no health insurance, so the "stakes for getting workers' compensation are much higher," she said.

"When it comes to health and safety, they're some of the most difficult areas for workers to exercise their rights . . . and the enforcement is really dismal," Vruno told *The Nation's Health*.

To advocate for workers, *"el Comite de Defense de los Trabajadores,"* or the Committee for the Defense of Workers, was formed about one year ago and consists of about 30 members, mostly Hispanic workers. Some employers assume they can exploit immigrant workers, who may not know their rights and are too afraid to stand up to an employer, Vruno said. The committee provides a place for workers to come together to try to improve the working conditions in Washington, D.C., by engaging rogue employers and putting pressure on them to abide by the law.

The D.C. Employment Justice Center is also home to *"El teatro de trabajadores,"* or Workers' Theatre, a troupe of low-wage, Spanish-speaking workers. Troupe members re-enact real stories they've heard through friends or the legal clinic at venues most likely to reach low-wage workers. After performances, the actors engage the audience about what they would do in certain work situations, Vruno said.

"Employers know this is a vulnerable work force—many of (the workers) have families at home dependent on this money—but employers assume that they can hold immigration status over people's heads," she said.

In New York City, the New York Committee for Occupational Safety and Health has been advocating for safe and healthy work places since 1976. The committee, a coalition of unions and health professionals, provides training to about 4,000 to 5,000 workers a year on occupational safety and workers' rights under the law and monitors the implementation of laws on the city, state, national and federal levels, according to APHA member Joel Shufro, PhD, the committee's executive director.

"The level of enforcement of OSHA generally is so poor . . . so it is not able to enforce its standards in a rigorous manner, especially when it comes to day laborers," Shufro told *The Nation's Health.*

The committee recently became part of a pilot program called the Queens Occupational Injury Prevention Project in collaboration with Queens College and Elmhurst Hospital. The initial phase of the project will target Hispanic immigrant workers living in Queens and will offer free occupational health screenings via a medical mobile unit. The project, which is slated to begin soon, grew out of an earlier project involving workers near the site of the Sept. 11, 2001, terrorist attacks in New York City, Shufro said.

During the clean-up efforts, a van was placed near the location of the former World Trade Center towers to monitor the health and safety of workers, mainly immigrant day laborers, who were cleaning buildings that were near the trade center towers. Investigations found that some workers were not being provided with respiratory equipment, not being trained on how to safely conduct clean-up and were not being paid, according to Shufro. About 400 workers went through the screening program near the towers site and about 99 percent of the workers, most of whom were Hispanic and living in Queens, had respiratory problems as a result of exposure to post-Sept. 11 clean-up. The New York Committee for Occupational Safety and Health is still trying to obtain workers' compensation for those clean-up workers, according to Shufro.

Knowing that many of those workers were living in Queens and were doing some of the most dangerous and dirty work in New York City, the committee wanted to continue providing health screenings, thus the conception of the Queens mobile clinic project. New York City's Elmhurst Hospital is providing a van two days per week as well as paying for an occupational health doctor to accompany the project, while staff from Shufro's organization educate participants on occupational health and the law and how to access workers' compensation.

"For Queens, where 65 percent of the workers are foreign-born, this is a major issue," Shufro said.

The committee also operates the Immigrant Worker Project, which began about four years ago, developing partnerships with community organizations that serve low-wage workers and day laborers, according to Beverly Tillery, coordinator of the project. For example, the project works with English-as-a-second-language teachers to develop curricula on occupational health and safety.

Tillery also works with community-based worker centers, places that often provide day-laborer pickup sites—a mechanism used to bring day laborers together to organize standards around work conditions and control the market to get a fair wage. The Immigrant Worker Project works with such centers to integrate occupational health and safety training into their programs, Tillery said.

"Once workers get to talk collectively, they realize that the problems are systemic," she told *The Nation's Health*.

Tillery said OSHA does not conduct nearly enough inspections, particularly at places where immigrants work. Common complaints she hears from day laborers are working without protections such as hard hats and gloves, working with chemicals in areas with no ventilation and working without respirators or safety training.

"You shouldn't be in a situation where you have to choose between your health and your job, but that's really where a lot of workers are at," Tillery said. "The reality is that the employers are not doing what they need to do to protect workers and they know they can get away with it."

For more information on disparities in occupational and environmental health among Hispanics, visit <www.cdc.gov>, <www.fwjustice.org> or <www.nycosh.org>.

Joining in the Conversation

1. What does Krisberg say contributes to the fatalities among Latino workers? What places pose the greatest threats to health for farmworkers? List several of the organizations that were created to help farmworkers. What is the specific goal of each group? How are the problems of the farmworkers attributed to racism?
2. Krisberg wrote this article for *The Nation's Health* magazine. Who do you think is the audience for this magazine? Would you have read it? Where do you think it will get a wider audience? Suggest some other magazines that you think the article would be appropriate for and that have a wider circulation than *The Nation's Health*.
3. Complete some research on the work of Cesar Chavez and discuss how his work helped bring attention to the farmworkers. For what issues is he well known? What did he help to create? Is it still in existence today?

Acculturation Is Bad for Our Health: Less Fast Food, More *Nopalitos*

JUANA MORA

Professor Juana Mora is a member of the Department of Chicano/a Studies at California State University, Northridge. Her area of expertise is in health and nursing. Mora has published other health-related articles, especially about Chicanas, and she wrote the following one for this book.

✦

WHAT IS THE HEALTH STATUS OF LATINOS IN THE U.S.?

What is the health status of Latinos in the United States? It is difficult to answer this question because (1) Latinos are a diverse population of cultural groups with different histories and cultural practices that influence health, and (2) health researchers until recently did not include Latinos in their studies. However, new studies that have focused on the health of Latinos are giving us a new understanding of the health and health care needs of Latinos. Based on these studies, we can summarize the health status of Latinos as follows:

Good News

- Immigrant Latinas give birth to healthy babies;
- Latina mothers have relatively low infant mortality rates (children of Latinas are less likely to die at birth compared to whites);
- Latinos have lower rates of heart disease, cancer, and stroke compared to non-Latinos (Hayes-Bautista, 2002; Myers & Rodriguez, 2003).

Bad News

- Latinos have higher death rates related to diabetes, HIV-AIDS, alcohol-related cirrhosis of the liver and homicide compared to whites;
- Latinos are more likely to receive health care in a hospital emergency room and are less likely than whites to have a regular health care provider;
- The longer Latino immigrants live in this country, the greater risk there is to their health due to increases in alcohol and other drug use, smoking, poor diets, and less physical activity (Hayes-Bautista, 2002; Vega et al., 1998; Myers & Rodriguez, 2003).

The last point is perhaps the most disturbing since we supposedly immigrate to the United States to better our lives and to create opportunities for our children. It seems, however, that from a health perspective, the health gains that are brought to the United States by immigrant populations are lost in the process of transitioning from the home culture to new cultural norms and environments. The gains in healthy births, for example, are at risk as U.S.-born or U.S.-raised Latinas increase their alcohol intake, other drug use, and smoking, and live more stressful lives. Zambrana et al. (1997) for example, found that women of Mexican origin who had higher levels of acculturation experienced more prenatal stress, which in turn was associated with preterm deliveries and lower-birth-weight babies. The impact of increased drug use and smoking may also lead to more instances of heart disease, cancers, and strokes. Some studies (Espino & Maldonado, 1990) have found an increase in hypertension among more acculturated, middle-aged Mexican Americans. And other studies (Vega et al., 1998) have found higher rates of psychiatric disorders, including major depression among U.S. born or raised Latinos. According to leading health experts, immigrants come to this country at some risk to their physical well-being and mental health. So what happens to an apparently healthy immigrant lifestyle after several years of residing and working in the United States?

WHY IS ACCULTURATION BAD FOR OUR HEALTH?

Part of the changes that occur as immigrants adapt to the United States are that their daily habits and environments change. For example, there is evidence that when immigrants, particularly immigrant children or the children of immigrants, grow up in the United States, they will be exposed to and eat more fast food, will not have access to home-grown foods that they may have had in their home countries, and are more likely to be raised in unsafe and unhealthy low-income neighborhoods where there is a disproportionate amount of fast food, alcohol, and tobacco advertising (Maxwell & Jacobson, 1989). These are not optimum conditions for healthy growth and prosperity. Apparently, upon arrival to the United States and for years after, there is a greater reliance on inexpensive fast food for survival. There is also less physical activity, particularly for immigrant children who remain indoors watching TV, often for many hours, because neighborhoods are unsafe or are not suitable for outdoor play. Scholars have for a long time described immigration as a dangerous, stressful journey with long-term effects on the family (Falicov, 1998; Igoa, 1995).

Our families bring us here to improve our educational opportunities and to live better lives. But they seldom know about the long-term effects of immigration such as the stress produced by learning a new language and culture, living in new and sometimes dangerous environments and having less time to raise and supervise children. In fact, experts have identified a series of disorders that can result from the immigration process alone. These include post–traumatic stress disorder, disturbed sleeping and eating patterns, depression, and so on. However, the long-term effects of immigration that include poorer diets, less physical activity, substance abuse, and unsafe neighborhoods are perhaps more disturbing and can have more of an affect on the long-term health of subsequent generations of Latinos. What else contributes to poor health outcomes for Latinos living in the United States?

INEQUALITY IN HEALTH CARE

Acculturation into U.S. health norms, including a greater reliance on fast food and poor environments, contribute to the poor health outcomes of Latinos, but the disparities in health between Latinos and whites can also be explained by a noted difference in the quality of health care. According to a report by the Institute of Medicine, (2003), racial and ethnic minorities tend to receive lower-quality health care than whites do, even when insurance status, income, age, and severity of conditions are comparable. The findings of this study are as follows:

- Minorities and persons of lower socioeconomic status are less likely to receive cancer-screening services and are more likely to have late-stage cancer when the disease is diagnosed.
- Minorities and patients of lower socioeconomic status are less likely to receive recommended diabetic services and are more likely to be hospitalized for diabetes and its complications.
- When hospitalized for acute myocardial infarction, Latinos are less likely to receive optimal care.
- Racial and ethnic minorities and persons of lower socioeconomic status are more likely to die from HIV.
- Being a member of an ethnic or racial minority is also associated with receiving more amputations and treatment for late-stage cancer.

Thus, in addition to changes in daily habits, poor quality of health care, even for Latinos who are insured, adds to the increasing negative health outcomes for Latinos.

POOR, UNSAFE NEIGHBORHOODS AND ENVIRONMENTS

The health status of Latinos is also affected by the environmental conditions of the places where they live, work, play, and raise their children. When immigrants arrive in this country, they most often are not able to afford homes in clean, safe neighborhoods or expensive, nutritious food. Studies (Igoa, 1995; Vega et al., 1998;

Maugh & McConnell, 1998) have found that because immigrant parents sometimes work more than one job, the care of the children is assigned to older siblings who resort to nearby, inexpensive fast food for themselves and the children in their care. The majority of Latino immigrants live in crowded urban environments associated with all the risks to health and safety that overconcentrations of liquor stores, air pollution from industrial facilities, and freeways bring to these environments. In Southern California, new studies (Morello-Frosh et al., 2002) examining the impact of environmental conditions on the health of Latino families and children are finding a disproportionate burden on the health of poor and ethnic minority communities that house more than their share of toxic waste, pesticide runoff, lead exposure from old housing, trash, graffiti, and air pollution. It has been estimated that environmental exposures contribute 10 to 20 percent to the causes of diseases, including respiratory illnesses such as asthma, developmental delays and learning disabilities, cancers, and birth defects. A report of the impact of power-plant pollution and the effects on Latino health issued by the League of United Latin American Citizens (LULAC) (Keating, 2004) reported that 71 percent of Latinos in the United States live in counties that violate federal air-pollution standards. Another study in New York found that children in low-income families are eight times more likely to be poisoned by lead exposure than children in high-income families (Cahn and Thompson, 2003). These environmental conditions are clearly hazardous to the health of Latino immigrant families and children. What can immigrant families do to prepare for the opportunities as well as the risks of immigration?

OUR CULTURE IS PROTECTIVE: LOOK FOR THE STRENGTHS

While the outlook for Latino health looks grim due to the triple threat of acculturation, lower-quality health care, and environmentally unhealthy living conditions in the United States, there are strengths within our culture that can be protective of health. We can maintain some of our traditions, including growing our own food even if there is only a small space in which to do so, we can listen to our *abuelos y abuelas* to learn about how they lived and stayed healthy, and we can advocate for safer, cleaner neighborhoods. In San Diego, the residents of Barrio Logan have come together to advocate for cleaner air and safer neighborhoods. In Los Angeles, community residents in some of the poorest neighborhoods organize community clean-up efforts. Families can grow their own food, even if they live in crowded spaces, by organizing community gardens. Even in crowded spaces, we must find the physical and spiritual space for maintaining and honoring those aspects of our culture and tradition that are protective and help us live better lives. I live in a suburb of Los Angeles. When I moved into my home, the first thing my mother did was to plant a *nopal,* oregano and *yerba buena* in my small back yard. This was her way of giving me her strength and knowledge. We can utilize our space, as small as it might be, in ways that maintain the positive aspects of our *cultura.* We no longer have to give up everything that is sacred and honored. And if maintaining a healthy diet that includes *frijoles y "nopales"* in our diets is part of what we want, then we can do that. After all, acculturation does not mean complete assimilation and loss of your culture. It allows for individuals to keep the best from their original culture and learn to positively adapt to the new culture.

Works Cited

Cahn, L., & Thompson, G. (2003). "The Politics of Poison." Pratt Area Community Council. New York: www.prattarea.org.

Espino, D. V., & Maldonado, D. (1990). "Hypertension and Acculturation in Elderly Mexican Americans: Results from 1982–1984 Hispanic HANES." *Journal of Gerontology,* 45, M209–M213.

Falicov, C. J. (1998). *Latino Families in Therapy: A Guide to Multicultural Practice.* New York: Guilford Press.

Hayes-Bautista, D. (2002). "The Latino Health Research Agenda for the Twenty-first Century." In M. Suarez-Orozco & M. Paez (eds.), *Latinos Remaking America.* David Rockefeller Center for Latin American Studies, Harvard University. Berkeley: University of California Press.

Igoa, C. (1995). *The Inner World of the Immigrant Child.* New Jersey: Lawrence Erlbaum Associates.

Institute of Medicine (2003). *Unequal Treatment: Confronting Racial and Ethnic Disparities in Healthcare.* Washington, D.C.: National Academies Press.

Keating, M. (2004). *Air of Injustice: How Air Pollution Affects the Health of Hispanics and Latinos.* Washington, D.C.: League of United Latin American Citizens.

Maxwell, B., & Jacobson, M. (1989). *Marketing Disease to Hispanics: The Selling of Alcohol, Tobacco and Junk Foods.* Washington, D.C.: Center for Science in the Public Interest.

Maugh, T. H., & McConnell, P. J. (1998). "Americanization a Health Risk," *Los Angeles Times*: Los Angeles.

Morello-Frosh, R., Pastor, M., Porras, C., & Sadd, J. (2002). "Environmental Justice and Regional Inequality in Southern California: Implications for Research," *Environmental Health Perspectives Supplements,* Vol. 110, No. S2.

Myers, H. F., & Rodriguez, N. (2003). "Acculturation and Physical Health in Racial and Ethnic Minorities." In K. M. Chun, P. B. Organista, & G. Marin (eds), *Acculturation: Advances in Theory, Measurement and Applied Research.* Washington, D.C.: American Psychological Association.

Vega, W. A., Kolody, B., Aguilar-Gaxiola, S., Alderete, E., Catalano, R., & Caraveo-Anduaga, J. (1998). "Lifetime Prevalence of DSM-III-R Psychiatric Disorders among Urban and Rural Mexican Americans in California." *Archives of General Psychiatry,* 55, 771–782.

Zambrana, R. E., Scrimshaw, S. C. M., Collins, N., & Dunkel-Schetter, C. (1997). "Prenatal health behaviors and psychosocial risk factors in pregnant women of Mexican origin: The role of acculturation." *American Journal of Public Health,* 87, 1022–1026.

Joining in the Conversation

1. List at least three ways that the health of Latinos deteriorates by immigrating to or living in the United States. How does the presence of advertising negatively affect the health of Latinos living in the United States? What suggestions does Mora make to help immigrant Latinos improve their health?
2. Although this is a persuasive article, Mora includes exemplification (examples), research information, description, and personal narrative. Analyze the article, finding the thesis or main idea first, then give examples of the ways Mora makes her point and evaluate how successful she is in making this a successfully persuasive article.
3. Select a single health issue that puts many Latin@s/Chican@s at risk in the United States Using Mora's article as a model, decide how you would persuade a good friend to change his/her lifestyle to avoid that particular health issue. Try to use the types of writing that Mora used, such as examples, research, and personal narrative to make your point.

"I Want to Live a Long Life": Starting Healthy Habits Early Program Helps Hispanic Children Learn to Stay Fit

ERIC BERGER

Eric Berger is the science reporter and staff writer for the Houston Chronicle. *Over the years, the "SciGuy," as Berger is often known, has focused on the environmental problems associated with pollution and global warming, as well as the damage caused by natural disasters. The following article appeared in the* Houston Chronicle *(October 24, 2004) and looks at the physical damage one's favorite foods may cause.*

✦

Rosa Molina used to give a predictable response when her mom offered a steaming bowl of broccoli at the dinner table: "ewww" or "ugh," followed by a recoil in disgust.

So innate was this disgust for the vegetable, in fact, Rosa had never tried it. Then a teacher suggested that broccoli wasn't so bad, and it was healthy, too. So Rosa tried it and no longer passes on broccoli at home. She's also taken up gymnastics to get fit.

"These were pretty easy decisions," said Rosa, a fifth-grader with a very slight weight problem who attends Schmalz Elementary in west Houston. "I want to live a long life."

This is one, arguably rare, success story amid an almost overwhelming rise in childhood obesity rates, especially for Hispanics. By the time Rosa reaches the 11th grade, she and other Hispanic girls are more than three times as likely as Anglo girls in Texas to be overweight. The Hispanic boys in her class won't be any better off.

The success comes in prevention, like getting Rosa to develop a taste for broccoli and exercise now, before she has to suffer

---

Source: Eric Berger, "'I Want to Live a Long Life': Starting Healthy Habits Early Program Helps Hispanic Children Learn to Stay Fit," *Houston Chronicle,* October 24, 2004, p. B1.

under major weight-loss programs. It's not an easy sell when kids are bombarded with ads for fast food and the latest video games.

But in a state where Hispanics will become the plurality population by 2015 or 2020, and a majority by 2050, the societal and economic consequences of ignoring the problem and creating an ever-larger, more-diabetic Texas are dire.

Because epidemiologists and health officials recognized the full scope of the obesity problem only in the past half-decade, researchers are just now beginning to ask why Hispanics seem to be more prone to gain weight and become diabetic.

"This, clearly, is an understudied area of science," said Texas Health Commissioner Eduardo Sanchez. "But I think we should be investing in things that can make a difference even as we try to figure out why this problem exists. If we spend all of our time trying to figure this out, we may lose out on our opportunity to intervene."

The program that led Rosa to try broccoli, Community Access To Child Health . . . , or CATCH, is one of many such interventions.[1] It is distinguishable from other programs, however, in one quantifiable way—it works.

The CATCH program combines increased activity in gym class, lessons for cafeteria workers to make leaner, healthier meals and classroom instruction for students on how to eat better and lead more active lives.

A study that followed 900 El Paso students, to be published later this year, found that boys and girls enrolled in the CATCH program maintained healthy weights, while many of their peers did not.

STUDY SHOWS RESULTS

At the beginning of the two-year study, 30 percent of the third-grade girls in CATCH were overweight or at risk of becoming overweight, according to national standards. By the fifth grade, that figure rose to 32 percent. In contrast, during the same time period, the percentage of their peers in El Paso schools who were overweight or at risk jumped from 26 percent to 39 percent.

The findings were similar for boys. The percentage of boys enrolled in CATCH with weight problems rose slightly between third and fifth grades, from 40 percent to 41 percent, while for boys not enrolled in the program it rose from 40 percent to 49 percent.

"The program increased their physical activity to recommended levels and gave them better food choices," said the study's lead author, Karen Coleman, an assistant professor in the Graduate School of Public Health at San Diego State University. "This will lead to their being more active as adolescents and adults and thus able to maintain a healthy weight."

QUESTIONS ABOUT DISPARITIES

Researchers know both genetics and behavior play a role in obesity.

But because human genes haven't changed much in the past four decades—and Americans have continued to get fatter—researchers believe environmental factors such as diet, exercise and socioeconomic status have driven recent increases.

To begin answering questions about Hispanic health disparities, the National Institutes of Health awarded a $7.5 million grant last year to the University of Texas School of Public Health at Houston and UT-Brownsville. The grant, the first NIH funding ever received by the Brownsville school, will focus on the threats from obesity, cardiovascular disease, diabetes and cancer in the lower Rio Grande Valley.

Scientists in Houston and Brownsville are finding they need to be creative when identifying fixes.

"We can't just ask people to eat more fruits and vegetables when they're on a tight food budget," said Steven Kelder, a UT-Houston researcher involved in the project. "It's much cheaper and quicker for them to go to a fast-food restaurant."

At Baylor College of Medicine, researchers have collected DNA from about 1,000 overweight Hispanic children in the Houston area to see whether they can identify genes that make people more susceptible to becoming overweight.

Many of these children already have developed serious complications, such as high blood pressure or blood sugar levels that could lead to Type II diabetes, said Nancy Butte, a Baylor professor involved in the study.

"It's really quite alarming," she said.

Researchers also are studying the diet and physical activity of the children, and have found a high intake of sweetened drinks such as Kool-Aid, soda and Tampico fruit punch, a top-selling brand that parents may not realize isn't juice at all, Butte said. Such sugar-sweetened beverages have been linked to diabetes and obesity in adults.

OBESITY LIKELY RUNS IN FAMILY

Another Baylor professor, Theresa Nicklas, is studying the eating and exercise habits of children enrolled in Head Start, a development program for preschool children in low-income families. Her study is a year or two away from producing results.

But already, she's found a link between overweight parents and children. In her study, Nicklas said 90 percent of the children who are at risk of being overweight, or already are, have a mother who is overweight.

This suggests that any intervention must include messages for parents, including the message that their children emulate them, researchers said.

"We need to change lifestyles during preschool," Nicklas said. "This is the time when children are developing their lifelong habits."

Few, if any programs, begin that early. Some components of CATCH start in kindergarten, but the bulk of the program, including classroom education and increases in moderate-to-vigorous physical activity, doesn't begin until the third grade.

CATCH is not new. First tried in 1991, researchers at UT-Houston and three other institutions conceived the program to control heart disease, before they recognized obesity as a major health problem. Although the program successfully reduced the fat content in school lunches and increased physical activity, it was only recently seen as a tool to fight obesity.

Now about 1,500 schools, or one-third of the state's elementary schools, have implemented some form of the program, Kelder said.

Sanchez and other health researchers say success requires a comprehensive set of programs—from public service announcements during Saturday morning cartoons to a subsidized discount on lowfat milk.

REVERSING THE TREND

As parents become aware of the problem of childhood obesity, they must also realize there is no quick fix, said Deanna Hoelscher, who directs the human nutrition center at the University of Texas School of Public Health at Houston.

The cultural trends that have led to the problem—video games, TV and junk food among them—have developed over decades, she said.

It will take combined efforts by schools, government and parents to reverse these trends. Rosa said her mother, Alma, suggested she try gymnastics—along with broccoli—when she was younger. Encouragement from a teacher helped Rosa overcome her fears.

"I was always scared of gymnastics because I thought you had to be very flexible to do flips," she said. "Now I am becoming flexible, and it's good for my body."

Endnote

1. CORRECTION: The Coordinated Approach to Child Health program is widely used in Texas to improve children's eating and exercise habits. This story . . . gave the wrong name for the CATCH program. Correction published 10/26/04.

Joining in the Conversation

1. What are the cultural forces driving obesity and the development of diabetes in older children that Berger discusses? In your response, do not consider just the types of foods children eat, but their habits as well.
2. Berger writes as the "SciGuy," a reporter interested in the scientific viewpoint of a problem. Look back through his article and discover the types of writing he uses to get his point across. Ask yourself if he was strictly scientific, giving figures and study results, or if he combined the scientific information with other forms of writing to get his points across in his article.
3. One point Berger makes particularly clear is that just telling someone to eat healthier foods such as broccoli often does not work because the family may not be able to afford such foods on a consistent basis. Imagine that you are the grocery shopper for a family that consists of you and a spouse plus a two-year-old and a fourteen-year-old. Your grocery allotment for the week is $75. Visit your local grocery store and make a list of all the foods you will need for one week for your family. How healthy were your food selections? Prepare a report for class describing the difficulties of keeping to a strict budget and still retaining a healthy menu for your family.

Latinos Re-Examine Pregnancy in Teens

Brian Feagans

Brian Feagans is a staff writer for The Atlanta Journal-Constitution. *Feagans writes about changes in demographics, health concerns,*

Source: Brian Feagans, "Latinos Re-examine Pregnancy in Teens: Limiting Births Contrary Concept for Immigrants," *Atlanta Journal—Constitution*, October 12, 2005, p. A1.

drug issues, multicultural concerns, and public issues. This article appeared in the October 12, 2006 issue of The Atlanta Journal-Constitution.

✦

LIMITING BIRTHS CONTRARY CONCEPT FOR IMMIGRANTS

Carolina Darbisi has a formidable task: getting Latin American immigrants to talk to their kids about sex. But she has found one statistic weighty enough to smash cultural taboos against discussing the subject.

Of every 10 Latinas in Georgia, she tells parents, six get pregnant before turning 20, according to the Georgia Campaign for Adolescent Pregnancy Prevention.

That gets their attention. "I say, 'How many daughters do you have?'" said Darbisi, who visits parents in schools and apartment complexes in Gainesville for the nonprofit group, which is known as G-CAPP. "They say, 'Oh yeah. So my daughters are [included] in that number.'"

Newcomers from Mexico and other parts of Latin America have made Georgia home to one of the nation's fastest-growing Latino populations over the past decade. Some have arrived from villages that place a high value on motherhood, even at a young age. Others, many in the United States illegally, find themselves in difficult circumstances far from support networks back home. Alarmed Latino activists say the result is something that can hamstring those families in America: a soaring teen pregnancy rate.

The pregnancy rate for Hispanics ages 15–19 leaped 58 percent between 1994 and 2003 in Georgia, even as the figure for both white teens and black teens fell more than 32 percent, according to the most recent data from the state Department of Human Resources. The pregnancy rate for Latinas in Georgia was second only to that in North Carolina in 2000, and is now about double the national average for the ethnic group.

The forces driving the increase are as diverse as the Latino community itself. Some immigrant parents work late, leaving their children unsupervised in the after-school hours. Some marry young. Many of the teens are Roman Catholic and less likely to use contraception. And a large portion of the newcomers are from rural Mexico, where young women often are encouraged to start families.

For decades the Mexican government urged women to have lots of children, who could help settle the sparsely populated desert region of northern Mexico, said Greg Bautista, a former G-CAPP worker who is now outreach Manager for AID Gwinnett, an HIV/AIDS service organization.

"We're combating over 100 years of . . . what is normal and appropriate for a family to look like in Mexico," Bautista told those attending G-CAPP's 10th annual meeting last month in Atlanta.

BETWEEN TWO CULTURES

Teenage mothers in the United States, married or unmarried, face greater hurdles to improving their education and finding successful jobs, advocates against teen pregnancy say.

Families settling into Georgia from all over Latin America often get stuck between two cultures, and early pregnancies result, said Maritza Pichon, a Colombia native and executive director of the Latin American Association in Atlanta.

"What has been a support system or safety net in the countries where they come from—family, peers, strong religious standards—is kind of upset once they come here," she said. "Back home they have much more parental control and a lifestyle that's more traditional. Here they may be working two jobs."

Girls like one Norcross High School junior who recently discovered she was pregnant are left to sort out competing cultural signals. The 17-year-old, interviewed between blood tests at the *Centro International de Maternidad* (International Maternity Center) in Norcross, asked not to be named because of the stigma associated with teen pregnancy.

Her parents, who moved to Atlanta from a hardscrabble suburb of Mexico City a decade ago, often work past 8 p.m. cleaning houses and laying carpet. But she made a point of signing up for the after-school sports and academic clubs that she says so many of her fellow Latinos avoid. An honors student who plans to study medicine, she says college is the key to success here.

But she also has felt the pull of her parent's culture and got married earlier this year at 16, the same age at which her grandmother wed and just a year younger than her mother was on her wedding day. She said she forgot to take her birth control pills a couple of times and, within her first month of marriage, was pregnant.

When she arrived at school this year with a bulging belly, she said it was as if everyone was looking at her like one of the statistics she had vowed to beat. Many of the teen moms she knows were involved in gangs, drugs or other risky behavior. That's why she hates those looks in the hallway.

"I'm like, 'I'm not another one,'" she said. "I'm not another one like that."

INFORMATION IS KEY

About one in six Hispanic girls ages 15–19 got pregnant in Georgia during 2003, according to the state figures. The same rate held in Cobb County. But the figure was substantially higher in several other metro Atlanta counties. Roughly one in five Hispanic girls in that age range got pregnant in DeKalb, Gwinnett and Clayton counties during 2003. In Fulton, the rate was nearly one in four.

Maria Francis, administrator of the Norcross maternity clinic and three other clinics north of Atlanta, said plenty of the girls who walk through her doors are struggling with addiction or depression. A baby gives them a sense of importance, Francis said. "A lot of them think it's cool," she said. "They say, 'My girlfriend has done it and she's only a year older than me.'"

Michael Basso, a former high school health teacher in Miami who lives in Sugar Hill, said Latina teens face another difficult challenge: the wide power gap between them and male suitors who are often much older. "The ability for [the teens] to say no or negotiate not having sex in that situation is very, very difficult," said Basso, now a first-response coordinator at the Centers for Disease Control and Prevention.

The key is for young students to get information on healthy relationships at the individual level, whether it's through a parent or a teacher, Basso said. That's why he decided to translate his 1997 book, "The Underground Guide to Teenage Sexuality," into Spanish. It was released last month.

Well aware that teen moms are more likely to drop out of school, the Latin American Association, a group that advocates for Latinos in Georgia, is trying to get young Latinas on a fast track to college rather than motherhood. The nonprofit operates after-school programs out of several apartment complexes in metro Atlanta. And it has established ballet programs for girls at two DeKalb County schools—Woodward Elementary and Cross Keys High.

Later this month at Norcross High the association will host a national forum of 1,000 teens designed to get students thinking about school activities, standardized tests and other important steps to college.

G-CAPP, meanwhile, is trying to connect with parents in Gainesville. The group will launch the first of many Spanish-language "home health parties" this fall. Parents identified as community leaders will host parties with other parents in two largely Latino apartment complexes, said Michele Ozumba, executive director of G-CAPP. The idea is to get them to talk candidly to their children about sex. "Things like if you know teens are sexually active, here are the services they need to seek," Ozumba said.

Dr. Jonathan Ehrlich, co-founder of the Norcross maternity clinic, said parents haven't had frank discussions with their children before they became sexually active. Ehrlich said he would like to see schools in Georgia expand their sex education programs, but he's not holding his breath. "The only people who would benefit are the kids," he said. "And they don't vote."

The pregnant 17-year-old Norcross High student said she intended to beat the odds and attend college after her child arrived. Her grandmother is coming up from Mexico to help with child care. And she draws hope from an unlikely source: those evenings she and her brothers were home alone. While many of her peers were getting help from their parents on science projects and term papers, she said she was figuring things out on her own.

"I felt kind of lonely," she said, "but it made me stronger."

Joining in the Conversation

1. Feagans discusses several forces that affect the pregnancy rate among Chican@ teenagers. Review the article and determine the various reasons for the increased pregnancy rates and the actions that Feagans thinks could change the rate increase.
2. Feagans begins his article from the perspective of the parents, but the focus of most of the article is from that of the teenagers and counselors. Does such a tactic add strength to his argument for lower pregnancy rates or would the article have gained more power if he had divided the focus equally among parents, students, and counselors?
3. For both married and unmarried teenagers, pregnancy is an important factor that affects decisions about continuing their education. Research your own campus to discover the programs and facilities available for students with children. Also interview faculty members about their own classroom policies regarding absences and late-work penalties due to child-care issues. If there are no programs available on your campus, propose one. Be prepared to present your findings or proposal to the class using a variety of methods.

For Younger Latinos, a Shift to Smaller Families

MIREYA NAVARRO

Mireya Navarro is a longtime writer for the New York Times. *The following article appeared in the December 5, 2004 issue.*

Rocio Yniguez grew up in a family of seven children in Jalisco, Mexico. She remembers how friends of her parents proudly displayed a clock in their living room with a picture of each of their 12 children, a son or daughter for every hour.

Ms. Yniguez, 35, a department store cashier who now lives in Redwood City in the San Francisco Bay area, said she could not imagine having more than the three children she has, not if she wants to educate them and ferry them to soccer games, dance lessons and play dates. And she does not want to diverge from the goal that brought her to this country.

"You need to work to get ahead, and with children it's too hard," she said. Her decision to stop at three has made her part of a trend that is catching some demographers by surprise.

Latina women are choosing to have smaller families, in some cases resisting the social pressures that shaped the Hispanic tradition of big families.

Latinos became the country's largest minority partly because they had the highest fertility rate among the major ethnic groups. But that fertility rate is on the decline as more women work at a younger age, achieve higher levels of education and postpone marriage, all of which affects when they will give birth and how often, sociologists who study Hispanic trends say.

In California, with the largest Hispanic population, state demographers recently scaled back their population projections for 2040 by nearly seven million people, citing as one major reason the continuing drop in the fertility rate of Latina women to 2.6 children

---

Source: Mireya Navarro, "For Younger Latinos, a Shift to Smaller Families," *New York Times*, December 5, 2004, Section 1, p. 1.

per woman in 2003, from 2.8 in 1997 and 3.4 in 1990. Nationally the fertility rates for Latinas dropped to 2.7 children in 2002 from 2.9 in the early 90's (although the rate has risen in some states with newer immigrant populations, like Georgia and North Carolina).

Demographers say the decline is significant because of the size of the Latino population—about 40 million—and the implications for long-term needs tied to population growth. In California, for example, the increase in the school-age population will not be as striking as was anticipated, some said.

"It means Latinos, men and women, are increasing their options of what kind of life they're going to have," said William Frey, a demographer with the Brookings Institution in Washington who studies race and ethnic change. Family may still come first, Mr. Frey said, but compromises may be necessary. Now, he said, "they're like everybody else."

Assimilation into the American lifestyle is certainly fueling the trend. Studies by the Public Policy Institute of California, a research organization in San Francisco, show that American-born Latinas have a much lower fertility rate (2.2 percent) than that of immigrant Latinas (3.1 percent) in the state.

But the studies also show that the rate for immigrant women has dropped 30 percent over the last decade, reflecting birth trends in home countries like Mexico.

Isis Moran, a 19-year-old from Santa Ana in Orange County, said she planned to have two or three children, even though her Mexican-born mother, Viviana Abalo de Moran, 42, warns her she might regret having that few. At her daughter's age Mrs. Moran was already married and pregnant with the first of her five girls. She is one of 11 siblings, all of whom, she said, had to work in the fields in Mexico and most of whom did not get past elementary school.

"I asked my mom, 'Why so many children?'" said Viviana Moran, who by 14 had left for California. "It was ignorance. They didn't know how to take care of themselves in those days. My mother started taking the pill after the 11th child."

Mrs. Moran, a nurse assistant, said she had five daughters while trying for a baby boy to please her husband. But she likes the idea of a full dinner table at Thanksgiving and Christmas, she said, and warns her daughters to think "how you'll feel with a table with just two children."

Her daughter, a sophomore at Cornell University who hopes to pursue a career in politics, said she would feel just fine. "It's not that the family is not a priority," Ms. Moran said. "It's just that there's other things involved. If I'm going to have the profession I'm looking into, it would be rough on a big family."

The resolve to limit their families has led some women to an extreme choice. Digna Campos said she would have been happy with only one child, her 9-year-old daughter. But when her contraceptive—the patch—failed, she found herself pregnant with her second baby. Last month Ms. Campos, 35, joined seven other Hispanic women attending a class on female sterilization at Kaiser Permanente Los Angeles Medical Center. The women watched a graphic video in Spanish that showed the actual surgery and a dramatization of its pros and cons.

"It's like saying goodbye to a part of myself," a woman in the video said in the melodramatic style of a *telenovela.*

There was not a wet eye in the room. Afterward the women, including Ms. Campos, signed the form consenting to a tubal sterilization after her second child is born.

"You want the best for your children, and I can give everything to two," explained Ms. Campos, a lobby attendant at a Los Angeles hotel, who emigrated from El Salvador in 1988. "More than two would be too difficult."

In their quest for smaller families, Latina women say, quality of life is paramount for those who came from big families themselves and felt crowded and neglected. Latinas still have higher fertility rates than non-Hispanic white and black women and other groups, and outreach workers say many women still contend with *machismo* and social and religious pressures to procreate.

Some agencies said that Latina women must still contend with poor access to health care because of the lack of health insurance or bilingual services.

"Latinas don't see health care providers as often as other women of color," said Silvia Enriquez, the director of the National Latina Institute for Reproductive Health in New York. "The structural barriers of not having health insurance and culturally appropriate health care are still there."

But the cultural and religious norms that once dictated larger families have also evolved. The Roman Catholic Church, for instance, opposes birth control, but few priests would press the issue from the pulpit or in the confessional, given the overwhelming rejection of such doctrine among Catholics, said the Rev. John Coleman, a sociologist and professor of social values at Loyola Marymount University in Los Angeles.

"Most Catholics practice birth control, and they don't see it as a stumbling block to being Catholics," Father Coleman said. Organizations like Planned Parenthood note that Latinas today have more access to a wider variety of contraceptives, and they are using them.

And while outreach workers for Planned Parenthood say they find Latinas who still believe that having children helps keep their men faithful, the men have become more receptive to family planning.

On a cold Monday morning in November, two of the outreach workers, Maria Lam and Delmy Cetino, were at the Wilshire Union Day Laborer Center in Los Angeles, demonstrating the use of a condom to about 30 construction workers waiting for jobs.

The men listened with a mixture of curiosity, amusement and embarrassment, but many said that they would have to limit the number of children they have.

Luis A. Santos, 28, said his girlfriend wanted to be sterilized after her third child is born, in a few months, even though he wants more.

But David Saenz, 27, said he and his girlfriend had agreed that they would have no children for now. Finding work is tough, he said, and "it's O.K. for me to go hungry but not the children."

Even among the Latinas who have decided to limit the size of their families, some speak almost wistfully about the "Brady Bunch" ideal, if they could afford it or if times were different.

Isis Moran said she confirmed there was a good side to being part of a big family when she went off to college and moved across the country. For a whole summer she had a room of her own. But instead of enjoying it she felt lonely.

She missed her sisters, who were her close friends. And she appreciated the "pretty neat" experience of pitching in with the younger ones, changing their diapers, teaching them how to ride a bike.

"In being independent, I also learned how important my family really is to me," she said.

Joining in the Conversation

1. List several reasons that Navarro cites for the decision to have smaller families. What does assimilation have to do with this decision? List at least two reasons why older Mexican American women had larger families than today's women.

2. What strategies does Navarro use in writing this article? Is she trying to convince or persuade the audience about a particular position or is she simply presenting information about a current debate? Explain what you see. Why does she use male voices in addition to the women's?
3. Navarro lists several elements in Latinas' lives that affect on their decisions about family size: the Catholic Church, their own families, Planned Parenthood, and so forth. Using several of the influences from the article, create a questionnaire and ask Latinas in your community about their feelings about family size and which of the influences listed have had an impact on their decisions. Return to class to share what you have found. Arrive at conclusions based on the class's findings. Are they the same as or different from what Navarro presents?

Additional Topics of Conversation

1. Individuals who are unfamiliar with *curanderos* and *curanderismo* often reject the positive effects such folk medicine frequently offers to patients. Using the Trotter-Chavira article as a starting point, complete further research about unconventional approaches to treating and curing diseases, their success rates, and how the traditional medical profession views these methods. Be prepared to present your findings to the class along with your own perspective of the *curanderos* and *curanderismo*.
2. Assume you have control of the U.S. Department of Health and Human Services, and you have just found out that your budget for next year has been cut by one-third. Where and to whom would you cut services so that you do not run out of money? Remember that your Department provides not only specific medical services but research and educational programs to the public as well.
3. Assisted living homes and nursing homes are topics that are frequently in the news; however, we hear very little from Chican@ voices about them. Visit several assisted living and nursing homes in your area and speak with administrators to find out the number of Chican@ elderly in their populations as well as the ethnicities of others. Also visit and interview families who have elected to keep their elderly at home. Determine how Chican@ families feel about elder care in general and specifically about their own family members. Be sure to differentiate between assisted living and nursing facilities through the use of definition.
4. Often scientific studies lead to differing outcomes on very serious topics. Look at two articles, "Acculturation Is Bad for Our Health: Less Fast Food, More *Nopalitos*" and "Workplace Health, Disparities among Hispanics," and determine how these two articles can arrive at two different views

as to stroke within the Hispanic community. Be sure to identify not only the main points for each article but the supports provided. Conclude your argument with your own evaluation as to which article provides the stronger argument.

5. Several articles you have read included the basic assumption that the schools, at all levels, should share in the responsibility of keeping students healthy. For example, consider the article by Berger, "I Want to Live a Long Life," and "Workplace Health Disparities among Hispanics." Look at how each automatically includes the schools within a program for health awareness. Do you agree with this basic assumption regarding the school's role in the students' lives, or should that issue be dealt with on a family basis or through another public agency? Support your position.

A

abuela, abuelita: grandmother; diminutive form of grandmother, usually used as a term of endearment

abuelo: grandfather

abuelos y abuelas: grandfathers and grandmothers

alto: stop

antepasados: ancestors

aprende: learn

la asociacion mexico-americana (anma): the Mexican-American Association

atravesados: those who cross, go across

B

barrio: neighborhood populated predominantly by Mexican Americans

Betty La Fea: *Ugly Betty*

bracero: migrant farmworker

brujos: male witches

C

campaxiuchil: marigold flowers

la carga: the cargo/freight/load

cargas: responsibilities

causa, la: the cause, referring here to the cause of the Chicano Movement

centavos: coins in Mexican money

chambelan: escort for the young woman celebrating her fifteenth birthday

charreada: Mexican rodeo

charro: Mexican cowboy

chino: Chinese

cholos/as: Mexican-American teenagers who are members of a street gang

Chorros, Los: The Streams

circulos: circles

cobarde: coward

compadre: godfather or best man; very close friend

conquistador: Spanish conquerors

corran: run (plural)
coyotes: smugglers; usually refers to individuals who smuggle people from Mexico to the United States for a very high price
criollos: individuals of Spanish heritage who were born in Mexico
crisis, la: the crisis
cucaracha/o: cockroach
cultura: culture
curanderismo: the practice of folk healing
curandero: male folk healer
curar: to heal, cure

D

damas: ladies
don, el: the gift of healing
Dora la Exploradora: *Dora the Explorer*

E

el cruzar del mojado: the crossing of the illegal
el movimiento: the Movement, generally used as a shortened form of The Chicano Movement
el siguiente año: next year/the following year
embrujado: hexed
empacho: indigestion
empapado: drunk; soaked with—a metaphorical term meaning to be completely taken with something
enganchadores: recruiters/smugglers
en las pastas y el: in the pastures or fields and the
enseñamela: show it to me
Español: Spanish
estrenar: to wear something for the first time

F

farolito: little light, sometimes refers to stars or lanterns
frijoles: beans
frontera, la: border
fuerenos: outsiders
fuerza: force

G

gabacho: negative term for a white male
gringos/as: Americans

H

hijita: little daughter
Hispano: Spanish speaker; Hispanic
hombre: man
Huitzilopochitli: the Aztec God of War

I

India/o: Indian
Infosel en linea: Infosel online
-ita: suffix making a work/noun diminutive and usually adding endearment

L

la fea: The ugly woman
La fea mas bella: The Prettiest Ugly Girl
la linea: the border
La Mañanitas: Happy birthday song, translated as The Little Mornings/Dawn
lo indio/a: adjective referring to that which is Indian
loroco: a Central American palm blossom
Los Chorros: restaurant name; *chorro* is a stream of water
los tres grandes: The Three Great Ones

M

mama: mama
machismo: manliness
macho: manly
maquiladoras: factories
mariachi: Mexican band and singers
mentiras: lies
mentirosa: liar (female)
menudo: spicy Mexican soup
mestizaje: group of interracial individuals, usually refers to Mexicans, the union between the Spaniards and the indigenous people
mestizo: an interracial individual, usually refers to Mexicans
Mexicanos/as: Mexicans
migra: immigration
mi'ja: contraction of "*mi*" and "*hija*"; a loving term that literally means my daughter. Connotatively, the term is one of endearment.
mojados: wetbacks, slang for people who cross the border illegally

molcajete: a mortar and pestle, usually made from lava rock
mural: mural
muro: wall
musica: music
musica, la: music
mutualistas: mutual aid societies

N

negocios: business
nopales: cactus plants
nopalitos: young cactus
Norteamericanos, Los: the North Americans
norte, el: the north, meaning north of Mexico
nosotros: we, us
No soy hispano, soy Cubano.: I am not Hispanic, I am Cuban.

O

ofrenda, una: an offering
orale: street langauge meant to get one's attention, as in "hey!" but with more frustration, more of an expletive
oyeme: listen to me

P

palabra: word
Pan de muerto: Bread of the Dead, usually baked for Day of the Dead festivities
paqueteros: Carrier or mule, slang
para: for
pasadores: smugglers
peso: paper currency in Mexico
plebe: plebian
plotas: plots
Poblanos: residents of Puebla, Mexico, a town and state not far from Mexico City
pobres, los: The poor
política; políticos: female politician; politicians
pollero: person who smuggles people across the border
presidio: garrison or fortress
pulquerías: saloons
pueblo: town

pupusas: Salvadorean spicy meat-filled pastry dish that is flat and fried in a skillet. The wrapping is similar to a thick corn or flour tortilla, and refried beans can be substituted for the meat.

Q

quinceañera: party for a 15-year-old girl that also introduces her to society as a young woman

R

raza, la: the people
regalos: gifts or blessings
Retorno, El: The Return
RióNueces: Nueces River
RióGrande: Rio Grande is the 1,885 mile river that begins in Colorado, flows through New Mexico, and acts as the border between Texas and Mexico.

S

sabor: taste, flavor
salsa: a spicy sauce and a kind of music
santo: holy
Se cayeron.: They fell down.
si: if
sí: yes
Si puede leer esta frase, podría tener una maravillosa carrera professional.: If you can read this sentence, you could have a marvelous professional career.
sitio, el: the site, the place
suavecito: street language for "real cool"
susto: fright

T

teatro: theater
Tejano: Tejano music is music that was found along the Texas–Mexico border and was influenced by the Europeans who moved to the United States in the early 1900s. It incorporates an accordion, a drum and a 12-string bass guitar from Spain. It also appropriates the beat of German music. For more information, see <http://www.ondanet.com/tejano/tejhistory.html>.
Tejanos: people living in the area that is now Texas before it was ceded to the United States

Telemundo: Spanish-speaking television station
telenovelas: soap operas
terreno: land
tocayola: a name-twin (and therefore a friend)
tortillas: flat bread fried without oil
trabajo: (specialized meaning in reference to *curanderismo*) magical work or hex
travasía: the crossing
tropical: tropical music coming from the Caribbean. It is fast, with a rhythmic tempo and is meant especially for dancing

U

universo: universe
urraca: black bird

V

la vida latina: Latin life
vieja: old woman

Z

Zorro: la espada y la rosa: *Zorro: The Sword and the Rose*

Phrases

A

A la cueva volveràn.: They will return to the cave.
"Ahora si ya tengo una tumba para llorar," dice Conchita . . .: *"Now I have a grave/tomb to cry on," says Conchita*
A ver . . . A ver que tienes! A ver que tienes!: Let's see . . . Let's see what you have! Let's see what you have!
Amor Prohibido: *Forbidden Love*
arroz con pollo: rice with chicken
Ay virgencita morena, mi madrecita, dame tu bendicíon.: Oh, little brown virgin, my little mother, give me your blessing.

C

Cállete, hombre.: Be quiet, man.
Centro Medico Excel: Medical Center Excel
Cinco de Mayo: Fifth of May, the day Mexican troops defeated the invading French Army in 1862
circulos de hombres: men's circles
Ciudad Futura: Future City

como la flor: like the flower
¿Cómo te llamas?: What's your name?
Con el destierro y el exilio fuimos desuñados, destroncados, destripados.: With the loss of the land and exile, we were stripped, truncated, and disposed [disemboweled].

D

del otro lado: from Mexico or from the other side
Dicen que cada mexicano siempre sueña de la conquista en los brazos de cuatro gringas rubias, la conquista del país poderoso del norte, los Estados Unidos. En cada Chicano y mexicano vive el mito del tesoro territorial perdido.: They say that each Mexican always dreams of the conquest in the arms of four blond women, the conquest of the powerful country to the North, the United States. In each Chicano and Mexicano lives the myth of the lost treasure land.
Diosmío, mija: My God, daughter

E

El cementerio estaba cercado.: The cemetery was close by.
El Comite de Defense de los Trabajodores: The Workers' Defense Committee
El Movimiento Estudiantil Chicano de Aztlán (MEChA): The Chicano Student Movement of Aztlan
El teatro de trabajadores: The Workers' Theatre
En 1521 nació una nueva raza, el mestizo, el mexicano.: In 1521 a new race was born, the *mestizo*, the Mexican.
en la cancíon "Amalia": in the song "Amalia"
enchiladas coloroados: red enchiladas
Enlaces América: Connections America
Enseñame la carga.: Show me the freight/cargo/load.
Entre a Mi Mundo: Come into My World
Era una india: She was an Indian; *India* adds the feminine gender suffix meaning that the speaker is speaking about an Indian woman, so the literal translation would be, she was an Indian woman.
es una herida abierta: it is an open wound
espiritús malos: bad spirits

F

frijoles y "nopales": beans and cactus

G

gente de razón: intelligent people; thinking people; civilized people

H

habla español: speak Spanish

L

La asociacion mexico-americana: The Mexican-American Association

la frontera, entre México y los Estados Unidos: the border, between Mexico and the United States

la migración de los pueblos mexicanos: the migration of Mexican towns

la mojada, la mujer indocumentada: the [female] wetback, the undocumented woman

La Paleteria Lulu: The Lulu Ice Cream Bar Cart

La tierra se puso bien seca y los animales conmenzaron a morirse de se'. Mi papá se murió de un **heart attack** ***dejando a mamá*** **pregnant** ***y con ocho hurecos,*** **with eight kids and one on the way.** ***Yo fui la mayor, tenía diez años.:*** The earth became very dry and the animals began to die of thirst. My papa died of a heart attack leaving mama pregnant and with eight kids and one on the way. I was the oldest; I was ten years old.

la vida Latina: Latin life

lo indio: the Indian; that which is Indian

los Estados Unidos: the United States

M

Mal Hombre: Bad Man

Mexicano del otro lado: Mexican from the other side/across the border

mi pueblo: my town

Mi pobre madre vieuda perdió two thirds of her ganado.: My poor widow mother lost two-thirds of her cattle.

Mundo Latino: Latin World

N

nació una nueva raza, el mestizo, el mexicano: a new race was born, the *mestizo,* the Mexican

No eres Mexicana: You aren't a Mexican; *Mexicana* adds the feminine gender suffix meaning that the speaker is speaking to a

Mexican woman, so the literal translation would be, you aren't a Mexican woman.

No hablaron ingles.: They did not speak English.

No hay trabajo.: There is no work.

P

panzas blancas: white stomachs

picosito: slang for a little spicy

Premio Casa de las Americas: House of the Americas Prize

Q

¿Qué creías?: What did you think?

Que Pasa, U.S.A.?: slang that is translated as What's Up, U.S.A. or What's Happening, U.S.A.?

Que tal loca no sabes . . .: Street language that literally translated does not mean what it is meant to say: Hey, crazy women, you don't know anything. It's meant to get the listener's attention.

Qué dicen muchachos a echársela de mojado?: What do you say, boys, to throwing yourselves into the wet?

quepasa: name made from two words—que and pasa—which is slang for what's happening?

S

salsa picante: stinging sauce (literal); hot sauce

***Se cayeron* in droves *en las pastas y el* brushland, *panzas blancas* ballooning to the skies. *El siguiente año* still no rain. *Mi pobre madre vieuda perdió* two-thirds of her *ganado.*:** The fell in droves in the pastures and in the brushlands, white stomachs balooning to the skies. The next year still no rain. My poor widowed mother lost two-thirds of her cattle.

Se enferma de los nervios, de alta presíon.: She gets sick from her nerves, from high [blood] pressure.

Se lo llevaron.: They took him.

Se lo llevaron sín un centavo al pobre. Se vino andando desde Guadalajara.: They took the poor man without a penny. He came back walking from Guadalajara.

Señor Dios: literally, Mr. God. An attempt to show respect to God while one is praying

Si, yo se.: yes, I know.

sin papeles: without documents, papers that prove he is a citizen or is in the United States legally

Soy Chino.: I am Chinese
su licensia y registre, por favor: your license and registration, please

T

tanto dolor me costó el alejamiento. . . . Tierra natal: so much pain the move away cost me. . . . Native land

U

Universidad Nacional Autonoma de Mexico: National Independent University of Mexico

V

valle de: valley of
Virgen de Guadalupe: the Virgin of Guadalupe
viva media: long live media

Y

y el ganado: and the cattle.
Ya estoy cansado de vivir.: I am tired of living.
Ya vez, se ve como Papá Tonio.: You see, she looks like Papa Tonio.
yerba buena: mint
Yo fui la mayor, tenía díez años.: I was the oldest, I was ten years old.
Yo quiero Taco Bell.: I want Taco Bell.

Poetry

Now let us go.
Tíhueque, tíhueque,
Vámonos, vámonos
Un pájaro cantó.
Con sus ocho tribus salieron
De la "cueva del origen."
Los aztecas siguieron al dios
Huitzilopochitli

* * *

Now let us go.
Tíhueque, tíhueque,
Let us go, let us go
A bird sang.
With his eight tribes they left
From the "cave of origin."

The Aztecs followed the god
Huitzilopochitli

Entonces corre la sangre
no sabe el indio que hacer;
le van a quitar su tierra,
la tiene que defender,
el indio se cae muerto,
y el afuerino de pie.
Levántate, Manquilef.

Arauco tiene una pena
más negra que su chamal,
ya no son los españoles
los que le hacen llorar,
hoy son los propios chilenos
los que le quitan su pan.
Levántate, Pailahuan.
Violeta Parra, "*Arauco tiene una pena*"

* * *

Then the blood runs
the Indian does not know what to do;
they are going to take away his land,
he has to defend it (her),
the Indian falls dead,
and the outsider on foot.
Get up, Manquilef.

Arauco has a sorrow
blacker than his blanket
it's not only the Spaniards
that make him cry
now it's the proper Chilenos
that take away his bread.
Get up, Pailahuan.
Violeta Parra, "Arauco has a sorrow"

Ya la mitad del terreno
les vendió el traidor Santa Anna,
con lo que se ha hecho muy rica
la nación americana.
Qué acaso no se conforman
con el oro de las minas?

Ustedes muy elegantes
y aquí nosotros en ruinas.
from the Mexican *corrido*
"Del peligro de la Intervencíon"

* * *

The half of the land
the traitor Santa Anna has sold to them
has already made them very rich
the American nation.
Which in case they don't conform
with the gold of the mines?
You very elegant people
and here, we in ruins
from the Mexican *corrido*
"From the Danger of the Intervention"

"Ahora si ya tengo una tumba para llorar,"
dice Conchita, upon being reunited with
her unknown mother just before the mother dies.
—from Ismael Rodriguez's film,
Nosotros los pobres

* * *

"Now I have a grave so I can cry,"
says Conchita, upon being reunited with
her unknown mother just before the mother dies.
—from Ismael Rodriguez's film,
We the Poor

Chapter 1

p. 2 Rodolfo F. Acuña, "Identity; We Owe History." Reprinted by permission of the author. This essay was written for this book.

p. 24 Ines Pinto Alicea, "'But Can She Cook?' Family Expectations Weigh Heavily on Latina Students," *The Hispanic Outlook in Higher Education,* Vol. 11, Issue 10 (February 26, 2001). Reprinted by permission of the publisher.

p. 35 Linda Rader Overman, "Family Pictures Shape Memory." Adapted by Linda Rader Overman from her essay "Conversations with Memory," *Talking River,* Issue #19 (2005), pp. 62–80. Reprinted by permission of the author.

p. 40 RosaMaria Chacon, "Changing Names and Making Connections: *¿Cómo te llamas?*" Reprinted by permission of the author. This essay was written for this book.

Chapter 2

p. 59 Regina R. Robertson, "Josefina Lopez: A writer's Life." This article appeared originally in *Venice,* July 2004 and was later reprinted in *Latin Style,* Issue Number 51, pp. 20–21. Reprinted by permission of the author.

p. 68 From *Chicano Popular Culture* by Charles Tatum. © 2001 The Arizona Board of Regents. Reprinted by permission of the University of Arizona Press.

Chapter 3

p. 90 From *Hunger of Memory* by Richard Rodriguez. Reprinted by permission of David R. Godine, Publisher, Inc. Copyright © 1982 by Richard Rodriguez.

p. 99 Maria C. González, "Proud to be a Product of Affirmative Action," Reprinted by permission of the author. This essay was written for this book.

p. 105 Copyright © 1997 by Sandra Cisneros. First published in *The Los Angeles Times,* October 26, 1997, Section M. Reprinted by permission of Susan Bergholz Literary Services, New York, NY and Lamy, NM. All rights reserved.

p. 108 Sarah Cortez, "Speaking Spanish," Reprinted by permission of the author. This essay was written for this book.

p. 115 Lucy Hood, "Where Do I Go with Spanish?" *Career World,* September 2005. Reprinted by permission of Weekly Reader Publishing Group.

Chapter 4

p. 125 From *Borderlands/La Frontera: The New Mestiza.* Copyright © 1987, 1999 by Gloria Anzaldúa. Reprinted by permission of Aunt Lute Books.

p. 142 Rolando Hinojosa, "A Sense of Place," *Texas Journal of Ideas, History and Culture,* Vol. 17, No. 1 (Fall/Winter 1994), pp. 18–21. Reprinted by permission of the author

p. 136 From Jonathan Kandell "Cross Purposes," *Smithsonian,* June 2005. Reprinted by permission of the auhtor.

p. 151 From Mary Jo McConahay, "They Die in Brooks County," *The Texas Observer,* June 1, 2007. Reprinted by permission of the author.

p. 166 Gregory Rodriguez, "La Nueva Orleans: Latino Immigrants, Many of Them Here Illegally, Will Rebuild the Gulf Coast—and Stay There." First published in *The Los Angeles Times,* September 25, 2005, p. M1. © 2005 by Gregory Rodriguez, The Wylie Agency.

Chapter 5

p. 199 Kim Krisberg, "Work Place Health Disparities Increasing among Hispanics," *Nation's Health*, Vol. 34, No. 2 (March 2004), pp. 11–12. Reprinted by permission of the American Public Health Association.

p. 206 Juana Mora, "Acculturation Is Bad for Our Health: Less Fast Food, More *Nopalitos*." Reprinted by permission of the author. This essay was written for this book.